fiction for youth

A Guide to Recommended Books

Third Edition

Lillian L. Shapiro
Barbara L. Stein

Neal-Schuman Publishers

New York   London

Published by Neal-Schuman Publishers, Inc.
100 Varick Street
New York, NY 10013

Printed and bound in the United States of America

Library of Congress Cataloging-in-Publication Data

Fiction for youth : a guide to recommended books / edited by Lillian
   L. Shapiro, Barbara L. Stein. — 3rd ed.
     p.   cm.
   Includes bibliographical references and index.
   ISBN 1-55570-113-2
   1. Children's literature—Bibliography. 2. Fiction—20th century—
Bibliography. I. Shapiro, Lillian L. II. Stein, Barbara L.
Z1037.F44   1992
[PN1009]
016.80883'083—dc20   92-33190
                                                                       CIP

Dedicated, as always, to my husband
Herman and my two remarkable
daughters, Dr. Susan Skea and
Prof. Judith Shapiro. It is also for Zazie.

LLS

Dedicated to Todd, Amy, and Julie

BLS

Contents

Fiction carries a greater amount of truth in solution
than the volume which purports to be all true.

William Makepeace Thackeray.
The English Humorists.

'Tis the good reader that makes the good book.

Ralph Waldo Emerson.
Society and Solitude.

Dort wo man Bücher
Verbrennt, verbrennt man auch am Ende Menchsen.
(Whenever books are burned men also,
in the end, are burned)

Heinrich Heine.
Almansor

Preface to the Third Edition

The preparation of this edition of recommended titles for *Fiction for Youth* offered me an opportunity to share with others many good, and some great, novels that have been published since 1986. It was also a welcome chance to be reminded of a few titles that had been overlooked in the second edition. I was delighted with the choice for the 1992 Pulitzer award for fiction because I had already discovered Jane Smiley's *A Thousand Acres* and found it one of the best novels I had read in a long time.

One hundred and twenty-five out-of-print titles had to be dropped since the second edition and 126 new titles have been added. Many women writers are among the new entries, including two women detective writers whose main characters are feisty female private investigators. A special effort was made to locate authors from varying ethnic backgrounds.

The introduction to the first edition of *Fiction for Youth* remains in this revised edition since it describes the original methodology and selection criteria that shaped the book. As in the previous editions, the great majority of recommendations are adult titles. Those titles which, by reason of style or theme, are for the most mature reader are starred. The so-called junior novels that are included are those which, in my opinion, are of lasting value. What has been avoided is the "problem" novel written by formula, usually of no high literary quality, which tends to either trivialize or glamorize the serious problems of young people.

Sexual explicitness or obscene language were not reasons for eliminating titles. On the other hand, books that I felt used sex or obscenity for sensation rather than the integrity of the novel, or—again in my opinion—exploited and applauded behavior that carried dangerous messages to adolescents, were not selected. It is not a question of censorship but rather a question of this editor's values. This does reflect personal taste as well as the predetermined criteria; every recommended list carries with it the philosophical view of the author of the list. Certainly such issues as drug addiction, pregnancy, incest, and anorexia face many young people; but it is not necessarily in juvenile fiction, or fiction with adolescent protagonists, that the wisest solutions can be found.

There is continuing concern about the mediocrity of American education and the resulting lowered capability of our students. Such reports as *A Nation at Risk: The Imperative for Educational Reform* (The National Commission on Excellence in Education) and Ernest L. Boyer's *High School: A Report on Secondary Education* (Harper) have been instrumental in bringing about some changes. Curriculum offerings have been strengthened, colleges are stiffening their requirements; and some parents are becoming more involved with the programs available in their children's schools.

When we read in *A Nation at Risk* that the average achievement of high school students on most standardized tests is now lower than decades ago; that over half the population of gifted students do not match their tested ability with their achievement in school; that for the first time in the history of our country the educational skills of one generation will not surpass, will not equal, will not even approach those of many of their parents, it is time for all the adults who are responsible for this generation to provide more guidance. And now in 1992 those adults—and the young people who have the right to vote—should look to those whom we elect to lead us and urge that they eliminate the economic inequality which adds to the disaster already affecting education. I think this means also taking a look at the influences that are keeping our youth at a level below that of which they are capable.

For today's youth the major attractions are the computer and television (these may also be the major diversions for their adult mentors). Television is valuable for some of its outstanding programs, especially those we are privileged to enjoy without the interruption of commercials on public television stations. (Unfortunately those are fighting for their continued existence.) Network television, which is too often the main diversion, is not without negative aspects. In a recent book entitled *The Age of Missing Information* by Bill McKibben (Random, 1992), the author reports on several months spent viewing tapes of two thousand hours of programs on cable in Fairfax, Virginia. He points out that we are overly optimistic to assume that television is a prime source of important and vital information. Programming consists largely of game shows and talk shows, which seem to emphasize personal problems rather than important issues affecting our lives, and commercials, many of which are so silly that one wonders to what audience they are directed.

The computer is another object of the attention of young people. There is no argument that it is valuable for many activities but too often is used more for playing games than for promoting education. In my own experience I have learned, unhappily, that there are some problems with computers—such as being quirky enough at times to devour a disk and being subject to viral infections that have a disastrous outcome. How careful one must be about worshipping the machine is the basis for a collection of stories called *Fairy Tales for Computers* (Eakins Press, 1969). The authors included are E. M. Forster, Franz Kafka, Theodor Herzl, Samuel Butler, Paul Valéry and Hans Christian Andersen.

What do we hope to gain in urging our young people toward these books that are in FFY which, incidentally, include science fiction, mysteries, and humorous stories? A teacher in one of the visits described in Boyer's report explains it succinctly.

> My background in literature is more useful than my psychology background in helping students understand human motivations and in making them more sensitive people. They need to feel, through literature, a relationship and kinship with the human family.

Another quote in the same report underscores the need for encouraging students to read such books as those listed in FFY.

> . . . television, calculators, word processors, and computers cannot make value judgments. They cannot teach students wisdom. That is the mission of the teacher, and the classroom must also be the place where the switches are turned off.
>
> Above all, the classroom should be the place where students are helped to put their own lives in perspective, to sort out the bad from the good, the shoddy from that which is elegant and enduring. For this we need teachers, not computers.

Some may question where there are such readers who would be attracted to the titles described in *Fiction for Youth*. I have frequently watched an outstanding program presented by the Close Up Foundation (44 Canal Center, Alexandria, Va. 22214)—a plus for television! High school students from a number of different high schools discuss with intelligence and insight issues of the day. These are certainly capable readers. What motivates them to read? It has always been my opinion that motivation emanates from adults who read. This means parents, teachers, and librarians who share their enthusiasms.

Some years back a book entitled *Why Johnny Can't Read* by Rudolf Franz Flesch was widely discussed. The original publication date was 1955 but *Books in Print* also lists an edition for 1986 so it is clear that the problem persists. More up-to-date than that is a provocative article in *The American Scholar* (Spring, 1992) by J. C. Furnas, entitled "Why Johnny Needn't Read." The theme of that article is the widespread use of crutches like Cliff Notes, Monarch Notes and other such outlines. I propose a remedy: teachers should stop asking for written book reports and employ instead such means as open discussion, book talks, or book clubs with some choice among titles to read and discuss. I confess that in my own reading of over 125 titles I considered for this edition some element of relaxation and pleasure was diminished by the constant thought in the back of my mind that I had to write an annotation for the book!

Sharing is the essence of enjoying what one reads. I would, therefore, recommend the book described below to all those readers who wish to be knowledgeable about the current question of what should be read by college students—and for high school students that means the near future for them. The book is *Debating P. C.—The Controversy Over Political Correctness on College Campuses*, edited by Paul Berman (and including Irving Howe, Barbara Ehrenreich, Dinesh D'Souza, Catherine R. Stimpson, George R. Will, Henry Louis Gates, Jr., et al.). The controversy pits Moderns against Ancients, as one of the essays in the book identifies the contributors to the book. All sides of this debate are represented. *I* think that it will make *you* think about where you stand on the issue.

Lillian L. Shapiro

Acknowledgments

Fiction for Youth: a Guide to Recommended Books, Third Edition, was a collaborative effort. Lillian Shapiro read, selected, and annotated the adult titles for this edition, as she did for the first two editions. Colleagues who helped select and annotate young adult titles include:

Pauletta B. Bracy, Associate Professor, School of Library and Information Sciences, North Carolina Central University.

Betty Carter, Assistant Professor, School of Library and Information Sciences, Texas Woman's University.

Frances McDonald, Professor, School of Library and Information Sciences, Mankato State University.

Beth Mashburn, Master of Information Science, School of Library and Information Sciences, University of North Texas.

Peggy Sullivan, Professor, Director of University Libraries, Northern Illinois University.

In addition, the editors thank the clerical staff of the School of Library and Information Sciences, University of North Texas, directed by Paula King.

Many publishers were forthcoming with preview copies. This was greatly appreciated in these increasingly tough economic times. We especially thank those publishers whose works were not selected for this edition but who graciously provided reading copies.

A debt of gratitude is owed to Margo Hart and Susan Holt of Neal-Schuman Publishers for making this edition possible.

Barbara L. Stein

Introduction to the First Edition

READING—WHO NEEDS IT?

In an article entitled "Why Johnny Can't Write" (*Newsweek*, December 8, 1975), Merrill Sheils writes as follows: "The spoken word, while adding indisputable richness and variety to the language as a whole, is by its very nature ephemeral. The written language remains the only effective vehicle of transmitting and debating a culture's ideas, values and goals." He continues with a quote from Lincoln Barnett's *The Treasure of Our Tongue:* "The written word is the link between the past and the future." For me this lays to rest the myth that the ability to read is an outmoded skill in our high-technology culture. The written word is certainly meant to be read.

The place of nonfiction in an information-oriented society is accepted as a sine qua non. Fiction, on the other hand, has to fight for its life (how often now have we mourned the passing of the novel?), and as a source of recreation, it has formidable competition in this era. Among the several problems ensuing from an overexposure to the visual modes of communication so ubiquitous in our time (and that produce mainly passive audiences) is the diminution of the power to imagine, to react in a thoughtful, personal way. The reading of fiction would appear to be a way of remedying that, as Nadine Gordimer points out in the preface to her book *Selected Stories.* She defines fiction as "a way of exploring possibilities present but undreamt of in the living of a single life."

RATIONALE FOR THIS LIST

Lists of recommended titles already exist in no small number, and we have examined many of them in the preparation of this one. They are noted in the section of this Introduction explaining our methodology. Their purposes vary according to the audience they wish to reach. Some of them include nonfiction and fiction and do not examine the fiction in depth; some of them are annual, with their selections changing according to trends in the popular culture; some of them include no fiction at all, as in the most recent edition of *Books for Secondary School Libraries;* some touch on fiction only minimally, as in the *Senior High School Library Catalog:* some list annotations but cover only about one hundred titles.

This fiction list is intended for the capable reader, often college-oriented, who would read more, and better, books if motivated or encouraged to do so. This is not said in a moralistic sense, but rather with the aim of providing alternatives to the fiction most often made available to such readers. We all remember the marginal books we loved in our youth. Some of us can recall the Nick Carter titles, the Bobbsey Twins series, the pulp magazines. They were not, however, in the school library or the English classroom—and with happy results. As adults who have had such guidance we are not hostage to the potboiler, often on the best-seller list, that is churned out quite specifically as a money-making "product." In short, the adults who were our mentors helped us to recognize and differentiate between the gold and the dross by bringing the former to our attention. There have been studies enough by now that have reported how important are teachers' expectations of achievement by their students. An article in the *Chicago Tribune* of April 6, 1979, reported the results of a survey of American teenagers 13 to 18 years old in which 45 percent of those questioned said that the work given them in high school was not hard enough.

The inability to read up to one's capability is a problem that does not go away. In the past several years there has been no dearth of reporting on the issue of illiteracy, but the problem is more multifaceted than that. The spectrum of readers with problems ranges from those who cannot even recognize monosyllabic words (many of our high school dropouts and unemployed) to those whose achievement has been affected by a lack of challenge (bright, able students who are not reaching the scholastic levels attained a mere two decades ago by students with the same capabilities). This decline in reading ability, along with other skills, among students admitted to college has caused some reevaluation of scholastic records recently by such universities as Harvard and Stanford that is expected to lead to a tightening of admission criteria.

Federally funded programs like those subsumed under the Library Services and Construction Act work with the illiterate. Committees of library associations or library systems are concerning themselves with producing lists called Hi-Lo (high interest level, low vocabulary level). Many of the titles on these lists are being written expressly for students with severe reading problems.

It is the capable, if unmotivated, reader whose interests seem to have been neglected—interests, we must admit, that lie fallow but could be stimulated by the enthusiasm of a parent, teacher, or librarian who reads. There has been, since the advent of television, little sharing by adults of loved or special titles with young charges. Ironically, it is by way of the showcase television provides that a title is often revitalized, and we all know how authors welcome the request to appear on talk-shows in order to promote a new book. It seems a shame that adults who work closely with youth in schools or at home have failed to make use of the various means available to them to encourage reading as a pleasurable, and not necessarily easy, lifetime pursuit. As television does, we should "showcase" our materials, whether in one-to-one discussions of enjoyable or provocative titles; book-talks to groups; book clubs that meet to discuss one specific book; programs that utilize drama, readings, and guest appearances to highlight a title; free time set aside in the school day to read; or the provision of books in classrooms, homerooms, and lunchrooms, as well as the library, and, of course, lots and lots of paperbacks.

There is a decline in the time spent reading among adults themselves. This is a particularly serious problem among some professional personnel who have lost a sense of their basic role and have found lay psychiatry or community-center activities the more appealing attraction. In this regard, the youngest readers are most fortunate, since story hours and the sharing of books are still fairly common practice among elementary-school personnel and children's librarians.

Not only the high school or college student but any adult can benefit from a reading program that is designed to celebrate sensitivity, stimulate thought, provoke controversy, and evoke laughter—and all of this is possible through the reading of worthwhile fiction. Another reason for this list is to remind readers of authors often forgotten or so overlooked that they have nearly reached the point of oblivion, otherwise known as being out of print. Fortunately, from time to time a publisher rescues such a title from the grave, and a few of the titles in this bibliography were brought back to life just as this manuscript was being completed. It is in the hope that more such titles will be rescued that the appendix lists twenty-two out-of-print titles that, in the editor's opinion, should be salvaged.

WHO IS THE YOUNG ADULT?

The definition of the young adult (a term perhaps not favored even by the group so identified) has been argued endlessly without any consensus being reached. It is rather difficult, therefore, to pinpoint exactly the reader we mean to reach. We have set the boundaries between the ages of 13 and 18. We are saying that the projected public consists of those young people who are in high school or beginning college. This is a very heterogenous group, emotionally, physically, and intellectually. The numerical description must be tempered with the reminder that a reader of 12 might be reading Hesse (remember the titles young people read when it was only the special collection in a family's library that was available?), while 20-year-old college students may, and do, enjoy the fantastic Middle Earth of Tolkien and the sophisticated science fiction of Heinlein. There is no accounting for taste, it has been said; but taste, defined as being able to appreciate the difference between something genuine and an imitation, is an ability worth acquiring.

For the lower end of our age range, we have included juvenile novels, that is, titles specifically written and marketed for a youth audience. We have tried to select those that make more than a transitory contribution to the enjoyment of reading and that even adults could enjoy. They represent, however, only 20 percent of the total number of titles listed. This is a ratio long considered most acceptable in a young adult library collection. The balance of the titles listed here comprises adult books of varying levels of difficulty that can be read by those capable readers I know exist among today's young people, whom we underestimate in many ways, except, perhaps, in terms of their sexual interests and activity. Novels for the most mature, indicated by an asterisk, present the most challenging themes, style, content, and length.

Practice makes perfect, or at least better. One learns to read with enjoyment even those books that require effort, and the effort becomes less onerous with constant application. Some youths will find this list valuable as a guide that they can use independently. The majority, it is safe to say, will take fire from a spark generated by that adult who wishes to share a treasure with another person.

CRITERIA

The criteria guiding the selection of titles for this list have been strict, and we have looked for qualities more important than popularity and current relevancy of topics. This does not indicate a disregard for the subjects that are important to youth. The subject index shows that we have paid attention to the great interest young people have in family relationships and problems, mysteries, science fiction, love stories, adventure, and so on. Our selections deal with important issues of our times, with struggles to survive, with excitement, and with loss. Many titles are well known, but some are not known to enough of our capable readers, and discovering them can be a memorable experience. Many of the books are of a high level of language, of powerful ideas, and challenging concepts. They are for the most mature reader. Some of the books contain passages that are sexually explicit or language that is rough, but in applying the criterion of literary quality we have tried to distinguish between integrity in the writing and specious catering to the current fashion.

We have not intended by our selections to censor anyone's reading. Much that the public reads may be of little literary value, of little permanent worth, and may even be salacious. Such books are available in bookstores, airports, and drugstores; these are outside the channels of guidance for which schools and young adult library collections exist. They are not precluded from being published and will be found without any intervention on the part of persons trained to give library service. The intention here is to call attention to books that add a worthwhile dimension to the lives of young people—and adults. We have also sought not to duplicate the efforts of other lists.

To recapitulate, then, the following are the criteria underlying the selection of the titles in this list:

1. Books must be fiction published in the twentieth century.
2. Subjects should represent interests pertinent to adolescence and youth but go beyond those to themes of universal import.
3. The majority of titles should be adult books.
4. Juvenile titles must have more than passing value.
5. Books must have literary quality.

Sexual explicitness or obscene language were considered within the overall impact of the book and were not reasons for eliminating a title. An indication of these in the annotation will help librarians judge the suitability of a title for their own communities.

METHODOLOGY

In preparing this bibliography it was important to get representation from as broad a geographical spread as possible on our committee. With the help of colleagues in the field, five people were asked to join in preparing the list. At the time of our first meeting, all of the committee members were in direct contact with young adults either as coordinators of programs in public library systems or as persons in charge of materials for that group. In addition to the editor, the committee members were:

> Betty Brown, Manager, Program Services (formerly Branch Materials Selection Coordinator), Dallas Public Library, Dallas, Texas
>
> Sari Feldman, Young Adult Services Librarian, Onondaga County Public Library, Syracuse, New York (formerly Assistant Librarian, Cook Memorial Library, Libertyville, Illinois)
>
> Bob Smith, Community Librarian, Garfield Heights Branch, Cuyahoga County Public Library, Garfield Heights, Ohio (formerly Coordinator, Young Adult Services, Cuyahoga County Public Library, Cleveland, Ohio)
>
> Elizabeth J. Talbot, Branch Head, Newark Public Library, Alameda County Free Library, Newark, California (formerly Senior Young Adult Specialist, Fremont Main Library, Fremont, California)
>
> Fannette Thomas, D.L.S. Program, University of Wisconsin Library School, Madison, Wisconsin (formerly instructor in children's literature at Emory University). Thesis subject: "The Genesis of Children's Service in the American Public Library from 1875 to 1907."

Each member of the committee was responsible for looking through specific selection tools, which included the following:

ALA *Booklist*. 1970-1980.

Books for the Teen Age. New York Public Library annual list, 1970-1980.

Books and the Teen Age Reader. G. Robert Carlsen. Harper & Row, 1971, 1980.

Books for Secondary School Libraries. National Association of Independent Schools. Bowker, 1971.

Books for You. National Council of Teachers of English. 1976.

Fiction Catalog and *Supplements*. H.W. Wilson, 1975-1979.

Junior High School Library Catalog. H.W. Wilson, 1975.

Kirkus Reviews. 1970-1980.

Kliatt Paperback Book Guide. 1976-1978.

Latino Materials. Daniel Flores Duran. Neal-Schuman, 1979.

School Library Journal, 1970-1980.

Senior High School Library Catalog. H.W. Wilson, 1977 and *Supplements*.

VOYA. 1978-1979.

YASD Annual Lists of *Best Books*, 1950-present.

In addition, discussions with colleagues provided other possible titles for inclusion.

The committee members submitted their suggestions, which were integrated into a composite list of about 900 titles. This list was sent to some experienced people in the field of young adult librarianship who gave their advice on the titles. We are especially grateful to:

> Helen Farah, Head Librarian, United Nations International School, New York
>
> Pamela D. Pollack, Editor of Book Reviews, *School Library Journal*

Lillian Morrison, Coordinator of Young Adult Services, New York Public Library

Lily Feinstein, Head Librarian, Bayside High School, Bayside, New York, until her recent and shockingly sudden death.

The combined recommendations resulted in the present list of 619 titles. For any omissions or entries with which librarians may disagree, I take full responsibility, since mine was the final decision about the titles that are included. Any list represents personal biases, and we are all aware that even prize-winning books, plays, or movies rarely, if ever, receive 100 percent of the judges' votes. A book like this will require subsequent editions; when they are in preparation, any suggestions from professional colleagues can be evaluated for possible inclusion.

We have limited our choices to books published in the twentieth century in order to make the project more manageable, and we have paid most attention to books published after 1920. Even that circumscribed area, however, is itself so large that it is possible that we have overlooked some gems. I am reminded of the dictum of a well-traveled friend who said, "Never go anywhere the first time. You are bound to overlook seeing something you should have visited."

All six members of the committee prepared the annotations, with each assigned an equal number. At the same time, each committee member suggested possible subject headings for those titles, which the editor then coordinated to achieve consistency.

Only books in print, either in hardcover or paperback, are included. Titles were checked in *Books In Print, 1979-1980* and *Paperbound Books in Print, December 1979*. Where the hardcover is out of print (o.p.), it is noted, but the bibliographic information is given in order to inform the librarian or reader about the original date of publication and publisher. When available, the Library of Congress number is given. The ISBN number is indicated for every title in print. Prices have not been quoted because of the suddenness with which they change. In some cases a paperback title has been issued by more than one publisher. We have indicated that by the symbol +.

It is our hope that you will find this bibliography a useful addition to your professional collection.

Books Arranged
Alphabetically By Author

Abe, Kobo. *Beyond the Curve*. New York: Kodansha International, 1991. 247pp. LC 90-49456. ISBN 4-770-1465-1.

These 12 stories by Abe are strange, surrealistic and mainly related to losing one's identity. In "An Irrelevant Death" a man returns to his apartment to find a dead man in it. Because he fears being suspected of being the murderer he begins to erase evidence, thus making his behavior more suspicious. In "Intruders" a large family usurps a man's apartment and forces him to become homeless. In "S Karma" the character's business card becomes the representation of his being. Characteristic of many of Abe's stories is the loss of all things like papers, keys, and names that would help the character know who he is. The endings leave the reader with questions rather than answers.

*Abe, Kobo. *The Woman in the Dunes*. Trans. from the Japanese by E. Dale Saunders, New York: Knopf, 1964. 239pp. LC 90-50625. (o.p.) New York: Random, pap. ISBN 0-679-73378-7.

An entomologist, off on an expedition to collect insects and hoping to find some unique specimen, wanders into a village where he is tricked into descending to the home of a solitary woman in the sand dunes. He finds himself a captive, needed to help the woman in a continuous struggle against the sand, which has almost the movement of water. The woman's battle against the sand is part of the survival system for the village; food and water are delivered only if the work to remove the sand continues. The man's efforts to escape are unsuccessful, and yet he continues to makes those efforts. Abe's novel is surrealistic and symbolic, and can be read on many levels.

Abrahams, Peter. *A Wreath for Udomo*. New York: Knopf, 1956. 356pp. LC 83-45608. (o.p.) New York: A M S, pap. ISBN 0-404-20001-X.+

Michael Udomo has long dreamed of freedom for Africa, and comes to London where he meets Tom Lanwood, a revolutionary writer, and other African nationalists. He is also introduced to Lois Bariow, a white woman who sympathizes with African revolutionaries and with whom he has an affair. Udomo returns to Africa where, after some years, he becomes Prime Minister and works cooperatively with two British government officials who sense the inevitability of freedom from colonialism. However, he fails to convince his Africans of the need to utilize the technical assistance of the white man. Udomo's strong convictions and efforts to push Africa into the future costs him his life. The interaction between British imperialism and African nationalism and tribalism make this a powerful and timely story.

Achebe, Chinua. *Anthills of the Savannah*. New York: Doubleday, 1987. 216pp. LC 87-18708. ISBN 0-385-01664-6. New York: Doubleday, pap. ISBN 0-385-26045-8.

Three young African men who have been friends follow differing careers but are together in West African Kangan. Chris Oriko is the Commissioner for Information; Ikem Osodi is a poet and the editor of the local newspaper. The third, however, having followed a military career, is now the leader of the state and becoming more distant from his two friends as his appetite for more and more power grows and needs feeding. This drive, fed by suspicion and jealousy, leads finally to his causing the death of Ikem and Chris. Language is sometimes that spoken by educated people, sometimes in the idiom of the village and city people. The few passages describing sexual encounters are important as character portrayal and not intended to be either gratuitous or titillating.

Achebe, Chinua. *Things Fall Apart.* New York: McDowell, 1959. 215pp. LC 59-7114. (o.p.) New York: Fawcett, pap. ISBN 0-449-20810-9.+

Integrating elements of Nigerian culture into the story of Okonkwo, a member of the Ibo tribe, Achebe tells of the changing tides that affect the private and public lives of a people when Europeans come on the scene as colonizers. Okonkwo wishes only to protect his wives and children, but the conversion of one of his sons to Christianity has a terrible consequence.

Adams, Richard. *Watership Down.* New York: Macmillan, 1974. 444pp. LC 73-6044. ISBN 0-02-700030-3. New York: Avon, pap. ISBN 0-380-00293-0.

Faced with the annihilation of its warren, a small group of male rabbits sets out across the English downs in search of a new home. Internal struggles for power surface in this intricately woven, realistically told adult adventure when the protagonists must coordinate tactics in order to defeat an enemy rabbit fortress. It is clear the author has done research on rabbit behavior, for this tale is truly authentic.

Agee, James. *A Death in the Family.* New York: McDowell, 1957. 339pp. (o.p.) New York: Bantam, pap. ISBN 0-553-27011-7.+

Six-year-old Rufus Follet, his younger sister Catherine, his mother, and various relatives all react differently to the unexpected announcement that Rufus's father has been fatally injured in an automobile accident. The poignancy of sorrow, the strength of personal beliefs, and the comforting love and support of a family are all elements of this compassionate novel.

Agnon, Shmuel Y. *Twenty-One Stories.* Ed. by Nahum N. Glatzer. New York: Schocken, 1970. 287pp. LC 71-108902. ISBN 0-8052-3350-4. New York: Schocken, pap. ISBN 0-8052-0313-3.

These stories, translated from the Hebrew, depict Jews in Poland and Israel. All the characters are strongly influenced by their orthodoxy, involved in family relationships, and marked by a penchant for the mystical. In "The Kerchief," an important gift from a husband to his beloved wife is given away by their son to a beggar. "A Whole Loaf" is almost Kafkaesque in its mixture of frustration and fantasy. "The Doctor's Divorce" chronicles painfully, step by step, the deterioration of what appeared to be a happy marriage that is relentlessly destroyed by an unappeasable jealousy. Agnon is a sensitive, perceptive writer of spiritual power, and he captures the uncertainty and pain of Jewish life.

*Allende,Isabel. *Eva Luna*. Trans. from Spanish by Margaret Sayers Peden, New York: Knopf, 1988. 304pp. LC 88-45272. ISBN 0-394-57273-4. New York: Bantam, pap. ISBN 0-553-28058-9.+

The young girl of the title of the book describes her life from girlhood to womanhood in households both poor and affluent. Her life intersects with that of Huberto Naranjo who becomes a rebel leader and guerilla fighter in a Latin American country, and with Rolf Carlé, an emigré from Austria to Latin America who becomes a controversial documentary film-maker. Like many other Latin American authors Allende writes with passion and political awareness.

*Amado, Jorge. *Gabriela, Clove and Cinnamon*. New York: Avon, 1988. pap. ISBN 0-380-075470-3.

Ilhéus, a Brazilian town near Bahia, is fortunate in the wealth it is realizing from its cacao crop. Money flows freely and is spent in cabarets, in bordellos, and on gambling during the period 1925-1926. As in American frontier towns, justice in Ilhéus is often administered personally, with a gun. While men find pleasure in each other's company, they also pursue women, their own and other men's. Adultery is a capital offense only for a wife, not when practiced by a husband. The removal of a sand bar blocking the harbor is the basis of this fascinating portrait of politics in a provincial Brazilian town. Amado also tells the love story of Nacib, the Arab owner of the most popular café in town, and Gabriela, a child of nature. Amoral rather than immoral, with skin the color of cinnamon and smelling of cloves, Gabriela gives her love readily and freely. Her skillful cooking makes her more valuable to Nacib as a mistress than as a wife. The atmosphere of this entertaining novel is lusty, sensual, and humorous.

Ambler, Eric. *Intrigue: Four Great Spy Novels*. New York: Berkley, pap. : *Background for Danger*. ISBN 0-425-06420-4. *Cause for Alarm*. ISBN 0-425-07029-8. *Journey into Fear*. ISBN 0-425-06391-7. (o.p.) *A Coffin for Dimitrios*. ISBN 0-425-06408-5. Mattituck, N.Y.: Amereon, pap. ISBN 0-89190-461-1.

This collection of four espionage novels includes *A Coffin for Dimitrios*, a story of bizarre occurrences in Istanbul; *Background for Danger*, which concerns London bankers, Rumanian oil interests, international agents, and a British journalist caught in their midst; *Journey into Fear*, which is about an English engineer returning from Turkey after the war; and *Cause for Alarm*, the story of the life, criminal record, and death of a Greek fig-packer.

Amis, Kingsley. *Lucky Jim*. Mattituck, N.Y.: Amereon, 1976. 256pp. ISBN 0-89244-069-4. New York: Penguin, pap. ISBN 0-14-001648-1.

James Dixon, junior instructor at a minor university in England, is desperate as the term ends and he still does not know whether he will be asked to teach the following term. He tries to ingratiate himself with the head of his department but somehow cannot stop from stealing the affections of the young woman who is engaged to the department head's arrogant son. All comes right in the end as Jim lives up to his name, "Lucky Jim."

*Anderson, Jessica. *Tirra Lirra by the River*. New York: Penguin, 1991. 160pp. pap. LC 83-13164. ISBN 0-14-099705-9.

Nora Roche dreams an imagined world, and perhaps a love, inspired by the lines from Tennyson's "The Lady of Shalott": "He flashed into the crystal mirror, Tirra Lirra, by the river sang Sir Lancelot." Feeling distant from both her mother and her sister, Nora seeks warmth in her friendship with Dorothy Irey. She escapes into a marriage that is cruel and bleak, and after a divorce she finds some companionship with others equally estranged from the world about them in London. A brief affair leads to an abortion, attempted suicide, and finally a return to Australia when she is old. There she picks up the life stories of the people she had known when she was young and, at last, comes to some understanding of the meaning of Sir Lancelot's song.

Anderson, Sherwood. *Winesburg, Ohio*. New York: Penguin, 1988. 256pp. pap. ISBN 0-14-043304-X.+

A series of 23 vignettes, *Winesburg, Ohio* is a character study of a small town. It highlights individual residents and scrutinizes who they are and why this reality often conflicts with their dreams. The short stories are linked through George Willard, a young newspaper reporter who is disenchanted with the narrow-mindedness of small towns.

Armstrong, William H. *Sounder*. New York: Harper, 1969. 128pp. LC 70-85030. ISBN 0-06-020143-6. New York: Harper, pap. ISBN 0-06-080975-2.+

Set in the South in the era of sharecropping and segregation, this succinctly told tale poignantly describes the courage of a father who steals a ham in order to feed his undernourished family; the determination of the eldest son, who searches for his father despite the apathy of prison authorities; and the devotion of a coon dog named Sounder.

Arnold, Elliott. *Blood Brother*. Lincoln, Neb.: Univ. of Nebraska Press, 1979. 454pp. LC 78-26788. ISBN 0-8032-1003-5. Lincoln, Neb.: Univ. of Nebraska Press, pap. ISBN 0-8032-5901-8.

Although this is a story of friendship, it is also a story of violence and bloodshed. In the conflict between American pioneers and the Indians, the great Apache chief Cochise leads his people in a fight to the death in order to stem the tide of white settlers. Unreasoning hatred becomes the rule of thumb until Tom Jeffords is put in charge of the mail route from Tucson. He seeks safety for the mail riders by way of a private agreement with Cochise, persuading the chief that some white men do not lie. Jeffords is instrumental, finally, in bringing about the peace that permits the settlement of whites in the Southwest.

Arnow, Harriette Simpson. *The Dollmaker*. Lexington, Ky.: Univ. Press of Kentucky, 1985. 560pp. LC 85-40073. ISBN 0-8131-1544-2. New York: Avon, pap. ISBN 0-380-00947-1.+

Gertie Nevels and her husband Clovis are untouched by city life until the outbreak of World War II. Then they are forced to abandon their Kentucky mountain home and travel to Detroit so that Clovis can participate in the war effort by repairing heavy machinery. Gertie's survival techniques are useless in an urban milieu. She resorts to whittling a Christ figure out of a block of cherry wood in order to lessen her loneliness and despondency. Neither she nor her children adapt easily, and they flounder in their new surroundings. In spite of the debasing effect of city life on her family, this remarkable woman maintains her faith in her fellow beings.

Asimov, Isaac. *The Foundation Trilogy*. Garden City, N.Y.: Doubleday, 1951, 1952, 1953, 684pp. LC 82-19919. ISBN 0-385-18830-7. New York: Ballantine, pap. ISBN 0-345-34088-4.+

Far in the future, the decadent galactic empire is rapidly crumbling. Along with the corruption, however, is the flower of an ancient society's science and culture. Must the galaxy be thrown back to mindless barbarism? Hari Seldon and his fellow psychologists conceive of a daring thousand-year plan to save the galactic empire and prepare for a new society. Using the statistical science of psycho-history, they hope to manipulate the planets of the galaxy toward a series of crises that will result in the future order.

Asimov, Isaac. *I, Robot*. Garden City, N.Y.: Doubleday, 1963. 218pp. LC 63-6943. ISBN 0-385-05048-8. (o.p.) New York: Bantam, pap. ISBN 0-553-29438-5.

These loosely connected stories cover the career of Dr. Susan Calvin and United States Robots, the industry that she heads, from the time of the public's early distrust of these robots to its later dependency on them. This collection is an important introduction to a theme often found in science fiction: the encroachment of technology on our lives.

Asimov, Isaac. *Nightfall and Other Stories*. Garden City, N.Y.: Doubleday, 1969. 343pp. LC 77-78711. ISBN 0-385-08104-9. (o.p.) New York: Ballantine, pap. ISBN 0-345-31091-8.

"Nightfall," the story of the first darkness in a world of eternal daylight, highlights this collection of Asimov's personal favorites. A brief anecdotal introduction precedes each story, giving an inside view of writing and publishing. The author's scholarly background, vivid imagination and readable style have produced a very satisfying short-story collection.

Atwood, Margaret. *Cat's Eye*. New York: Doubleday, 1989. 446pp. LC 88-24345. ISBN 0-385-26007-5. New York: Bantam, pap. ISBN 0-553-28247-6.

Elaine Risley, a Canadian artist, returns to Toronto for a retrospective of her work. Retrospection is also the novel's method for intertwining

Elaine's past and present. We see the family relationships and the very different kind of family hers is as compared to that of her elementary school classmates. We learn about her lovers, her marriage and, most important, about Cordelia whom she considers her best friend and, perhaps, her cruelest one. While the alternation between past and present will be a bit challenging, the mature reader will gain a sense of how values change.

*Atwood, Margaret. *The Handmaid's Tale*. Boston: Houghton, 311pp. LC 85-21944. ISBN 0-395-40425-8. (o.p.) New York: Fawcett, pap. ISBN 0-449-44829-0.

In a novel that forecasts a cruel dictatorship after a nuclear disaster, we read of a frightening prediction describing how a cadre of ruthless men overtake the government and destroy the refinements and civilized living once enjoyed by the people. Most horrendous is the status of women prescribed by those in command. Women are chattels divided into categories that determine their roles. They are Wives (mostly sterile), Marthas (houseworkers), Angels (young girls compelled into arranged marriages), and Handmaidens. The last group are used as instruments for procreation, their ability to produce children for—and by way of—the commander of their household. Their ability to produce offspring determines their safety, in fact their very lives. This is a futuristic and horrifying story for the most mature reader.

Baker, Dorothy. *Young Man With a Horn*. Boston: Houghton, 1938. 243pp. (o.p.) Repr. Larchmont, NY: Queens, 1977. ISBN 0-89244-025-2.

Rick Martin is not interested in school but is intrigued by music. Learning how to play the jazz trumpet from black musicians, Rick becomes a genius in the art of "swing" and quickly rises to fame in the Phil Morrison orchestra. The inability to cope with success, as well as a bad marriage and gin, lead to his fatal end.

Baldwin, James. *Go Tell It on the Mountain*. Garden City, N.Y.: Doubleday, 1953. 256pp. ISBN 0-385-27019-4. New York: Dell, pap. ISBN 0-440-33007-6.+

During his early adolescence John Grimes confronts all of the psychological traumas of growing up, plus the impact of being part of a strict black God-fearing family. Under these conditions John makes his rite of passage into young adulthood. Interwoven with his story are the reflections of his parents and his aunt as they cope with the pressures of their own lives.

Baldwin, James. *If Beale Street Could Talk*. New York: Doubleday, 1974. 224pp. ISBN 0-385-27066-6. (o.p) New York: Dell, pap. ISBN 0-440-34060-8.+

Tish, aged 19, and Fonny, 22-years old, are in love and pledged to marry, a decision hastened by Tish's unexpected pregnancy. Fonny is falsely accused of raping a Puerto Rican woman and is sent to prison. The families of the desperate couple search frantically for evidence that will prove his innocence in order to reunite the lovers and provide a safe haven for the expected child. There is some explicit sex but it is not treated in a sensational manner, nor is the use of street language gratuitous.

Bambara, Toni Cade. *Gorilla, My Love*. New York: Random, 1972. 177pp. LC 81-51024. ISBN 0-394-48201-8. (o.p.) New York: Random, pap. ISBN 0-394-75049-7.

This collection of short stories conveys 15 images of the black experience in America. When her children object to her enjoying a dance and a good time with Bovanne, who is blind, their mother decides that "My Man Bovanne" is for her anyway. In "Mississippi Ham Rider," a blues singer decides to leave the South for a possible recording career. "The Johnson Girls" decide to share their knowledge of the womanly arts to help Inez reclaim her boyfriend. Writing in the black English idiom, the author captures the ethos and the pathos that characterize black living, whether in a rural or an urban environment.

Banks, Russell. *The Sweet Hereafter*. New York: HarperCollins, 1991. 257pp. LC 90-56404. ISBN 0-06-016703-3.

Dolores Driscoll has driven the school bus for the town of Sam Dent for years and then a snowy morning and the need to avoid what looks like a small animal causes her to swerve and the bus crashes down a steep embankment. Fourteen children are killed, and several are injured, among them one beautiful teenager who is left handicapped. The events and what happened to the town as an aftermath are described through the words of Dolores, and Billy Ansel, the father of twins who were killed, Nichole Burnell, the teenager whose life is permanently changed from popular cheerleader to wheelchair confinement and Mitchell Stephens, a sharp New York City lawyer who urges several families to sue the local authorities. In each of the four segments we learn about the private lives of these narrators as well as their connection with the accident. This is an unforgettable and heartbreaking book.

Barnard, Robert. *Death of a Mystery Writer*. New York: Dell, 1980. 224pp. pap. ISBN 0-440-12168-X.

Sir Olive Fairleigh-Stubbs—a writer with a vast public who loved his best-selling mystery novels and a small circle of family and friends who despised him as an obese, overbearing bully—dies with distinction while sipping a special liqueur in his luxurious library on the occasion of his 65th birthday. What a surprise to discover that the son who hated him most has been bequeathed the lion's share of his father's fortune and that Sir Oliver's final manuscript, probably worth millions, has vanished. The demise of this famous mystery writer is clearly a case of murder. The readers of one Barnard mystery are likely to become addicted.

Barrett, William E. *Lilies of the Field*. Garden City, N.Y.: Doubleday, 1962. 92pp. LC 62-8085. (o.p.) New York: Warner, pap. ISBN 0-466-31500-1.

Homer Smith is an amiable Southern black man. Driving through the Southwest after getting out of the Army, he stops to help four German refugee nuns build a church. After teaching them English and survival skills, he disappears, leaving behind the legend of his faithful help.

Bassani, Giorgio. *The Garden of the Finzi-Continis*. San Diego, Ca.: Harcourt, 1977. 200pp. pap. LC 77-77261. ISBN 0-15-634570-6.

The Finzi-Continis, a wealthy Jewish Italian family, lived in a beautiful and seemingly secure environment and enjoyed intellectual pursuits. The narrator remembers the family, his unrequited love for the beautiful but cold Micol, and his friendship with her brother, Albert. The novel describes the assimilation of Jews into Italian society and then the changes effected when fascism overtakes Italy and anti-Semitism destroys the family.

Beach, Edward Latimer. *Run Silent, Run Deep*. New York: Holt, 1955. 364pp. LC 85-21801. ISBN 0-03-026645-9. (o.p.) Repr. Annapolis, Md.: Naval Institute Press, 1986. 304pp. LC 85-21801. ISBN 0-87021-557-4. New York: Zebra, pap. ISBN 0-8217-2408-8.+

Commander Beach describes the unique war experiences of the fictious submarine Walrus and its crew, fighting underwater battles in the Pacific during the years 1941-1946. A survivor of ten Pacific patrols, the author constructs a realistic picture of the relationship between men and their war machines.

Beagle, Peter S. *A Fine and Private Place*. New York: Viking, 1960. 272pp. (o.p.) New York: New Amer. Lib., pap. ISBN 0-451-45096-5.+

Mr. Rebeck has lived in a cemetery for 19 years and can talk to ghosts. He has been supplied with food by a cranky and hilariously funny raven who scavenges the city not only for food but for information of the world outside, so that Mr. Rebeck can remain cloistered. A living companion enters his life when Mrs. Kapper, a Bronx widow, begins to make regular visits to the grave of her deceased husband. Rebeck becomes involved also in the growing relationship between two ghosts, a young professor and a bookstore clerk, neither of whom was honest with himself or herself or others until death allowed them that freedom. This fantasy, rich with characters and situations, takes a less grim look at death than we usually encounter.

Beagle, Peter S. *The Last Unicorn*. New York: Viking, 1968. 218pp. (o.p.) New York: New Amer. Lib., pap. ISBN 0-451-45052-3.+

According to legend, unicorns are immortal creatures who reside alone in forests, protecting wildlife from harm. The unicorn in this story overhears hunters discussing the fact that she is probably the last remaining unicorn. Dismayed and disbelieving, she sets off to uncover the truth and luckily encounters Schmendrick the Magician, who accompanies her on her quest.

Beckman, Gunnel. *Admission to the Feast*. Trans. from the Swedish by Joan Tate. New York: Holt, 1971. 114pp. (o.p.) New York: Dell, pap. ISBN 0-440-90312-2.

Frightened, nauseated: that is Annika Hallin. At the age of 19 she discovers that she is dying of leukemia. In a letter to her friend Helen, who lives in the United States, Annika gives vent to all the emotions that the knowledge of her death brings to her. In poetic prose, the author has captured the horror and the panic, as well as the resolve, that comes with one's acceptance of death.

*Begley, Louis. *Wartime Lies*. New York: David McKay, 1991. 198pp. LC 90-53429. ISBN 0-679-40016-8.

Maciek, a young Jewish boy, lives in a small town in Poland. His aunt Tania rules the household after his mother's death and it is she who will be responsible for saving their lives as Hitler's Germany overruns Poland. When Jews are arrested, deported, or killed, Maciek begins his "wartime lies" as he and his family, actually assimilated Jews, are forced to buy safety from Polish neighbors who may or may not betray them. A German officer who becomes Tania's lover risks his life to help them but loses in the end. The descriptions of escalating danger and hideous brutality are terrifying. For Maciek, even as he passes as a Catholic, there is the need for constant vigilance since the fact that he is circumcised can bring about his death. Even after the war, many of the Poles sought the extermination of Jews.

Bell, Clare. *Ratha's Creature*. New York: Atheneum, 1983. 259pp. LC 83-13875. ISBN 0-689-50262-1. (o.p.) New York: Dell, pap. ISBN 0-440-97298-1.

This story is as much an allegory of freedom and tyranny as it is a fantasy set in a time millions of years ago. Ratha is part of a clan of wild cats called the Named. They are intelligent herders and are warred upon by the Un-Named, raiders who are devoid of the keen intelligence of Ratha's clan. There is, however, a totalitarian aspect to her clan: the absolute obedience shown to their leader, Meoran. When Ratha discovers fire (Red Tongue) as a source of power, she is forced by Meoran to flee her clan and becomes part of the Un-Named. Her sole protection among them is Bonechewer, who is different from the rest and becomes her mate. This unusual story, which portrays loyalty, courage, lonely exile, and conflict of values comes to a dramatic climax that has significance for us today who live with the threat of a force more powerful than fire.

*Bellow, Saul. *Mr. Sammler's Planet.* New York: Viking, 1970. 313pp. LC 76-58850. ISBN 0-670-49322-8. (o.p.) New York: Penguin, pap. ISBN 0-14-007317-5.

Artur Sammler, in his seventies and an escapee from the horrors of Nazi atrocities and the memory of having had to dig himself out of his own grave, theorizes about the possibility of finding a similar escape from the assaults of life in New York City, its muggings, crime, dirt, noise. Living with his bizarre daughter, Shula, also saved from death in Europe but somewhat deranged, perhaps the result of traumas suffered, is not possible, and living with his niece Margotte also has its drawbacks. The most important person to Sammler is his nephew Elya, by whose generosity Sammler and Shula are able to exist. But Elya's escape from the horrors of his own life—his son Wallace's irresponsible behavior and his daughter Angela's sexually promiscuous behavior— is by way of death. For our desire to find relief from the outrages of life in this decade, Bellow has made a metaphor of man's desire to go to the moon.

Benford, Gregory, and Eklund, Gordon. *If the Stars Are Gods.* New York: Ace, 1981. 224pp. (o.p.) New York: Bantam, pap. ISBN 0-553-27642-5.+

Expanded from a shorter Nebula-award-winning work, this is an episodic novel of the mystery of alien contact and the secrets of the cosmos. Sixty-nine years are covered in the startling life of Bradley Reynolds, scientist, explorer, and philosopher. He is sole survivor of the famed 1992 Martian expedition. Twenty-five years later he is called upon to establish contact with the aliens inhabiting a vast starship that appears near the moon. Finding only enigmas, Reynolds returns to earth and lives as an ascetic recluse in the desert. When he is called upon again some 35 years later, he achieves his destiny in a spiritual-metaphysical conclusion.

Bennett, Arnold. *The Old Wives' Tale.* Garden City, N.Y.: Doubleday, 1908. 612pp. (o.p.) New York: Penguin, pap. ISBN 0-14-018255-1.+

In this novel that takes place in the nineteenth century, Sophia and Constance Baines are sisters who are very unlike each other both in temperament and in terms of their goals. This difference keeps them apart most of their adult lives. Abandoning their family shop as soon as possible, Sophia, the rebellious one, elopes with Gerald Scales, a weak and unreliable man, to live in Paris, sometimes lavishly but eventually in impoverished circumstances; she finally becomes the owner and manager of a pension. Constance, remaining behind in England, marries quiet, unimaginative Samuel Povey, a clerk. The marriages of both sisters are failures. Constance does have a son, Cyril, upon whom she lavishes affection, but she gets little in return. In fact, he does not even return from a trip abroad to attend his mother's funeral at the novel's conclusion. This is a very human story of two sisters and the contrasts in their lives as girls, wives, and widows.

Berger, Thomas. *Little Big Man*. New York: Dial, 1964. 447pp. (o.p.) New York: Delacorte, 1979. ISBN 0-440-05165-7. (o.p.) New York: Amereon, ISBN 0-8488-0429-5. New York: Dell, pap. ISBN 0-440-34976-1.+

The author purports to write the story of Jack Crabb, adopted Cheyenne, gunfighter, buffalo hunter, and survivor of Custer's last stand, whom he has located at the Marville Center for Senior Citizens. In the few months before his death at the self-professed age of 111, Crabb recounts *his* version of life in the Old West.

Blos, Joan W. *A Gathering of Days: A New England Girl's Journal 1830-32*. New York: Scribner, 1979. 144pp. LC 79-16898. ISBN 0-684-16340-3. New York: Scribner, pap. ISBN 0-689-70750-9.

Written in diary form, this is a moving and vivid picture of life on a New Hampshire farm in the early 1830s. Catherine Hall, not quite 14, is responsible for looking after her family, which consists of herself, her widowed father, and a younger sister. We watch her go about her chores and share her friendship with Cassie Shipman, whose death is a poignant episode in the journal. There are descriptions of farm activities, days in the schoolroom, a wedding, and the help given by Cath and Cassie to a runaway slave. The integrity of the author's style, written in the cadence and the vocabulary of that historical period, adds much to the inherent goodness we see reflected in the lives of these people and the values they respected.

Bograd, Larry. *Los Alamos Light*. New York: Farrar, 1983. 168pp. LC 83-11638. ISBN 0-374-34656-9.

At 16 Maggie Chilton is upset and angry when her father, a physicist, tells her that they are leaving Boston to go to New Mexico. She must leave her friends and a happy time at a school where she has a favorite English teacher. That teacher encourages Maggie to look upon the move as an opportunity to discover new talents within herself. With names like Oppenheimer and Teller mentioned, the reader knows that the mysterious project at Los Alamos will result in the world's most awful weapon, but for Maggie it remains a mystery until the final test. Her personal gains are in establishing a friendship with an American Indian girl and a young Mexican man—and also in coming to understand and love the New Mexican surroundings.

*Borges, Jorge Luis. *The Aleph and Other Stories, 1933-1969*. Trans., from the Spanish by Norman Thomas de Giovanni. New York: Dutton, 1970. 286pp. (o.p.) New York: Dutton, pap. ISBN 0-525-47539-7.

This collection displays the full range of Borges's skill as a short-story writer. "The Circular Room," which looks at the dreams of man, and "The Immortals," a horror story about immortality, are particularly noteworthy. The volume contains an autobiographical essay plus notes on each story. Those notes are especially valuable in assisting the reader to understand the stories and the origins of Borges's ideas.

Borges, Jorge Luis, et al., eds. *The Book of Fantasy*. New York: Viking, 1988. 384pp. LC 88-40100. ISBN 0-670-82393-7. New York: Carroll & Graf, pap. ISBN 0-88184-656-2.

This collection of 81 stories ranges from very brief (two lines) to full length "short" stories. The selections come from all the literatures of the world—some predating the twentieth century. A number of the entries are by authors well known to readers of fantasy—Ballard, Bradbury, Poe, and Jacobs (for the unforgettable "Monkey's Paw"). Some stories require serious thought; some are just scary. The introduction by Ursula Le Guin is an added attraction.

Borland, Hal. *When the Legends Die*. Philadelphia, Pa.: Lippincott, 1963. 288pp. (o.p.) New York: Bantam, pap. ISBN 0-553-25738-2.

Thomas Black Bull, a Ute Indian, is being reared in the traditional Native American way when his parents are forced to flee from the world of the white man. After the death of his parents Tom is returned to the white world, where he suffers the disintegration of his native heritage and traditions as he experiences school, sheep herding, and rodeo life. Following a serious accident at a rodeo he returns to the mountains and is drawn back into his past.

Bosse, Malcolm. *Ganesh*. New York: Harper, 1981. 192pp. LC 80-2453. ISBN 0-690-04102-0.

Jeffrey Moore, called Ganesh after an elephant-headed god, leaves the country he is used to, India, to come to America. Living with his Aunt Betty, he now has to learn about his real heritage among Americans to whom Hinduism, yoga, and mantras are alien. In a conflict about whether the government can force his Aunt to vacate her house in order to make way for a new highway, Ganesh introduces his school friends to an Indian way of taking action.

Boulle, Pierre. *The Bridge Over the River Kwai*. Trans. from the French by Xan Fielding. New York: Vanguard, 1952. 224pp. ISBN 0-8149-0072-0. (o.p.) Repr. Mattituck, N.Y.: Amereon, ISBN 0-89190-571-5. New York: Bantam, pap. ISBN 0-553-24850-2.

In 1942 the Japanese military under the command of Col. Saito orders its British prisoners of war to construct a bridge over the 400-foot-wide River Kwai in the Siamese jungle. Complications arise when prisoner Col. Nicholson insists that officers not be treated like regular lower-class soldiers. Medical officer Clipton is much more humane, and this difference brings the two fellow prisoners into frequent conflict. When the bridge is finally completed, a British demolition team prepares to destroy it.

Boulle, Pierre. *Planet of the Apes*. Trans. from the French by Xan Fielding. New York: Vanguard, 1963. 246pp. LC 63-21843. ISBN 0-8149-0060-7. (o.p.) New York: Dutton, pap. ISBN 0-451-16016-9.+

Ulysse Mérou writes of his experiences on an unusual planet where the roles of humans and apes are reversed. Gorillas wear clothing and run businesses, while humans are caged in zoos and are the subjects of scientific experiments. In the year 2500 a vacationing couple cruising through space spot a bottle-encased message, retrieve it, and soon become absorbed in Mérou's tale.

Bowen, Elizabeth. *The Death of the Heart*. New York: Knopf, 1939. 418pp. ISBN 0-394-42172-8. (o.p.) New York: Penguin, pap. ISBN 0-14-018300-0.

Portia, an innocent young girl, is taken in by her half-brother and sister-in-law after the death of her parents. She had been the issue of a middle-age male fling and had grown up on the Continent, drifting aimlessly with her parents. Lacking sophistication and social graces, she is not welcome in her new home. To some, she is an innocent child; to others, particularly her sister-in-law, she is an observer and a judge of the behavior of the middle class. Portia learns the games of social survival as she matures. The author has drawn characters beautifully and has used an uncomplicated story line to tell this tale of British middle- and upper-class people.

Boyle, T. Coraghessan. *If the River Was Whiskey*. New York: Penguin, 1989. LC 89-29956. (o.p.) New York: Penguin, pap. ISBN 0-14-011950-7.

Boyle is a master story teller. In this varied collection of short stories he shows himself to be literate, satiric, timely, irreverent and wickedly humorous. "Sorry Fugu" is about a chef who learns how to get around a food critic whose review can destroy a restaurant; "Modern Love" is a response to the current fear of AIDS; "The Devil and Irv Cherniske" retells the danger of making a deal with Satan. The characters in the stories are generally not admirable but they are credible in their various sinful and human behaviors.

*Boyle, T. Coraghessan. *World's End*. New York: Viking, 1987. 414pp. LC 87-40023. LC 87-32827. ISBN 0-670-81489-X. New York: Penguin, pap. ISBN 0-14-029993-9.

Three families are entangled in a history of New York State that begins in the seventeenth century and continues into the twentieth. The Van Warts, Dutch settlers, are wealthy landowners and oppressive rulers; the Van Brunts, also Dutch, are tenant farmers and ill-treated by the patroons; the Mohawks are the Native Indians who have been robbed of their land. The novel swings back and forth not only in time periods but also in the lives of the three families. It is a novel filled with violence, loveless sex and easy seduction by drugs and drunkenness. Walter Van Brunt is the pivotal character whose father Truman may have been either a patriot or a traitor. An important event is the Peekskill riot of 1949 when local people, driven by bigotry and hatred, attack those who have come to a peace-oriented concert featuring Paul Robeson. This is a wild chronicle of betrayal and failure and a challenge to those who have read and appreciated William Faulkner.

Bradbury, Ray. *Fahrenheit 451*. New York: Simon & Schuster, 1967. 192pp. ISBN 0-671-23977-5. (o.p.) New York: Ballantine, pap. ISBN 0-345-34296-8.+

Bradbury writes of a grim future when human creativity is stifled and there is no freedom to read. Books are considered dangerous and are therefore used as fuel for fires, while television screens grow in size to encompass whole walls. Those who care about the riches to be found in books commit whole tomes to memory in order to preserve a literary tradition.

Bradbury, Ray. *The Illustrated Man*. Garden City, N.Y.: Doubleday, 1958. 251 pp. ISBN 0-385-05060-7. (o.p.) New York: Bantam, pap. ISBN 0-553-27449-X.+

Eighteen chapters are structured as separate science fiction stories, each focusing on a specific image viewed by a wanderer whose trail crosses that of a unique tattooed man. The diverse topics that are broached include rocket travel, the atomic bomb, racism, and religion.

Bradbury, Ray. *The Martian Chronicles*. Garden City, N.Y.: Doubleday, 1950. 222pp. LC 72-94171. ISBN 0-385-03862-3. (o.p.) Repr. New York: Doubleday, 1990. LC 58-8207. New York: Bantam, pap. ISBN 0-553-27822-3.+

Martians in the years A.D. 1999-2026 are upset by the unexpected appearance of citizens from the planet Earth who are fleeing full-scale war in their homeland. Bradbury dissects the inhumanity of technology on earth, where machines have become more important than the humans who created them.

Bradbury, Ray. *Something Wicked This Way Comes*. New York: Knopf, 1962. 215pp. LC 82-48732. ISBN 0-394-53041-1. New York: Bantam, pap. ISBN 0-553-28032-5.

We read here of the loss of innocence, the recognition of evil, the bond between generations, and the purely fantastic. These forces enter Green

Town, Illinois, on the wheels of Cooger and Dark's Pandemonium Shadow Show. Will Halloway and Jim Nightshade, two 13-year-olds, explore the sinister carnival for excitement, which becomes desperation as the forces of the dark threaten to engulf them. Bradbury's gentle humanism and lyric style serve this fantasy well.

Bradford, Richard. *Red Sky at Morning*. New York: Harper, 1968. 256pp. LC 68-11272. ISBN 0-397-00549-0. (o.p.) Repr. New York: Harper, 1986. LC 86-45309. ISBN 0-06-091361-4.

Joshua Arnold and his mother move to their summer home in Corazon Sagrado, New Mexico, when the father joins the Navy during World War II. Josh copes with the Mexican and Anglo customs and is concerned with his mother's drinking. When his father dies in the war, he takes responsibility for his mother, his own life, and his father's business.

Bridgers, Sue Ellen. *Home Before Dark*. New York: Knopf, 1976. 176pp. LC 76-8661. ISBN 0-394-83299-X. (o.p.) New York: Bantam, pap. ISBN 0-553-26432-X.+

Stella Mae Willis has always lived on the road, in one battered car after another, as she and her family follow the crops to eke out a living. When Stella is 14 her father takes the family back to his family home, a tobacco farm in North Carolina. Stella knows immediately that she wants to stay here forever, but her mother, who has never known any life except that of a migrant, is unhappy staying in one place. The tragic events that dog the life of the Willis family continue to pursue them, but a chance for happiness appears—if they are able to take it up.

Bridgers, Sue Ellen. *Permanent Connections*. New York: Harper, 1987. LC 86-45491. ISBN 0-06-020711-6. New York: Harper, pap. 0-06-447020-2.

In trouble in school in New Jersey and escaping his pain with drugs, sullen Rob Dickson has no choice but to stay on the North Carolina family farm to help when his Uncle Fairlee breaks his leg. Irritable Grandpa, agoraphobic Aunt Coralee and assorted mountain folk offer no help to troubled Rob. Only Ellery, another unhappy newcomer, connects with Rob but her own troubles interfere with the close relationship that develops. Rob escapes to drugs again, but a court date and family crisis force him to begin to understand that his behavior could destroy everyone around him.

*Brooks, Terry. *The Sword of Shannara*. New York, Ballantine, 1977. LC 76-53925. ISBN 0-345-24804-X. (o.p.) Repr. New York, Ballantine, 1991. 736pp. LC 90-43727. ISBN 0-345-37143-7. New York: Ballantine, pap. ISBN 0-345-31425-5.

This is an epic, Tolkien-like evaluation of good versus evil. Shea Ohmsford, a half-elfin youth, is slowly drawn into a universe-shaking war against the forces of Darkness led by the horrible Warlock Lord. Shea, descendant of a noble race, is the only being alive who can control the Sword of Shannara, the sole weapon that can prevail against the spreading evil. Trolls, wizards, goblins, and all manner of weird creatures participate in Shea's journey, on which he is accompanied by his intrepid allies. This action-packed and violent novel is a prime example of the "sword and sorcery" genre.

*Brookner, Anita. *Brief Lives*. New York: Random, 1991. 260pp. LC 90-38904. ISBN 394-58548-8.

One critic compared this writer to Jane Austen for her perceptions about the personalities of the characters in her novels. Brookner's narrator in this book is Fay Langdon, longtime friend of Julia Morton whose husband Charles and Fay's husband Owen are business partners. It is this connection more than any real affection Fay has for Julia that maintains the friendship. When Owen dies Julia's husband approaches Fay in search of an intimate relationship which she welcomes. The novel examines the loneliness of unattached women who, for the most part, seem to have no commitment to anything outside of their personal lives. Even as they age they seem unable to find pleasure in the company of other lonely women.

Brown, Dee. *Creek Mary's Blood*. New York: Holt, 1980. 401pp. LC 79-9060. ISBN 0-03-044281-8. (o.p.) New York: Pocket, pap. ISBN 0-317-56791-8.

Through the words and memories of Dane, grandson of Creek Mary (or Akusa Amayi), we follow the history of the men, children, and grandchildren in the life of that indomitable exemplar of the American Indian. The action—and there is plenty of it—takes place in the period after the Revolutionary War and continues through the nineteenth century. The customs, rituals, courting, fighting, and celebrating are all described in detail. One of the most painful sections of the book depicts the forced removal west of the Mississippi of Indian tribes. This journey was called the Trail of Tears because so many Indians died in the exodus. The greed of the white man for land—to build roads, to look for gold, to dig for coal—was always a reason to drive various tribes into narrower and narrower confines, where their ability to find food, and thus to exist, was threatened. The relationships among the various tribes—Creek, Cheyenne, Cherokee, and others—is of great interest. Many famous names are recalled, among them Tecumseh, Andrew Jackson, Teddy Roosevelt, and the great chiefs Crazy Horse and Sitting Bull.

Brown, Harry. *A Walk in the Sun*. Mattituck, N.Y.: Amereon. 192pp. ISBN 0-88411-075-3. Repr. New York: A M S, LC 83-45721. ISBN 0-404-20045-1. New York: Carroll & Graf, pap. ISBN 0-88184-117-X.

This is a nearly perfect short novel about World War II. A platoon of soldiers lands on a beach in Italy. After their lieutenant and sergeant are killed, the men know only that they are supposed to take a farmhouse six miles up the road. Keeping to the limited objective, the story conveys the uncertainty felt by the courage of the common footsoldier in the face of unknown odds.

*Brunner, John. *Stand on Zanzibar*. Garden City, N.Y.: Doubleday, 1968. 586pp. (o.p.) Repr. Cambridge, Mass.: Bentley, 1979. ISBN 0-8376-0438-9. New York: Ballantine, pap. ISBN 0-345-34787-0.

Extrapolating from current politics, social and sexual mores, the communications revolution, the use of computers, brainwashing, drug use, psychology, philosophy, and sociology, Brunner has fashioned a mammoth work that is an intricate tapestry depicting a possible future. The dozens of characters interspersed in a complex fashion make the novel difficult to read but well worth the effort. Brunner's brand of cynicism and radical social commentary may not appeal to the taste of all readers, but in the time that has elapsed since the publication of the book, we have seen changes that bear startling similarities to several of Brunner's predictions.

Buchan, John. *The Thirty-nine Steps*. New York: Doran, 1915. 231pp. LC 89-46194. (o.p.) New York: Penguin, 1991. 128pp. pap. ISBN 0-14-001130-7.+

A bored, well-to-do Englishman, Richard Hannay, returns home to England after growing up in South Africa. Drifting between his club and the sights of London, he is drawn into the confidences of a secret agent in the thick of espionage. The agent is murdered in Hannay's apartment and Richard finds himself on the run from Scotland Yard and the cult of the "Black Stone."

Buck, Pearl S. *The Good Earth*. New York: Day, 1931. (o.p.) 375pp. Repr. New York: Crowell. ISBN 0-381-98033-2. (o.p.) Repr. Cutchogue, N.Y.: Buccaneer Bks., 1981. 421pp. ISBN 0-89966-299-4. New York: Oxford Univ. Press, pap. ISBN 0-19-581035-X.+

The saga of Wang Lung, his rise from the peasantry to membership in the land-owning class, is a tale of life in prerevolutionary China. In his quest for land, Lung leaves behind tradition, religion, and family. The cycle of life and nature's authority over Wang Lung's financial success show that no one ever really owns the land. The next generation comes upon the scene without respect for the land, and chooses power and wealth as its gods.

Burdick, Eugene, and Wheeler, Harvey. *Fail-Safe*. New York: McGraw-Hill, 1962. 286pp. ISBN 0-07-008927-2. (o.p.) New York: Dell, pap. ISBN 0-440-12459-X.

With mounting tension this gripping thriller tells of a possible nuclear holocaust. An American attack squadron is accidentally and irretrievably launched to obliterate Moscow. The frantic U.S. president and the Russian premier begin a dramatic hotline race against time to halt the bombers' flight and prevent disaster. The crisis is seen through the eyes of several characters, and their differing perceptions provide an effective story-telling technique. *Fail-Safe* is chilling in its credibility at this time of nuclear weaponry and international tension.

*Burgess, Anthony. *A Clockwork Orange*. New York: Norton, 1963. 184pp. ISBN 0-393-02439-3. New York: Ballantine, pap. ISBN 0-345-35443-5.

In this near-future satire, which is often compared to Orwell's *Nineteen Eighty-four*, the author creates a violence-dominated teenage society where inhabitants speak a language that is a mixture of Russian and Anglo-Saxon slang. Alex, the central character, is a delinquent facing reform treatment, which consists of viewing violence and rape to the point of inducing nausea in the viewer. As a result of these draconian measures, Alex is transformed into an automaton. The book continues to stir controversy and is unforgettable.

Burnford, Sheila. *The Incredible Journey*. Boston: Little, 1960. 145pp. ISBN 0-316-11714-5. Repr. New York: Bantam, 1990. ISBN 0-553-05874-6. Repr. Mattituck, N.Y.: Amereon, ISBN 0-88411-099-0. New York: Bantam, pap. ISBN 0-553-10220-6.

A half-blind English bull terrier, a sprightly yellow Labrador retriever, and a feisty Siamese cat have resided for eight months with a friend of their owners, who are away on a trip. Then their temporary caretaker leaves them behind in order to take a short vacation. The lonely trio decides to tackle the harsh 250-mile hike across the Canadian wilderness in search of home, despite the human and wild obstacles the group will encounter.

Burns, Olive Ann. *Cold Sassy Tree*. New York: Ticknor & Fields, 1984. 392pp. LC 84-8570. ISBN 0-89919-309-9. New York: Dell (Laurel), 1986. ISBN 0-440-51442-8.

Young Will Tweedy lives in a small Georgia town called Cold Sassy in the early 1900s. He is hard working (when pushed) because he has chores to do at home and work to do at his Grandpa Blakeslee's store. That still leaves him time to plan practical jokes with his pals and to overhear family dramas. The biggest drama begins when Grandpa, only three weeks after the death of his wife whom he had dearly loved, marries Miss Love Simpson—young enough to be his daughter. Miss Love has to face not only the town gossip, but also rejection from Will's Mother and Grandpa's other daughter. The story has humor, excitement, and realistic family confrontations.

*Cain, James M. *The Postman Always Rings Twice*. New York: Knopf, 1934. 188pp. (o.p.) Repr. Laurel, N.Y.: Lightyear, 1981. 457pp. ISBN 0-89968-234-0. New York: Random, pap. ISBN 0-679-72325-0.

Cora is a young and discontented wife, and Frank Chambers is a drifter who has taken temporary employment in a roadside stand owned by

Cora and her husband, whom the two plot to kill. When suspicion rightly falls upon the pair, a clever lawyer manipulates matters to engineer their acquittal. Retribution comes the second time around, however, when Frank is convicted of a crime he has not, in fact, committed. This book is an example of the realistic, hard-boiled fiction that was written in the 1930s.

Camus, Albert. *The Plague.* Trans. from the French by Stuart Gilbert. New York: Knopf, 1948. 278pp. LC 90-50477. ISBN 0-394-44061-7. New York: Random, pap. ISBN 0-679-72021-9.+

Using an epidemic of bubonic plague in an Algerian city as a symbol for the absurdity of man's condition, Albert Camus has in this novel articulated his firm belief in mankind's heroism in struggling against the ultimate futility of life. The plague makes everyone in the city intensely aware both of mortality and the fact that cooperation is the only logical consolation anyone will find in the face of certain death. Though each character, from doctor to priest, represents some aspect of mankind's attempts to deal with the absurd, none is a cardboard figure. The reader cares what happens to the men depicted here. One takes pleasure in the moments of deep human connection that leave us with the conviction that men are, on the whole, admirable.

Camus, Albert. *The Stranger.* Trans. from the French by Stuart Gilbert. New York: Knopf, 1946. 154pp. LC 83-48885. ISBN 0-394-53305-4. New York: Random, pap. ISBN 0-394-70002-3.+

Meursault, an ordinary little clerk living in Algiers, leads a quiet and unemotional life. He commits a senseless murder and is convicted, his lack of emotion toward his mother's death weighing against him. As he contemplates his execution, he considers the value of life and is on the verge of exhibiting feeling.

Canfield (Fisher), Dorothy. *The Bent Twig.* Cutchogue, N.Y.: Buccaneer, 1915. 334pp. ISBN 0-89966-343-5.

Growing up in an unconventional but scholarly family in the Midwest, Sylvia Marshall, daughter of a poor university professor, develops a taste for the riches of life, a taste that reflects the way of life of her aunt. When the opportunity arises to pursue her dreams, she discovers the shallowness of her goals.

Canin, Ethan. *Emperor of the Air*. Boston: Houghton, 1988. 190pp. LC 87-22540. ISBN 0-395-42976-5.

Nine stories present a variety of portrayals that describe how lives are led by characters ranging from young people to elderly ailing adults. In "Emperor of the Air" a 69-year-old man with a sick heart tries to save his 200-year-old elm tree whose heart may be destroyed by red ants. "American Beauty" illustrates differences in two brothers, one of whom is constantly breaking laws and the other whose moral base is stronger. "Where We Are Now" is about a marriage between a woman seeking to have more materially while her husband is content with less. Canin's descriptions of how families survive—or disintegrate—are unforgettable.

Capote, Truman. *The Grass Harp*. New York: Random, 1951. 181pp. (o.p.) *The Grass Harp and A Tree of Night and Other Stories*. New York: Dutton, pap. ISBN 0-451-16177-7.+

After the death of his parents, Collin goes to live with his two aunts, Verna and Dolly. The former is wealthy and practical, the latter, whimsical and romantic. Dolly produces a cure for dropsy that she bottles and sells through the mail. Verna is ready to take over the operation and realize a large profit. To avoid this scheme, Collin, Dolly, and Catherine, a servant, go off to live in a treehouse, where they are joined by other eccentric characters. When Dolly dies, Collin is ready for his independence, having learned a valuable lesson about love and nonconformity.

Caputo, Philip. *Horn of Africa*. New York: Holt, 1980. 528pp. LC 79-27513. ISBN 0-03-042136-5. (o.p.) New York: Dell, pap. ISBN 0-440-33675-9.

The author, with his own experiences as a Marine and a captive of Palestinian guerrillas, writes with authenticity of the terrible reality of war and the hunger for power that triggers war. Three men, two

Americans and one Englishman, embark on a mission as mercenaries in Africa, involving gun-running and clandestine warfare. Their capacity for violence is related to events and drives in their own lives. Nordstrand, the most amoral of them, is a character that is indelibly drawn as are the horrible experiences lived through in desert treks. This author has been compared to Joseph Conrad and Graham Greene in his exploration of the deepest recesses of man's soul. There are echoes of the brutalities described here in reports of adventurers today who fight under any flag or train even terrorists in order to gain wealth or power.

Carr, J.L. *A Month in the Country.* Chicago, Ill.: Academy, 1984. 111pp. ISBN 0-89733-124-9.

This small gem of a novel celebrates art and those who care about it. Birkin, a British veteran of World War I, is hired to restore a painting in the local church. His living quarters are minimal and he depends on the people of the town for much of his nourishment. When he meets the wife of the Reverend Keach there is a feeling of rapport which becomes, at the end, a painful case of what might have been.

Carter, Alden R. *Up Country.* New York: Putnam, 1989. 224pp. ISBN 0-399-21583-2. New York: Scholastic, pap. ISBN 0-590-43638-4.

Feeling trapped in a world made undesirable by an alcoholic and promiscuous mother, 16-year-old, straight-A student Carl Staggers copes by subscribing to his created "Plan" which will ultimately culminate in a secure middle class lifestyle—characteristically comprising a career in engineering, a suburban home, a wife, and a BMW. In the meantime, he repairs stolen stereos for a teen gang as a means to finance his college education—the starting point of the "Plan." Both the dreams and the productive repair business are shattered when his mother is arrested in a drunken hit-and-run accident. Subsequently, Carl is sent to live with somewhat unfamiliar relatives in the country after the court orders his mother to a recovery program. In his new environment, he begins to address his problems honestly and candidly and gain fresh new insights on love, friendship, family, and the painful predicament of children who have alcoholic parents.

*Cary, Joyce. *The Horse's Mouth.* New York: Harper, 1950. 368pp. LC 90-55051. ISBN 0-06-092021-1. New York: Harper, pap. ISBN 0-06-080046-1.

The concluding novel of Cary's trilogy, of which *Herself Surprised* and *To Be A Pilgrim* are the first two parts, can stand alone as a tale of Gulley

Jimson's old age. Jimson is an artist newly released from prison. At 67, he has finally gained some critical acclaim. His aspirations to paint and live comfortably off the fruits of his achievements are thwarted, however, by his own desire to change artistically and by his accidental killing of a former model, Sara Monday. Gulley is a charming and humorous hero, constantly spouting his ideas on art and London and vividly describing the people around him. The story is lively, but the language, the themes of aging, and references to William Blake's poetry make this a serious novel for the mature reader.

Cary, Joyce. *Mister Johnson*. New York: New Directions, 1989. 228pp. pap. LC 88-35710. ISBN 0-8812-1174-6.

Johnson, a black native, is a clerk in the British colonial service in Africa. He lives in the reflected glory of working for the government and enjoys a feeling of importance. He spends money he does not have, gives parties that he cannot afford and never sees life as it really is. His judgment is unreliable and leads him to commit a crime that will bring about a final punishment. Cary has written this out of his own experiences in the British colonial service in Nigeria.

*Casey, John. *Spartina*. New York: Knopf, 1989. 384pp. ISBN 0-394-50098-9. New York: Avon, pap. 1990. ISBN 0-380-79104-4.

Dick Pierce is an angry man because he has seen property belonging to his family in his fishing village in Rhode Island bought up by affluent people for their summer homes. He works hard, not really making enough for his family, going out for crabs, lobsters, and swordfish. Pierce's relationship with is wife and his two sons is uneasy and his love for the boat he is building (Spartina—named for the tough grass that thrives on salt in marshy water) crowds out all other considerations. His discontent and need for money lead him to dangerous disregard for the law and into a passionate affair with Elsie Buttrick, an unconventional and independent young woman. A stunning episode in the novel is Pierce's exposing his new boat to the force of a violent hurricane because there is no safe harbor for it. Frank sexuality in Dick and Elsie's affair makes this a book for the mature reader.

Cassedy, Sylvia. *Behind the Attic Wall*. New York: Harper, 1983. 315pp. LC 82-45922. ISBN 0-690-04336-8. New York: Avon, pap. ISBN 0-380-69843-9.

Maggie Turner, orphaned early in life, has been in any number of foster homes from which she has either run away or in which she has deliberately made herself unloved by her behavior. She is finally sent to live with two elderly great-aunts in a home that looks and feels like an institution. The aunts are most interested in rules for deportment and nutrition and are constantly appalled by Maggie's actions. There is, however, another relative, Uncle Morris, whose strange conversation and easy manner begin to break down Maggie's feelings of distrust. But it is a strange phenomenon of hearing certain voices that leads Maggie to a place behind the attic wall and some dolls that become a substitute family for her.

Cather, Willa. *My Antonia*. Boston: Houghton, 1954. 272pp. ISBN 0-395-07514-9. (o.p.) Boston: Houghton, pap. ISBN 0-395-08356-7.

Told by Jim Burden, a New York lawyer recalling his boyhood in Nebraska, the story concerns Antonia Shimerda, who came with her family from Bohemia to settle on the prairies of Nebraska. The difficulties related to pioneering and the integration of immigrants into new culture are clearly portrayed.

Chase, Joan. *During the Reign of the Queen of Persia*. New York: Harper, 1983. 224p. LC 82-48680. ISBN 0-06-015136-6. (o.p.) New York: Ballantine, pap. ISBN 0-345-31525-1.

This story follows the lives of three generations of women on a farm in northern Ohio in the 1950s. We follow the women's courtships, the tyranny of a selfish matriarch, Gram (referred to as the Queen of Persia), and the approaching death of one of the sisters in the family. Although their settings are different, this story has been compared to *A Tree Grows in Brooklyn* because of its portrayal of family drama and relationships.

Childress, Alice. *A Hero Ain't Nothin' But a Sandwich*. New York: Putnam, 1973. 100pp. LC 73-82035. ISBN 0-698-20278-3. New York: Avon, pap. ISBN 0-380-00132-2.

At the age of 13 Benjie Johnson is hooked on "horse." He believes that he can break the habit whenever he is ready. When two of Benjie's teachers realize that he is on drugs, they report him to the principal of the school. Then begins his seesaw battle to break his addiction. Using Black English, the author draws a picture of the urban drug scene.

Christie, Agatha. *And Then There Were None*. New York: Dodd, 1940. 264pp. (o.p.) Repr. New York: Putnam, 1985. 218pp. ISBN 0-399-15018-8. New York: Berkley, pap. ISBN 0-425-12958-6.+

Ten individuals are abducted and taken to a secluded island off the coast of England as guests or employees of an unseen host. One by one they are murdered to the tune of an old nursery rhyme about ten little Indians while a taped voice reminds them of some crime in their past. Since the island is inaccessible, it is clear that the murderer is one of them—but which one?

Christie, Agatha. *Murder on the Orient Express*. New York: Dodd, 1960. 254pp. ISBN 0-396-05777-2. (o.p.) Repr. New York: Putnam, 1981. ISBN 0-396-08575-X. New York: Harper, pap. ISBN 0-06-100274-7.+

On a train traveling from Istanbul to Calais a man is murdered. The famous detective Hercule Poirot is there to unravel the mystery. There are several persons aboard the train who have a strong enough motivation to have committed the crime, as is usually the case in Christie's novels. Also as usual, the ending is a stunning surprise.

Clark, Walter Van Tilburg. *The Ox-bow Incident*. Magnolia, Mass.: Peter Smith. ISBN 0-8446-0060-1. New York: Dutton, pap. ISBN 0-451-52386-5.+

Rustlers are systematically stealing cattle near Bridger's Gulch, Nevada, in the late 1800s. After a cattleman is killed, an illegal posse is formed to apprehend the criminals. In a remote valley they surprise three men, hold a makeshift trial, and hang the three. Soon afterward it is discovered that the wrong men have been punished. This is a western with psychological insight.

Clarke, Arthur C. *Childhood's End*. San Diego, Ca.: Harcourt, 1963. 216pp. LC 53-10419. ISBN 0-15-117205-6. New York: Ballantine, pap. ISBN 0-345-34795-1.

The Overlords come to earth to aid in the technological progress and peace-keeping abilities of humans, but are unwilling to reveal their own purpose or even their appearance. After decades of nurturing the planet, the Overlords' moment of revelation comes. Their physical form shakes the foundation of Christian beliefs. Despite this, their work continues, and humankind is helped to take the next step in its metaphysical destiny.

Clarke, Arthur C. *Rendezvous with Rama*. New York: Bantam, pap. ISBN 0-553-28789-3.

A vast ship approaches earth, neither sending nor responding to signals. Bill Norton leads an exploration party to Rama to answer questions raised by the ship's presence. Clarke, one of the prime exponents of "hard" science fiction, which extrapolates from known scientific principles and possibilities, sets this story in the year 2130 to consider humankind's reaction to the existence of alien intelligence.

Clarke, Arthur C. *The Sentinel*. New York: Berkley, 1983. 303pp. ISBN 0-425-06183-3. (o.p.) New York: Berkley, pap. ISBN 0-425-09389-1.

This collection of nine science fiction stories represents a sampling of some of Clarke's best. Each story is preceded by an informal and informative introduction by the author telling when it was first written and when it appeared and, in some cases, how it led to a longer work such as *2001* or *Childhood's End*. Some of the stories included are "Breaking Strain," in which tension builds up between two men in a space ship as oxygen fails and only one man can be allowed to continue the journey; "Wind from the Sun," which describes a race among sun yachts; "A Meeting with Medusa," which tells of an amazing discovery of a form of life on Jupiter. Clarke's style makes for credibility so that we truly feel that these are *science* fiction and not fantasy.

Cleaver, Vera and Bill. *Where the Lilies Bloom*. Philadelphia, Pa.: Lippincott, 1969. 176pp. LC 75-82402. ISBN 0-397-31111-7. New York: Trophy, pap. ISBN 0-06-447005-9.

On his deathbed Roy Luther gave a number of charges to his daughter, Mary Call. She was not to give him a formal funeral or to tell anyone that he was dead. At all costs she was to keep the family together and out of the county's hands. Furthermore, she was not to allow their neighbor, Kiser Pease, to marry her sister, Devola, whom Roy Luther believed to be a bit retarded. At 14 years of age Mary Call found herself at the head of a family with a number of injunctions to follow, the natural elements to fight, and a living to earn as a wildcrafter in the mountains of North Carolina.

*Coetzee, J.M. *Foe*. New York: Penguin, 1987. LC 86-40267. ISBN 0-670-81398-2. (o.p.) New York: Penguin, pap. 1988. ISBN 0-14-009623-X.

The well-known story of Robinson Crusoe is here imaginatively extended with Susan Barton (later calling herself Mrs. Crusoe) as the heroine. Cast overboard by mutineers, she lands on Crusoe's island where she lives for a year with him and his mute slave, Friday. They are rescued, but Crusoe dies aboard ship and only Susan and Friday reach England. The novel then continues with Susan's vain efforts to get a writer, Mr. Foe, to write the story of Crusoe's island. Foe's opposition to so "dull" a story becomes Coetzee's philosophical explanation of how writers are inspired to use ideas, intermingling truth with an adornment thereof.

Coetzee, J.M. *The Life and Times of Michael K*. New York: Viking, 1985. 192pp. pap. LC 83-47860. ISBN 0-14-007448-1.

Born with a harelip and brought up in an uncaring orphanage, Michael K. struggles through a desperate life in South Africa. When his sick mother persuades him to bring her back to her homeland, he must endure not only the terrible journey, pulling her in a cart he has made, but also risk the dangers of military checkpoints since he does not have the necessary permits. His undying attachment is to the land, but he is not allowed to remain the gardener he wishes to be. The details of Michael's suffering in camps, hospitals, and labor gangs are harrowing and underscore a courage that never forsakes him.

Cole, Brock. *Celine*. New York: Farrar, 1989. 216pp. LC 89-45614. ISBN 0-374-31234-6. New York: Farrar, pap. ISBN 0-374-41082-8.

Sixteen-year-old artist Celine Morienval lives in an awkward situation with her new 22-year-old stepmother, Catherine, while her father is away one a European lecture tour. Her spirited life fluctuates between innocence and maturity and is populated by an array of interesting characters who unknowingly help shape her adolescent philosophy of life. Most important of these is seven-year-old Jake, a neighbor of divorce, whom she is forced to babysit. It is through her close relationship with him that they both grow, gaining self-actualization and exploring the ironies of life.

*Colegate, Isabel. *The Shooting Party*. New York: Viking, 1980. 195pp. LC 80-54194. ISBN 0-670-64064-6. (o.p.) New York: Penguin, pap. ISBN 0-14-014730-6.+

The time is October 1913, the place an estate in Oxfordshire where Sir Randolph Nettleby and his wife are hosting the biggest shoot of the season. Brought together are the privileged in pursuit of pleasure. For these guests shooting is a special ritual with the shooters, gamekeepers, beaters, and servants all playing specific roles, and the sport is marvelously and meticulously described. Woven through the story are the portrayals of the gentry, the allusions to romantic and adulterous affairs, the relationship between the classes, and the feeling of the vast changes soon to overtake the Edwardian period. The rising tension that accompanies the final hours of the shooting on this day explodes into unexpected tragedy.

Collier, James Lincoln, and Collier, Christopher. *My Brother Sam Is Dead*. New York: Four Winds, 1974. 251pp. LC 74-8350. ISBN 0-590-07339-7. (o.p.) New York: Four Winds, 1984. 224pp. LC 84-28787. ISBN 0-02-722980-7. New York: Scholastic, pap. ISBN 0-590-42792-X.

In 1775 the Meeker family lived in Redding, Connecticut, a Tory community. Sam, the eldest son, allied himself with the Patriots. The youngest son, Tim, watched a rift in the family grow because of his brother's decision. Before the war was over the Meeker family had suffered at the hands of both the British and the Patriots.

Condon, Richard. *The Manchurian Candidate*. New York: Random, 1959. 320pp. Repr. New York: McGraw-Hill, 1991. 320pp. LC 91-12801. ISBN 1-56287-020-3. New York: Jove, pap. ISBN 0-515-09441-2.

Raymond Shaw, a Korean War hero, is brainwashed and programmed by enemy agents to effect a political assassination. His stepfather, a politician, is on the move and is being manipulated by Shaw's mother. The F.B.I. attempts to discover the key to Shaw's actions and to stop the assassination.

Conford, Ellen. *The Alfred G. Graebner Memorial High School Handbook of Rules and Regulations.* Boston: Little, 1976. 220pp. ISBN 0-316-15293-5.

Through the eyes of Julie Howe and her circle of friends we share the problems marking the daily life of high school students. Typical of the experiences are a schedule with three classes of Home Ec, lunch at third period, gym as a first-period class, and six courses under the top-ranking bores in the school. The complaints are immediately recognizable to the high school student anywhere, even though there may be some exaggeration for the sake of humor.

Connell, Evan S. *Mrs. Bridge.* Berkeley, Ca.: North Point Press, 1981. 256pp. LC 81-81514. ISBN 0-86547-056-1.

India Bridge is a country club matron in Kansas City. Her husband, a successful lawyer, is seldom home so Mrs. Bridge copes—not too well—with her children, who are very different from one another. Ruth, the eldest, keeps aloof; Douglas, the youngest, is mostly off on his own projects and not interested in the fine rules of behavior that Mrs. Bridge finds essential. She seems able to communicate most easily with Carolyn, the middle child. We follow the family as the children grow. Mrs. Bridge, eager to be a proper upper-middle-class wife and mother, finds no happiness despite her affluence and good intentions. As one reviewer described it, this is a painfully sad and very touching "portrait of a lost lady."

Conrad, Joseph. *Lord Jim.* New York: Doubleday, 1900. 417pp. LC 44-22843. ISBN 0-385-04265-5. (o.p.) Repr. New York: Knopf, 1992. ISBN 0-679-40544-5. New York: Penguin, pap. ISBN 0-14-043169-1.+

Jim is an outcast and a wanderer. As chief mate aboard an old steamer he is disgraced when he abandons ship with the crew, deserting the passengers, although the ship does not go down as he thought it would.

Searching for ways to overcome his self-hatred, he settles in Patusan, becomes a veritable god to the Malay natives, and regains some personal honor.

Cooper, J. California. *Family*. New York: Doubleday, 1991. 231pp. LC 90-36996. ISBN 0-385-41171-5. New York: Doubleday, pap. ISBN 0-385-41172-3.

Clora is a slave in pre-Civil War days. Regarded as available property, she is used sexually by the master and gives birth to several children, four of whom survive. When Clora alone dies as a result of an attempt to kill her children and herself, she continues to watch over them like a guardian spirit. Always is the name of the youngest child, who, in turn, produces offspring fathered by the Young Master. The family becomes the source of four generations that are interracial because white fathers have sired children who could pass as white. The descendants in various parts of the world achieve success and Clora thinks of them as part of some universal human family. The novel shows the brutality and inhuman face of slavery, but it is also a testament to the courage and endurance of those who lived it.

Cooper, Susan. *Seaward*. New York: Macmillan, 1983. 167pp. LC 83-7055. ISBN 0-689-50275-3. New York: Macmillan, pap. LC 86-23234. ISBN 0-02-042190-7.

West and Cally have both experienced the loss of family and, strangers to each other from two different countries, they meet in a world that is mysterious. They are in danger from a powerful figure, Lady Taranis, but are befriended by her counterpart, Lugan, from time to time. The two young people must overcome fear through their own courageous hearts, aided by the faith instilled in them by their parents, whom they are trying to reach as they travel seaward. In addition to these four main characters there are two others who are unforgettable: Ryan, who helps Cally escape from the Stonecutter, and Peth, an alien creature who is as endearing as E.T.

Cormier, Robert. *After the First Death*. New York: Random, 1979. 233pp. LC 78-11770. ISBN 0-394-94122-5. New York: Dell, pap. ISBN 0-440-20835-1.

A busload of children is hijacked by a band of terrorists whose demands include the exposure of a military brainwashing project. The narrative line moves from the teenage terrorist Milo to Kate the bus driver and the involvement of Ben, whose father is the head of the military operation, in this confrontation. The conclusion has a shocking twist.

Cormier, Robert. *The Chocolate War.* New York: Pantheon, 1974. 272pp. LC 73-15109. ISBN 0-394-82805-4. New York: Dell, pap. ISBN 0-440-94459-7.

In the Trinity School for Boys the environment is completely dominated by an underground gang, the Vigils. During a chocolate candy sale Brother Leon, the acting headmaster of the school, defers to the Vigils, who reign with terror in the school. Jerry Renault is first a pawn for the Vigils' evil deeds and finally their victim. The readers of *Lord of the Flies* will appreciate this, another story that debates good and evil.

Cormier, Robert. *I Am the Cheese.* New York: Pantheon, 1977. 224pp. LC 76-55948. ISBN 0-394-83462-3. New York: Dell, pap. ISBN 0-440-94060-5.

In a compellingly mysterious journey, Adam finds himself pedaling furiously on an old-fashioned bike, trying to get from Massachusetts to Vermont. He is not sure how much of the journey is real, for he is searching through snatches of memories to try to find a key to his past. He remembers a happy childhood that was jarred from time to time by a nagging mystery involving his father. He struggles to recall some terrible truth that is just outside his consciousness but that must not be remembered if he is to survive. The shattering climax leaves the reader wondering what is reality and what is illusion.

Cozzens, James Gould. *The Just and the Unjust.* San Diego, Ca.: Harcourt, 1942. 434pp. LC 42-17992. ISBN 0-15-146577-0. (o.p.) San Diego, Ca.: Harcourt, pap. ISBN 0-15-646578-7.

As we follow the day-by-day events in a murder trial being held in a small Eastern city, we get to know much about the life of lawyers and the ambiguities of the law. Abner Coates, assistant district attorney and descendant of a family of lawyers, works with and admires District Attorney Martin Bunting, whom Coates may succeed in office if he decides to run. The techniques used by both prosecuting and defending attorneys, the competitiveness that extends to local politics, the range of cases that fall to the responsibility of a district attorney to prosecute—from simple infractions of the law to a community-upsetting indictment against a high school teacher on a morals charge—are the major emphases of the novel. There are also cameo portraits of the town inhabitants and a mild romance between Abner and Bonnie Drummond.

Craven, Margaret. *I Heard the Owl Call My Name.* Garden City, N.Y.: Doubleday, 1973. 166pp. LC 73-10800. ISBN 0-385-02586-6. (o.p.) Repr. Cutchogue, N.Y.: Buccaneer Bks., 1991. 250pp. ISBN 0-89966-854-2. New York: Dell, pap. ISBN 0-440-34369-0.

When Mark Brian's Bishop learns that the young priest is dying of a terminal illness, he assigns Mark to an outpost in British Columbia with the Kwakiutl Indians. Through his experience among these people, Mark comes to an understanding and an acceptance of death as a normal part of one's existence. When he knows that the owl has called his name, he faces the reality of death without fear.

Craven, Margaret. *Walk Gently This Good Earth.* New York: Dell, 1981. 192pp. pap. ISBN 0-440-39484-8.

Against a background of the Pacific Northwest and Montana, this family chronicle covers the years from the 1920s to the present. Judge Westcott, helped by a loving housekeeper, Maria, brings up his four children and an adopted son, Neal, to respect the values of their pioneer forebears. The family lives through the strictures of the Depression and World War II, during which Neal serves in the military. He returns to marry Cathy Westcott, and they continue to instill in their children those same values that the judge had handed down to them.

Crichton, Michael. *The Andromeda Strain.* New York: Knopf, 1969. 295pp. LC 69-14731. ISBN 0-394-41525-6. New York: Dell, pap. ISBN 0-440-10199-9.

In these days of interplanetary exploration, this tale of the world's first space-age biological emergency may seem uncomfortably believable. When a contaminated space capsule drops to earth in a small Nevada town and all the town's residents suddenly die, four American scientists gather at an underground laboratory of Project Wildfire to search frantically for an antidote to the threat of a world-wide epidemic.

Crichton, Michael. *The Great Train Robbery*. New York: Knopf, 1975. 288pp. ISBN 0-394-49401-6. (o.p.) New York: Dell, pap. ISBN 0-440-13099-9.

Edward Pierce, a Victorian prince among rogues, meticulously plans the theft of £12,000 in gold bullion from the London-Paris train. The story is based on an actual heist that rocked Victorian England more than a century ago.

Crichton, Michael. *Jurassic Park*. New York: Knopf, 1990. New York: Ballantine, 1990. 399pp. LC 90-52960. ISBN 0-394-58816-9. New York: Ballantine, pap. ISBN 0-345-37077-5.

In a novel that portrays the arrogance as well as the responsibility of some humans—perhaps especially scientists—an affluent man whose hobby has always been an interest in dinosaurs plans an entertainment park featuring living dinosaurs. Hammond has hired computer experts, engineers, a scientist interested in genetic engineering, and enlisted information from paleontologists. With their help 15 different species of prehistoric dinosaurs are cloned from cells found in insects preserved in amber. The plan is a secret until one animal escapes from the park and bites a child. The descriptions of the behavior of the species, the hair-raising escapes, perhaps too incredible, and the information regarding the various kinds of dinosaurs make this a special kind of thriller. While interest among young people especially remains high, there is a lesson in the story that warns humans about tampering with nature.

Crichton, Michael. *The Terminal Man*. New York: Knopf, 1972. 247pp. ISBN 0-394-44768-9. (o.p.) New York: Ballantine, pap. ISBN 0-345-35462-1.

Harry Benson is a dangerous man. His violent paranoia has twice led to his attempting to kill. In an experimental operation, wires are attached to points in Benson's brain. From then on, a computer is to regulate his behavior by means of shocks and stimulation. This turn of events is ironic because Benson has always regarded machinery with hatred and distrust. When he escapes from the hospital, the computer connections cause him to have seizures, and Benson decides his only means of escape is to fix the central computer. With chilling detail, Crichton has projected mind control in the not-too-distant future.

Crispin, Edmund. *The Moving Toy Shop*. Mattituck, N.Y.: Amereon, ISBN 0-8488-0104-0. New York: Penguin, 1958. 208pp. pap. ISBN 0-14-008817-2.

Mystery fans ever on the lookout for a new detective hero will find Gervase Fen an unpredictable sleuth. Although this eccentric character is actually an Oxford professor of English language and literature, he finds that calling far less interesting than amateur detecting. In this case he sets out to solve the murder of a gray-haired old lady whom Fen's friend, Richard Cadogan, stumbles upon in a toyshop that seems to disappear and reappear. This is a story that can be enjoyed as much for its humor as for its mystery.

Cronin, Archibald Joseph. *The Citadel*. Boston: Little, 1937. 401pp. ISBN 0-316-16158-6. Boston: Little, pap. ISBN 0-316-16183-7.

In 1921 Andrew Manson, newly graduated at the top of his medical-school class, accepts his first position as assistant to a dying physician in an impoverished Welsh mining town. Hard-working and conscientious at first, Andrew is promoted to a more socially desirable post in London, where he abandons his principles. A faulty operating-room procedure magnifies his increasing incompetence and jolts him back to a career of integrity.

Cronin, Archibald Joseph. *The Green Years*. North Pomfret, Vt.: David and Charles, 1944. 210pp. ISBN 0-575-00479-7. (o.p.) Repr. Boston: Little, 1984. 320pp. ISBN 0-685-09439-1. Boston: Little, pap. ISBN 0-316-16193-4.

Robert Shannon, an Irish Catholic boy, found life hard when he was sent to live with his Scottish Presbyterian grandparents. The stinginess of his grandfather and the inability of his grandmother to show him affection because of the burdens of her own life left Robert little happiness except for the love shown him by his great-grandfather, braggart and drinker though he was. In high school Robert's friends were Gavin and Alison, but the joys of those friendships were short-lived also. Gavin's death in an accident triggered a loss of faith in Robert's heart, resulting in his decision not to consider entering the priesthood. Alison's decision to move to London was another loss. It was his great-grandfather who again saved something of the future for Robert.

Cross, Amanda. *The Question of Max.* New York: Ballantine, pap. ISBN 0-398-35489-3.

This is a mystery with a leisurely pace whose style emphasizes literary references and wit rather than violence and gore. Professor of English Kate Fansler suspects Max Reston, her polished and elegant colleague, of having committed a crime. Her interest in the matter motivates her to do some research during a visit to Oxford University. The theory she evolves from her readings is fascinating—but wrong. The real solution soon occurs to Kate, along with a close call in which her life is in danger. Cross's mysteries are always intellectual, and a delight for the thoughtful reader.

Crutcher, Chris. *Stotan!* New York: Greenwillow, 1986. 192pp. LC 85-12712. ISBN 0-688-05715-2.

"The magic wasn't in gritting your teeth and enduring the pain with no show of emotion. It was in letting go; accepting reality; what *is* as they say." The high school swimming coach tells his team that as they gear up for the Washington state competition. Walker Dupree, team captain, whose diary provides this story of their senior year, learns about reality from many sources: the racist bully who's a classmate; a team member and friend who's a victim of abuse; another who soars to heights of independence, and a fourth member of the team who becomes terminally ill. This well-written novel includes some pretty gross conversation of the kind that can be heard in almost any high school corridor, but it depicts the swimmers and their lives effectively. The coach's Stotan Week of grueling activity not only makes them winning swimmers, but bonds them into a formidable team.

Dahl, Roald. *Kiss, Kiss.* New York: Knopf, 1953. 308pp. ISBN 0-394-43202-9.

These eleven stories of the macabre, with their surprise endings, will provide quick entertainment. The boarder in "The Landlady" becomes the next stuffed pet for a kindly, insane old lady who lets rooms. The widow in "William and Mary" finds that her husband is dead in body only, his brain and one eye remaining alive. She relishes the opportunity to torture him in semi-death as he tortured her in life. Dahl writes with wit, imagination, and a bizarre sense of humor.

Davies, Robertson. *Fifth Business*. New York: Penguin, pap. ISBN 0-14-004387-X.

In the year 1908 in the Canadian Midwest, a woman is struck by a poorly aimed snowball. Her son is born prematurely as a result of her fright. Dunstan Ramsay describes his connection with four of his friends whose lives were affected by the incident: Boy Staunton, who threw the snowball; Mrs. Amasa Dempster, who was hit by it; Paul, the son born prematurely; and Leola Cruikshank, a local beauty whom Staunton marries. The intertwining of their lives spans 60 years, three continents, and two wars.

Degens, T. *Transport 7-41-R*. New York: Viking, 1974. 171pp. ISBN 0-670-72429-7. (o.p.) New York: Puffin, pap. ISBN 0-14-034789-5.

A 13-year-old German girl, bitter that her family has sent her away so they would have one less mouth to feed during the difficult days immediately following World War II, travels from the Russian zone to Cologne in a cattlecar, which had been the usual mode of transportation for those who had been sent to concentration camps and death. Having decided to avoid becoming involved during the journey with other people, who could only use her or hurt her, she is at first unwilling to befriend the Lauritzens, a storekeeper and his wife. When Mrs. Lauritzen dies on the journey, her husband and the girl determine to fulfill the woman's dying wish to be buried in Cologne. With unexpected flashes of humor, the author has depicted the struggle they have in keeping the promise.

Deighton, Len. *Berlin Game*. New York: Knopf, 1983. 345pp. LC 83-48104. ISBN 0-394-53407-7. (o.p.) New York: Ballantine, pap. ISBN 0-345-01071-X.

Bernard Samson, a member of the British Secret Service, married to a woman who also works for that agency, goes to East Berlin to communicate with a special agent, Brahms Four. That agent wants out, but the

British agency wants to keep him in operation longer. There are complications that lead to an inescapable conclusion—there is a double agent at London Central. Deighton is a skillful writer, not depending on violence and blood, but keeping us in suspense as we near the final disclosure of who the double agent really is.

Deighton, Len. *The Ipcress File.* New York: Simon & Schuster, 1963. 287pp. (o.p.) New York: Ballantine, pap. ISBN 0-345-01014-0.

A British secret-service agent is assigned to help recover a kidnapped biochemist. The international intrigue, involving brainwashing, spies, and counter-spies of uncertain loyalties, takes the agent from London to the Far East, to an atomic test site in the Pacific, and behind the Iron Curtain.

Deighton, Len. *SS-GB: Nazi-Occupied Britain.* New York: Knopf, 1979. 344pp. LC 78-14563. ISBN 0-394-50409-7. (o.p.) New York: Ballantine, pap. ISBN 0-345-31809-9.

The King of England is a prisoner in the Tower, the Queen and Princesses have fled to Australia, Winston Churchill has been executed by a German firing squad, and the SS is in charge of Scotland Yard. Detective Superintendent Douglas Archer has started work on what seems to be a routine murder case until an SS official from Himmler's own staff comes to supervise the investigation. Archer finds himself involved in a resistance effort involving wealthy collaborators, high-level scientists, rivalry between the German military and the SS factions, and an attempt to remove King George from the Tower of London to the United States.

Desai, Anita. *Baumgartner's Bombay.* New York: Knopf, 1988. 230pp. LC 88-25753. ISBN 0-394-57229-7. New York: Penguin, pap. ISBN 0-14-013176-0.

Hugo Baumgartner, a German Jew, leaves Germany and the Nazis to work in India. He finds moderate success and comfort in Calcutta but when Britain and Germany become enemies he is interned as a German alien by the British in India. After six years of captivity he is freed and tries to return to some normal life but has to go on to Bombay. There he lives in squalor and poverty, befriending stray cats and befriended by

Lotte, a fellow German. In a final irony Baumgartner befriends a young German drifter who has neither heart nor gratitude but only a frenzy to get money for drugs. Like a Greek tragedy this German brings Baumgartner's story to an end. The author, daughter of a German mother and an Indian father paints a grim picture of India in the mid-twentieth century.

Desai, Anita. *Clear Light of Day*. New York: Harper, 1980. 183pp. LC 80-7603. ISBN 0-06-010984-X. (o.p.) New York: Harper, pap. ISBN 0-14-008670-6.

Tara, who is married to a diplomat in India, spends most of her time in a fairly sophisticated world. When she returns to her home in Old Delhi she tries to understand the years she spent before in this dusty, shabby house, remembering the benign neglect that she, her older sister Bim, and brother Raja suffered from their parents. Only when the fourth child Baba is born—not quite normal in physical and mental health—do the other children begin to feel some affection with the arrival of their aunt Mira. Her entire life has been devoted to caring for others. In this vivid portrayal of middle-class Indian life we see India during the period of post-partition and the inflammatory issue of the separation of Pakistan from India. Most important, however, is our insight into the lives of the central characters and the relationships among them.

*De Vries, Peter. *The Tunnel of Love*. New York: Penguin, pap. ISBN 0-14-002200-7.

Isolde and Augie Poole wish to adopt a child, and they submit their neighbors' names as character references. Dick, the neighbor, is a magazine art-editor given not only to making outrageous puns but also to flights of romantic fancy. Worried about endorsing Augie as a suitable parent because of his unsound financial position, Dick grows more uncertain as he learns of Augie's amorous escapades, behavior that would certainly disqualify him with the adoption agency. The hilarious path by which Augie finally comes to adopt his own illegitimate child is described in a rib-tickling way.

Deuker, Carl. *On the Devil's Court*. Boston: Little, 1988. 252pp. LC 88-13432. ISBN 0-316-18147-1.

Joe Faust's father is an outstanding professor in the field of genetics and his mother is a sculptor. They have high hopes for Joe's future but for Joe the only future he longs for is to be proficient in basketball. When the family moves from Boston to Seattle, Joe wishes to finish his last year in high school at the local public school, where he has observed good players whom he would like to join. His father, however, insists on a private school where Joe finds that they also have a moderately effective team. When the story of Doctor Faustus is assigned in Joe's English class he is tempted to do what the character in that story had done to win power—make a pact with the devil for skill at basketball. How that affects Joe's game, his family and his relationship with his peers makes for a fast-moving story with authentic details about Joe's favorite sport.

Dexter, Colin. *The Wench Is Dead.* New York: Saint Martin's Press, 1989. ISBN 0-312-04444-5. New York: Bantam, 1991. ISBN 0-553-29120-3.

The detective in this mystery is the British inspector Morse of TV fame. In a style reminiscent of Josephine Tey's classic mystery, *The Daughter of Time*, Morse becomes interested in trying to reconstruct a murder that had happened in the nineteenth century. Hospitalized for what might be serious surgery, the detective tries to divert himself by reading a book about this crime—an account of a young woman traveling alone by boat in the company of a crew of four men who seem very unsavory. When her body is found in the Canal, the men are arrested. In fine literary style and ingenious plot development, Morse satisfies his opinion about the validity of that nineteenth-century murder trial by way of twentieth-century research methods.

Dick, Philip K. *Collected Stories, Vol. 4.* New York: Carol, 1991. 380pp. LC 87-50158. ISBN 0-8065-1276-8.

Eighteen stories by a master sci-fi writer range from prophetic to ironic. "Autopac" and "Service Call" illustrate machines taking over from humans; "Minority Report" is a frightening example of data being improperly interpreted; "Stand-by" lampoons union featherbedding while it shows a government run by a homeostatic system and "The Mold of Yancy" demonstrates the power of media turning ordinary citizens into uniform non-thinkers. The notes at the back of the book add interesting commentary in the author's words.

Dick, Philip K. *The Man in the High Castle.* Boston: G.K. Hall. ISBN 0-8398-2476-9. (o.p.) New York: Berkley, pap. ISBN 0-425-10143-6.

What might American life be if the Axis powers had won World War II? It is many years now past the event, and America is divided into three areas: a primarily German one, a Japanese territory, and an amorphous confederation of free states. Wartime animosities have faded but a new culture of conqueror and conquered has arisen. Against this background of intrigue and drama we observe a quite believable world.

*Dickey, James. *Deliverance*. Boston: Houghton, 1970. 278pp. (o.p.) Repr. New York: Armchair Det. Lib., 1991. 256pp. LC 91-10975. ISBN 0-922890-96-X. New York: Dell, pap. ISBN 0-440-31868-8.

A relaxing down-river hunting trip in a wilderness area of the South is taken by a group of four businessmen whose personalities are revealingly different from each other. The planned vacation turns into a nightmare when one man is shot and killed by an elusive local man and the other three must fight for their lives. A brutal homosexual rape scene and strongly realistic descriptions make this a novel for the more mature reader.

Dickinson, Peter. *Eva*. New York: Doubleday, 1989. ISBN 0-385-29702-5. New York: Dell, pap. ISBN 0-440-20766-5.

Eva has been horribly, irreversibly injured in a car accident. Her father, in charge of a scientific study of chimpanzees in a controlled laboratory, makes an incredible decision in order to save Eva's life. Her human intelligence is transferred into the body of Kelly, one of the chimps. Since Eva has always spent much time among these human-like animals, she adjusts to their behavior patterns but is only able to communicate with humans with a word keyboard. She begins to feel that in the overpopulated world in which she lives and because of the destruction of the environment, the future may lie with a renewal of the evolutionary process and presses for a small group of chimps to live free away from the controlled environment of the laboratory.

Dickinson, Peter. *Tulku*. New York: Dutton, 1979. 286pp. LC 78-11461. ISBN 0-525-41571-8. (o.p.) New York: Ace, pap. ISBN 0-441-82630-X.

When his missionary father and the mission itself are destroyed in the Boxer Rebellion, Theo is propelled into a strange and dangerous adventure. He joins, albeit unwillingly, a Mrs. Jones, brash, unflappable, and quick on the draw, whose great passion is botany. Her lesser one, though strong enough, is Lung, a young Chinese convert. This trio reaches Tibet after many exciting events. There the religious community is convinced that the child Mrs. Jones is carrying (fathered by Lung) is the reincarnated Tulku, their spiritual head. In addition to the suspenseful happenings, the book has a continuing theme: the testing of Theo's own faith.

Dinesen, Isak. *Seven Gothic Tales.* New York: Modern Lib., 1934. 420pp. (o.p.) Repr. New York: Random, 1980. 420pp. LC 39-27353. ISBN 0-394-60496-2. New York: Random, pap. ISBN 0-394-74291-5.

Distinguished by a romantic style and an aura of mystery, these tales of nineteenth-century aristocratic life in northern Europe remain favorites of a wide audience. A major plot device in some stories is the revealing of illegitimacy (sometimes of legitimacy), while a strong element of the supernatural is to be found in others. People become involved in events they cannot control, as in "The Poet," which deals with a love triangle. In "Supper at Elsinore" two sisters who have unwillingly become old maids because their brother fled from his wedding wait unceasingly for his return.

Doctorow, E.L. *The Book of Daniel.* New York: Random, 1971. 303pp. LC 78-140700. ISBN 0-394-46271-8. New York: Fawcett, pap. ISBN 0-449-21430-3.+

The trial of Julius and Ethel Rosenberg in 1950-51 for espionage was a cause célèbre during the fifties. The justice of administering the death penalty to that pair is still argued, particularly by the sons of the Rosenbergs. In this novel, which is based on that case, Daniel Isaacson tells of the effect of that execution on his childhood, marriage, and career. The whole period of pre-World War II radicalism, the tyranny of the McCarthy era, the peace march on the Pentagon in 1967, the nature of left-wing politics in the United States are the elements that make this a provocative sociopolitical novel.

*Doctorow, E.L. *Ragtime.* New York: Random, 1975. 288pp. LC 75-9613. ISBN 0-394-46901-1. New York: Fawcett, pap. ISBN 0-449-21428-1.+

The lives of an upper-middle-class family in New Rochelle; a black ragtime musician who loses his love, his child, and his life because of bigotry; and a poor immigrant Jewish family are interwoven in this early-twentieth-century story. There are cameo appearances by well-known figures of that period: Houdini, anarchist Emma Goldman, actress Evelyn Nesbit, Henry Ford, and J.P. Morgan, whose magnificent library plays an important part in the story. The book mingles fact and fiction in portraying the era of ragtime.

Doerr, Harriet. *Stones for Ibarra*. New York: Viking, 1984. 214pp. LC 83-47861. ISBN 0-14-007562-3. New York: Viking, pap. ISBN 0-14-011218-9.

When Sara and Richard Everton pack up their belongings and mortgage themselves to leave California for a small village in Mexico, their friends think they are crazy. Many of the Mexican natives in the village of Ibarra also consider the two gringos incredible. While Sara restores the house that had belonged to Richard's grandparents, Richard restores a copper mine that had been his family's, and thereby gives employment to many of the villagers. We learn that Richard has leukemia and has been given just a few years to live, but it is the lives of the villagers that are more full of tragedy, religious commitment, and reliance on talismans and prayers. There is a strength among these people and an acceptance of all that life brings which make them memorable. Learning from them, perhaps, Sara finally accepts the inevitability of her husband's death.

Doherty, Berlie. *White Peak Farm*. New York: Orchard, 1990. 128pp. LC 89-23060. ISBN 0-531-05867-0.

Generally change comes slowly to White Peak Farm, but during Jeannie Tanner's senior year it enters with the force of a stampede. First her beloved Gran packs for a sudden trip overseas, an all too flimsy excuse for her move to a rest home for the terminally ill. Next, Jeannie's sister marries a neighboring farmer, the son of Mr. Tanner's lifelong nemesis, and is banished from the home. Another Tanner dream departs when older brother Martin, heir apparent to the family business, enrolls in art school. And even Jeannie isn't immune to change: should she stay at White Peak Farm and marry, or strike out on her own for her still ill-formed dreams at the university.

Donovan, John. *Family*. New York: Harper, 1976. 148pp. LC 75-37409. ISBN0-06-021722-7.

A group of apes are collected to be used in some experimental studies. Sasha, a male ape, has participated in other scientific experiments and has, as a result, forebodings about the current one. When Sasha communicates this to the rest of the group, a number of apes escape and live as a family for a while, providing protection and care for each other.

Donovan, John. *I'll Get There. It Better Be Worth the Trip*. New York: Harper, 1969. 189pp. LC 69-15539. ISBN 0-06-021718-9.

The year Davy Ross turns 13, the conscientious grandmother who raised him from age five dies. Compounding his difficulties with a divorced, hard-drinking mother and a distant, overregulated father, Davy's brief, intense attraction to another boy is swelled out of proportion by his mother's mishandling. An adolescent's guilt, grief, and self-doubt are honestly and forcefully conveyed in a novel that does not underestimate readers or the toughness of the trip to maturity.

Donovan, John. *Wild in the World.* New York: Harper, 1971. 94pp. LC 74-159044. ISBN 0-06-021702-2.

John Gridley has dropped out of high school after the first year and is the last surviving member of his clan of mountaineers in Vermont. Alone is this locale, on Rattlesnake Mountain, he is joined by a wolf who becomes his companion. So close is the relationship between the two that the derelict animal, driven off by neighbors, comes back to sleep in John's bed when the boy dies of pneumonia.

Dorfman, Ariel. *Widows.* Trans. from Spanish by Stephen Kessler. New York: Penguin, 1983. 146pp. pap. LC 88-23183. ISBN 0-14-011659-1.

Written by a man whose works were banished in Chile, it describes a gripping, devastating situation known to us in books of fact about repression and in the film "Missing." Thousands of people in many countries have been taken away by authorities in totalitarian countries and never reappeared. In this novella, the writer has used Greece as a locale for a universal condition. All the men are gone and mothers, wives, lovers and daughters mourn their loss. When a corpse washes up on the river bank, Sofia Angelo—strong and unmoving—courageously fights the military regime for permission to bury the body. In the end, another corpse is claimed by 37 women in an incredible stand against the threat of death for all of them.

Dorris, Michael. *Yellow Raft in Blue Water.* New York: Holt, 1987. 343pp. LC 86-26947. ISBN 0-8050-0045-3. New York: Warner, pap. ISBN 0-446-38787-8.

Three American Indian women of three generations tell their stories in a reverse chronology. Rayona, her mother Christine, and her grandmother of Ida, share with the reader their troubled lives and Native American culture. Rayona, whose father was black, perhaps has more obstacles to face than her forebears. Although she is the first narrator, the succeeding two chapters explain how she came to be abandoned by her mother and why her mother, Christine, had so difficult a relationship with her own mother, Ida. Christine's brother, Lee, and his best friend, Dayton, are important characters in this compelling story.

*Dos Passos, John. *Manhattan Transfer*. New York: Grosset, 1925. 404pp. (o.p.) Repr. Cambridge, Mass.: Bentley, 1979. LC 79-010459. ISBN 0-8376-0433-8. Boston: Houghton, pap. ISBN 0-395-08375-3.

Dos Passos creates a portrait of New York City in the first quarter of this century by telling the stories of many people. They include the daughter of an accountant, who loses hope for any future happiness when her first love commits suicide; a milkman who rises in status to become a union boss; and an immigrant sailor who starts as a bartender and becomes a wealthy bootlegger during Prohibition. There are happy and unhappy endings to these stories, but always the city plays an important role.

Dreiser, Theodore. *An American Tragedy*. New York: World, 1948. 874pp. (o.p.) Repr. Cambridge, Mass.: Bentley, 1978. LC 78-55741. ISBN 0-8376-0424-9. New York: Dutton, pap. ISBN 0-451-52204-4.

Clyde Griffiths, product of a poor and pious home, is driven by ambition to acquire money and social status. He is loved by Roberta, a factory coworker, but is dazzled by Sondra, who would be a passport to the country-club set. When Roberta, pregnant and no longer desirable, becomes an obstacle to Clyde's fulfilling his dream, he plans her death, for which he is caught and convicted.

Dreiser, Theodore. *Sister Carrie*. New York: Modern Lib., 1900. 557pp. (o.p.) Repr. Cambridge, Mass: Bentley, 1972. 472pp. LC 78-183140. ISBN 0-8376-0401-X. New York: Oxford Univ. Press, pap. ISBN 0-19-282742-1.+

Carrie Meeber, leaving her small hometown in Wisconsin to find fame in Chicago, meets a flashy salesman, Charles Drouet. A few weeks later, when her stingy sister sends her away, she goes to live with him on the strength of his promise of marriage. While Drouet is absent on business, Hurstwood, who has been asked by Drouet to look after Carrie, visits her and falls in love with her. Hurstwood's wife divorces him and he persuades Carrie to go off to Montreal with him. Carrie expects to be rich and happy in this marriage, but discovers that she must find work when Hurstwood returns some money he has stolen. She works as a chorus girl, leaves Hurstwood, and becomes a well-known actress, but happiness continues to elude her.

Drury, Allen. *Advise and Consent.* New York: Doubleday, 1959. 616pp. LC 59-9137. ISBN 0-385-05419-X.

Robert A. Leffingwell, a liberal intellectual, is nominated by the President of the United States to be Secretary of State. The lives of four politicians are affected by the fight for his approval in the Senate. A suicide, a surprise witness at the hearings, a vote of censure, and some chicanery highlight the Washington political scene depicted in this novel.

DuMaurier, Daphne. *Rebecca.* New York: Doubleday, 1938. 357pp. ISBN 0-385-04380-5. New York: Avon, pap. ISBN 0-380-00917-X.

Rebecca, lovely and charming wife of English aristocrat Maxim de Winter, dies unexpectedly, and the mystery surrounding her death haunts all who remain at the Manderley country estate. Eight months after the sailing accident in which Rebecca lost her life Maxim remarries. Through his new wife's writing, the reader learns the truth about Rebecca's death and character.

*Durrell, Lawrence. *Alexandria Quartet.* (Includes *Justine, Balthazar, Mountolive,* and *Clea*). New York: Dutton, 1962. 884pp. pap. ISBN 0-525-47795-0. (o.p.) Repr. New York: Penguin, 1991. pap. ISBN 0-14-015317-9. Titles also available separately. New York: Penguin, pap. *Justine.* ISBN 0-14-15319-5. *Balthazar.* ISBN 0-14-15321-7. *Mountolive.* ISBN 0-14-15320-9. *Clea.* ISBN 0-14-15322-5.

In *Justine,* a richly evocative novel set in Alexandria, Egypt, we are introduced to the cast that figures in the quartet: Justine and her husband, Nessim, Clea, Pursewarden, Scobie, and others. In *Balthazar,* their lives are told from a different perspective by a psychiatrist, Balthazar, as if this were a correction or explanation of the first volume. *Mountolive* leads us into the political turmoil of the Middle East and the interest that Justine and her husband have in the formation of a Jewish state. In *Clea,* the circle of friends is viewed from the point of view of an Englishman, Darley, who has an affair with Clea. The quartet is demanding and mature reading, but worth the effort. If the complete quartet seems too overwhelming, any single volume will provide an unusual reading experience.

*Eco, Umberto. *The Name of the Rose*. San Diego, Ca.: Harcourt, 1983. 512pp. LC 82-21286. ISBN 0-15-144647-4. New York: Warner, pap. ISBN 0-446-35720-0.

A Franciscan monk, William of Baskerville, is sent on an important mission in 1327 by the Holy Roman Emperor, Louis of Bavaria. This leads him to a Benedictine abbey in northern Italy where a meeting is to take place between a group of Franciscan theologians who are supported by the Emperor and representatives of Pope John XXII. The differences between them in interpreting church doctrine is the theme running through this erudite novel, but there are also several murders in the abbey that William will have to solve. This book is for the reader with an interest in fourteenth-century philosophy, the history of the church, and the conflict between a passion for knowledge and unquestioning faith—and with the patience to stay with a novel that demands thought and introspection.

Edmonds, Walter D. *Bert Breen's Barn*. Boston: Little, 1975. 270pp. ISBN 0-316-21166-4. (o.p.) Repr. New York: Syracuse Univ. Press, 1991. 280pp. ISBN 0-8156-0255-3.

Tom Dolan, son and grandson of ne'er-do-wells, is determined to overcome the poverty that his mother has battled all her life. With her support, Tom gets a job in a feed mill and plans to rehabilitate the old farm on which the family lives. He decides to buy the abandoned barn on Widow Breen's land and move it to his own land. Rumors that Bert Breen had treasure hidden there make the barn even more desirable an acquisition.

*Ellison, Ralph. *Invisible Man*. New York: Random, 1952. 439pp. ISBN 0-394-52549-3. (o.p.) New York: Random, pap. ISBN 0-394-60338-9.+

Acclaimed as a powerful representation of the lives of blacks during the Depression, this novel describes the experiences of one young black man during that period. Dismissed from a Negro college in the South for showing one of the founders how Negroes live there, he is used later as a symbol of repression by a Communist group in New York City. After a Harlem race riot, he is aware that he must contend with both whites and blacks, and that loss of social identity makes him invisible among his fellow beings.

Emecheta, Buchi. *The Slave Girl*. New York: Braziller, 1977. 176pp. LC 79-25651. ISBN 0-8076-0952-8.

Ojebeta, a daughter whose birth was welcomed by her parents, grows up with two older brothers in Ibuza, a small town in Nigeria. When her father and mother die and her older brother has gone off to the large city, Lagos, her younger brother Okolie is left with the responsibility for her care. He refuses to give her to the care of her aunt, who wants her, and instead sells Ojebeta to get enough money for a rite-of-passage ritual for himself. The girl's new owner is an affluent African woman of another tribe, Ma Palagada; and her life is not bad among the other slave girls, although the discipline administered by Pa Palagada could be severe. As the years pass and she reaches marriageable age she is selected to become the wife of Ma Palagada's son but decides that would make her still a slave. She flees back to her own people to a better marriage and a happy ending. The book is rich in the description of the daily lives and customs of Africans in East Africa in the early twentieth century.

Engdahl, Sylvia Louise. *Enchantress from the Stars*. New York: Atheneum, 1971. 275pp. LC 74-98609. ISBN 0-689-20508-2. (o.p.) Repr. Magnolia, Mass.: Peter Smith, 1991. ISBN 0-8446-6448-0. New York: Macmillan, pap. ISBN 0-02-043031-0.

Realizing that the planet of Andrecia is in danger, the Federation gives the assignment of saving it to a team of its field agents. Illegally a part of the team, Elana is pressed into service when one of the original members is killed. When Elana encounters the Younglings, they consider her an Enchantress. Through their contact with Elana, the Younglings and the Federation defeat the colonizing efforts of the Imperials.

*Fairbairn, Ann. *Five Smooth Stones*. New York: Crown, 1966. 756pp. ISBN 0-517-50687-4. (o.p.) Repr. Cutchogue, N.Y.: Buccaneer, 1991. 766pp. ISBN 0-89966-805-4. New York: Bantam, pap. ISBN 0-553-25203-8.

Although born in poverty in New Orleans, David Champlin, a young black man, escapes this dreary background with the help of devoted grandparents, a Danish professor, and a scholarship to a Midwestern college. The book details his successful legal and diplomatic career and his love affair and marriage with Sara Kent, a white classmate. David becomes involved also in the Civil Rights movement. The book concludes on a triumphant but tragic note.

Farmer, Philip Jose. *To Your Scattered Bodies Go*. Boston, Mass.: G.K. Hall. ISBN 0-8398-2620-6. (o.p.) New York: Berkley, pap. ISBN 0-425-10334-X.+

The fabulous Riverworld, site of the resurrection of every human being who has died, is one of the great fictional creations. Sir Richard Burton, Victorian explorer and rogue, finds himself reborn and sets off on an epic journey to learn the truth of its existence.

Farris, John. *When Michael Calls*. New York: Trident, 1967. 184pp. (o.p.) New York: Tor, pap. ISBN 0-8125-0356-2.

Helen Connelly is shaken by phone calls from a boy whose voice sounds like that of her nephew Michael, who had died in a blizzard some years before. Terror and murder follow. Psychologist Craig Young, Michael's brother, deranged by long-felt guilt and anger, is eventually exposed as the caller.

Fast, Howard. *April Morning*. New York: Crown, 1961. 184pp. ISBN 0-517-50681-5. (o.p.) New York: Bantam, pap. ISBN 0-553-27322-1.

The spirit of the Revolutionary War, a country coming of age, and the life of a boy passing into manhood are captured in this historical novel. Fast focuses on one day in the life of Adam Cooper as his family and the community of Lexington rise to the events of April 19, 1775. Adam at first is caught up in the excitement, but by the end of the first skirmish the death of his father has brought home the horror and reality of war.

*Faulkner, William. *Absalom, Absalom!* New York: Random, 1936. 378pp. ISBN 0-394-41400-4. (o.p.) Repr. New York: Random, 1991. 336pp. LC 90-50211. ISBN 0-679-73218-7. New York: Random, pap. ISBN 0-394-71780-5.+

During the summer of 1910, prior to Quentin Compson's leaving the South for his first year at Harvard, old Rosa Coldfield insists upon a private conference with the youth to divulge her recollections of Thomas Sutpen. Driven by a great plan to become a Southern aristocrat, Sutpen builds a mansion, only to see his life ruined. The title of the book reveals the story's basic tragedy: Sutpen's disappointment in his children. One is a spinster and thus has no offspring to continue the family lineage; the other is a son who has disappeared. Sutpen himself falls victim to a murder for retribution. Faulkner depicts the South before and after the Civil War in this powerfully written novel.

Faulkner, William. *Intruder in the Dust*. New York: Random, 1948. 247pp. ISBN 0-394-43074-3. New York: Random, pap. ISBN 0-394-71792-9.+

When Lucas, an elderly Negro, is accused of murdering a white man, Charles, a 16-year-old white boy, works to save him from being lynched. Charles gets the help he needs in his sleuthing from an old aristocratic lady and a young black boy. The trio visits the church graveyard at night to dig up the corpse of the supposed victim. The book can be read as a mystery and, on a deeper level, as a social commentary on the South.

Fenton, Edward. *The Refugee Summer*. New York: Delacorte, 1982. 272pp. LC 81-12593. ISBN 0-385-28854-9.

The time is 1922; the place is Kifissia, a suburb of Athens. Greece is at war with the Turks in Anatolia but that seems far away to Nikolas until he is asked to read the journal of a dead Greek soldier to the soldier's bereaved family. The arrival of two families, who have rented nearby villas for the summer, changes Nikolas' life. Especially influential is Oliver, a young boy from Boston, who presses his young companions to form a secret society dedicated to noble causes. Both political and social crises make this a story that offers excitement, humor, and courage and portrays young people from widely different cultures.

Ferber, Edna. *Cimarron*. Garden City, N.Y.: Doubleday, 1930. 388pp. LC 30-8609. ISBN 0-385-04069-5. (o.p.) Repr. Mattituck, N.Y.: Amereon, ISBN 0-88411-548-8.

Yancey Cravat was a big, handsome man who quoted Shakespeare and the Bible and knew the law. He started a newspaper in Wichita, Kansas, in whose pages he protested the government's treatment of the Indians. Against the wishes of her family he married Sabra Venable, daughter of an aristocratic Southern family. Then, lured by the newly opened frontier, he took off with her to help settle Oklahoma, where he was instrumental in establishing law and order. Although he could have been governor of the state, his restlessness took him away for weeks, months, and finally years, leaving Sabra with the responsibility for the newspaper. In the lives of these two strong-willed people, and of their son, Cim, Ferber has captured the drama, conflicts, and rewards of life in pioneer America.

Ferber, Edna. *Giant*. Garden City, N.Y.: Doubleday, 1952. 447pp. LC 52-10412. ISBN 0-385-04163-2. (o.p.) Repr. Cutchogue, N.Y.: Buccaneer, 1991. 392pp. ISBN 0-89966-806-2.

In Texas, where accomplishments seemed to be evaluated only in terms of size, Leslie Benedict was an outsider. She had grown up in Virginia and traveled to Reata Ranch as the bride of its immensely rich owner, Bick Benedict. Only after rearing two children and enduring numerous hostile onslaughts did Leslie begin to understand the land's giants.

Fields, Jeff. *A Cry of Angels*. New York: Ballantine, 1979. pap. LC 73-91623. ISBN 0-345-28204-3.

Orphaned Earl Whitaker, 14 years old, lives with his great-aunt and an odd assortment of golden-agers in a rundown boarding house in Ape Yard, the black quarter of a dying Georgia quarry town during the mid-1950s. Jayell Grooms, an erratic and visionary young architect, hears the "cry of angels" within him and is spurred on by Em Jojohn, a drunken Indian giant, to battle a villainous black undertaker for the souls of Ape Yard and the life of the town.

Finney, Jack. *Time and Again*. New York: Simon & Schuster, 1970. 399pp. (o.p.) New York: Simon & Schuster, pap. ISBN 0-671-24295-4.

The opportunity of going back in time to the 1880s is offered to Simon Morley if he will be a subject in a secret government study. Self-hypnosis is the key to the vague and unexplained technique Morley learns for entering the past. The historical information, rich details, and photographs Finney provides enrich this novel. Simon's encounter with a simpler time in the past and a young girl of that period makes him less anxious to remain part of the twentieth century and continue the project. The Dakota, a unique apartment house in New York City, is an important part of the story.

Fitzgerald, F. Scott. *The Great Gatsby*. New York: Scribner, 1925. 182pp. ISBN 0-684-16498-1. New York: Collier ISBN 0-02-019960-0.+

The story takes place in the period from the First World War to the Depression. Nick Carraway, the narrator, comes to New York to make his fortune on Wall Street and becomes involved in the lives of his cousin Daisy Buchanan and her husband, Tom. Their marriage is failing and becomes even more endangered when Daisy reencounters Jay Gatsby after a long separation. Gatsby is now wealthy, with an income reputed to be derived from racketeering. He and Daisy had known and loved each other when they were younger, in the Midwest. When Tom's jealousy is aroused, there is a serious argument between him and Gatsby, with tragic consequences.

Forbes, Esther. *Johnny Tremain*. Boston: Houghton, 1943. 256pp. ISBN0-395-06766-9. New York: Dell, pap. ISBN 0-440-94250-0.+

Johnny, an orphan, works as a favored apprentice to an aging silversmith until he burns his hand severely while working on an important project. During the Revolutionary War he serves as a dispatch rider for the Committee on Public Safety, meeting such men as Paul Revere and John Hancock. An outcast for a time, he finally learns on the battlefield of Lexington that his crippled hand can be put to use.

Forbes, Kathryn. *Mama's Bank Account*. New York: Harcourt, 1943. 204pp. (o.p.) San Diego, Ca.: Harcourt, pap. ISBN 0-15-656377-0.

When a family of Norwegian immigrants first settles in San Francisco during the early 1900s, Mama takes charge of financial matters. Money is scarce but there is the wealth of love to support them, and the children are especially proud of their "bank account" downtown, which contains a cache of dollars for extreme emergencies. Heartwarming anecdotes abound in this story. Only after 20 years does one daughter discover that Mama's bank account existed only in the minds of the family.

Forester, C.S. *The African Queen*. New York: Modern Lib., 1940. 307pp. (o.p.) Repr. New York: Queens, 1977. ISBN 0-89244-065-1. Boston: Little, pap. ISBN 0-316-28910-8.

At her brother's death Rose Sayer is left alone in an isolated African mission. She is determined to fight against the Germans, who have taken her brother's black converts into custody. She joins forces with a Cockney, Alnutt, and they take a long and dangerous trip down-river in Alnutt's dilapidated launch in order to reach the German boat they intend to blow up. The journey points up the differences between this ill-matched pair, and their bravery as well.

Forster, E.M. *A Passage to India*. New York: Harcourt, 1949. 322pp. LC 43-1812. ISBN 0-15-171141-0. San Diego, Ca.: Harcourt, pap. ISBN 0-15-671142-7.+

Politics and mysticism are potent forces in India just after World War I. Ronald Heaslop, magistrate of Chandrapore, has asked his mother, Mrs. Moore, to visit him along with his fiancée, Adela Quested. To add to their knowledge of the real India, Dr. Aziz, a young Moslem doctor, offers to take them to the Marabar Caves outside the city. The visit is a shattering experience. Mrs. Moore is struck by the thought that all her ideas about life are no more than the hollow echo she hears in the cave. Adela, entering another cave alone, emerges in a panic and accuses Dr. Aziz of having attacked her in the gloom of the cave. The trial that results from her accusation divides the groups in the city so acutely that a reconciliation appears impossible.

Forsyth, Frederick. *The Day of the Jackal*. New York: Viking, 1971. 380pp. (o.p.) New York: Bantam, pap. ISBN 0-553-26630-6.

Dissident OAS officers hire a mercenary, known by the code name "Jackal," to assassinate General Charles deGaulle. The officers hope to cash in on the political chaos that would follow. The methodical, ingenious preparations of "Jackal" are paralleled by the attempts of the combined French law-enforcement agencies to uncover and stop the plot. The suspense is acute.

Forsyth, Frederick. *The Odessa File*. New York: Viking, 1972. 336pp. (o.p.) New York: Bantam, pap. ISBN 0-553-25525-8.

Young German reporter Peter Miller comes upon the diary of a survivor of a World War II extermination camp at Riga. Its revelations lead him into the deadly pursuit of Commandant Roschmann, known as the Butcher of Riga. Roschmann is engaged in an international scheme to destroy the Jewish state. The plan is promoted by the Odessa, a secret organization that protects the identities and fortunes of former SS members. Miller infiltrates the organization to find and expose Roschmann.

Forsyth, Frederick. *The Shepherd*. Ill. by Lou Feck. Mattituck, N.Y.: Amereon, ISBN 0-88411-563-1.

A young pilot in the Royal Air Force is on his way home from Germany on Christmas Eve. Once airborne, his instrument panel and all communications systems cease to function. To worsen his situation, he encounters a heavy fog, and his chance for survival seems slim. Out of the fog appears a plane of the type that had been used in World War I that shepherds him to a safe landing on a no-longer-used air field. He hears a strange story from a man who keeps a solitary post there.

*Fowles, John. *The Collector*. Boston: Little, 1963. 305pp. ISBN 0-316-29096-3. New York: Dell, pap. ISBN 0-440-31335-X.

Frederick Clegg, a collector of butterflies, becomes obsessed with the idea of capturing a young, attractive art student, as he does insects. He finds the perfect, isolated spot for this adventure, and there ensues a tale of horror and suspense. It is told first by Frederick and then by Miranda, as she struggles valiantly, with intelligence and determination, for her freedom, to no avail. The novel requires a reader who can endure the terror and nightmarish qualities of the plot.

Fowles, John. *The French Lieutenant's Woman*. Boston: Little, 1969. 467pp. LC 77-86616. ISBN 0-316-29099-8. New York: New Amer. Lib., pap. ISBN 0-451-13598-9.

The clash of social systems and ethical standards of Victorian England are epitomized in the love triangle of Ernestina Freeman, a spoiled, shallow daughter of a merchant prince; Charles Smithson, a well-fixed and well-born amateur scientist; and Sarah Woodruff, whom the citizens of the town scorn because of a brief affair she had with a French sailor.

Fox, Paula. *The Slave Dancer*. New York: Bradbury, 1973. 176pp. LC 73-80642. ISBN 0-02-735560-8. New York: Dell, pap. ISBN 0-440-40402-9.

Thirteen-year-old Jessie Bollier is kidnapped from New Orleans and taken aboard a slave ship. Cruelly tyrannized by the ship's captain, Jessie is made to play his fife for the slaves during the exercise period into which they are forced in order to keep them fit for sale. When a hurricane destroys the ship, Jessie and Ras, a young slave, survive. They are helped by an old black man who finds them, spirits Ras north to freedom, and helps Jessie return to his family.

Francis, Dick. *Comeback*. New York: Putnam, 1991. 320pp. LC 91-23903. ISBN 0-399-13670-3.

Peter Darwin, a British First Secretary, is on his way to his new post in England and falls in with an elderly couple also going to England. When they ask for his help on the journey he winds up in Gloucestshire and becomes deeply involved in some murders and the treatment of several race horses who mysteriously die when they were already making satisfactory recoveries. The veterinarian, Ken McClure, is the target for suspicion of bad medical attention until Darwin begins to unearth a conspiracy with old roots. As usual Dick Francis gives the reader a bang-up finale.

Francis, Dick. *Trial Run*. New York: Harper, 1978. 246pp. LC 78-20204. ISBN 0-06-011383-9. (o.p.) New York: Fawcett, pap. ISBN 0-449-21314-5.

Randall Drew, an expert steeplechase rider who is no longer able to ride because he wears glasses and cannot tolerate contact lenses, is persuaded to go to Moscow for the Olympics. He is asked to do this in order to insure the safety of a member of the Royal Family who is supposed to ride in the Olympics. There follows a suspenseful story of danger and pursuit. Francis's tautly written books appeal not only to mystery fans but also to those interested in horses and racing.

Francis, Dick. *Twice Shy*. New York: Putnam, 1982. 307pp. LC 81-15814. ISBN 0-399-12707-0. (o.p.) New York: Fawcett, pap. ISBN 0-449-21314-5.

Jonathan Derry, a physicist, is handed some cassettes, apparently Broadway musical scores, by a friend who then meets a violent death. The cassettes turn out to be a computer program for handicapping horses—guaranteed to make the user a rich man. When Jonathan tries to track down the tapes' rightful owner he becomes involved with a rough man and his violent son. The latter is brought to justice by Jonathan and then, after his release, he tries to avenge himself on Jonathan's brother. Computer buffs as well as mystery fans will enjoy this one.

Francis, Dick. *Whip Hand*. New York: Harper, 1979. 293pp. LC 79-3408. ISBN 0-06-011384-7. (o.p.) New York: Fawcett, pap. ISBN 0-449-21274-2.

Sid Halley, top-ranked jockey, is forced to give up a career in racing because of an accident that has cost him his left forearm and hand. His knowledge of racing and horses, however, makes him an excellent investigator into the deaths of four outstanding thoroughbred horses. He is involved in a parallel investigation to help his ex-wife out of a swindling operation she has stumbled into. The book contains moments of breathless suspense, much information about the sport of kings, and perceptive insights into Halley's character that explain some of the reasons for the breakdown of his marriage.

Frank, Pat. *Alas, Babylon*. New York: Bantam, 1976. 320pp. pap. ISBN 0-553-27883-5.+

Survival after a submarine nuclear attack is the focus of this story of a small group of people in Fort Repose, Florida. Rationing food, re-establishing law and order, and pondering whether there will be any future for the survivors are some of the concerns of organizer-leader Randy Bragg.

Franklin, Miles. *My Brilliant Career*. New York: Saint Martin's Press, 1980. 232pp. LC 80-52658. ISBN 0-312-55599-7. (o.p.) New York: Pocket, pap. ISBN 0-671-45915-5.

Sybylla Melwyn is the heroine in this novel, which was written in 1901 but describes a strongly independent young woman who might have lived in 1980. In her Australian farm home she and her family struggle for survival against a terrible drought. Syb does not mind the drudgery as much as the complete absence of any cultural enrichment such as art, music, or literature. When she is invited to stay with her maternal grandmother her life becomes wonderful. Her aunt Helen even transforms her plain looks, which Syb considers ugliness, into quite an attractive appearance. There are a few would-be suitors, especially Hal Beecham, but she cannot bring herself to consider marriage, which she sees as enslavement and loss of freedom even when that freedom may mean economic hardship.

Freedman, Benedict, and Freedman, Nancy. *Mrs. Mike*. Cutchogue, N.Y.: Buccaneer, 1981. ISBN 0-89966-396-6. New York: Berkley, pap. ISBN 0-425-10328-5.

At 16, Boston-reared Katherine Mary O'Fallon is sent north to Alberta, Canada, to find relief for the pleurisy from which she has been suffering. While residing with her Uncle John, she falls in love with Mike, a handsome Canadian Mounted Policeman. Life in the wilderness in the early 1900s is harsh, but the newly married couple finds joy and challenge in their adventures.

French, Michael. *The Throwing Season*. New York: Delacorte, 1980. LC 79-53598. ISBN 0-440-08600-0.

Henry Chevrolet is known as Indian by his high school classmates because his father is a Native American. He has heard of the many difficulties faced by his father because of prejudice, and that becomes part of his determination to succeed in his main interest in life—shot-putting. When he is approached and threatened by a gambler who wishes to fix a contest, he refuses and is physically assaulted. His continuing obsession with this special sport, plus his competing against Golly, who is also striving to attain a put of more than 70 feet, makes an exciting climax to the story.

Fuller, Iola. *The Loon Feather*. San Diego, Ca.: Harcourt, 1967. 462pp. pap. ISBN 0-15-653200-X.

Oneta was the daughter of the great Indian Tecumseh and the grand-daughter of the chief of the Loon tribe of the Ojibways. After her father's death, Oneta's mother married Pierre, a Frenchman living on Mackinac Island, a fur-trading center. When her mother died of typhoid, Oneta and her half-brother Paul left Mackinac to live with Pierre and his mother in Detroit. Learning French and the ways of the white man did not erase Oneta's Indian heritage. Although conflict over fur trading and fishing rights intruded into her life, she found happiness in the love of Martin Rawlings, a young doctor from Boston who respected the age-old wisdom of Indian customs.

Gaines, Ernest J. *The Autobiography of Miss Jane Pittman*. Garden City, N.Y.: Doubleday, 1971. 244pp. ISBN 0-385-27009-7. (o.p.) New York: Bantam, pap. ISBN 0-553-26357-9.

In the epic of Miss Jane Pittman, a 110-year-old ex-slave, the action begins at the time she is a small child watching both Union and Confederate troops come into the plantation on which she lives. It closes with the demonstrations of the sixties and the freedom walk she decides to make. This is a log of trials, heartaches, joys, love—but mostly of endurance.

Gaines, Ernest J. *A Gathering of Old Men*. New York: Knopf, 1983. 224pp. LC 83-49000. ISBN 0-394-51468-8. New York: Random, pap. ISBN 0-394-72591-3.

The story opens with the murder of Beau Boutan, a Cajun farmer, on the Louisiana plantation of Candy Marshall, a headstrong white owner. She claims to have done the shooting because she wished to protect one of her black workers, Mathu, who has been like a guardian to her following the death of her parents. In the plan to stand between Mapes, the local sheriff, and Mathu, Candy has set into motion an idea that has brought together a group of old black men with shotguns (unloaded), all claiming to have done the shooting. The threat of the South's way of punishing blacks by lynching hangs over the story like a pall. It meets opposition from Beau's young brother who has been friends with a black fellow-student and team-mate at his university. This is a suspenseful story with unforgettable characters and confrontations.

Gallico, Paul. *The Snow Goose*. New York: Knopf, 1941. 58pp. ISBN 0-394-44593-7.

In 1930 Philip Rhayader, a hunchbacked painter, moves to an abandoned lighthouse, where he devotes himself not only to his painting but to maintaining a bird sanctuary. Rejected by the world, he is a recluse until Fritha, a young girl, brings him a hurt Canadian snow goose to care for and heal. The bird becomes a bond in their deepening relationship. When Philip is killed in aiding the rescue at Dunkirk, Fritha continues to care for his birds until the lighthouse is destroyed.

Galsworthy, John. *The Forsyte Saga*. (Includes *The Man of Property, In Chancery, To Let*.) New York: Scribner, 1933. 921pp. ISBN 0-684-17653-X.

These novels of Victorian life focus on a middle-class English family. Two cousins—Jolyon, an artist and a rebel, and Soames, who prizes possessions and material goods—are juxtaposed to present the values of the times. Soames's marriage to Irene is a failure but he derives happiness from Fleur, the daughter he has with his second wife, Annette Lamotte. Fleur's love for a young man is doomed when she learns of the family relationship that exists between them. The story is rich in characterizations, details, and interpersonal relationships, as individuals struggle to become whole human beings.

Gann, Ernest K. *The High and the Mighty*. New York: Morrow, 1953. 342pp. LC 53-5252. ISBN 0-688-01786-X.

A commercial airplane with 20 passengers on its way from Honolulu to San Francisco loses a propeller just after passing the point of no return. The crew and the passengers face possible death. Love, hate, jealousy, and faith emerge among the passengers and the crew as the plane fights for survival.

Gardner, John C. *Grendel*. New York: Knopf, 1971. 174pp. ISBN 0-394-47143-1. New York: Random, pap. ISBN 0-394-74056-4.

Grendel, the dread monster of *Beowulf*, becomes an emotionally moving hero as he tells his side of the story. Although the short novel may be most appreciated by those who have read *Beowulf*, Gardner has much to say about monsters as people's inventions and about the futility of war. The author maintains the spirit of Anglo-Saxon sagas, enriching the story with beautiful language and authenticity.

Garfield, Brian, ed. *The Crime of My Life; Favorite Stories by Presidents of the Mystery Writers of America*. New York: Walker, 1984. 192pp. LC 83-40389. ISBN 0-8027-0761-0.

Each story in this collection is by a different mystery writer who has chosen one of his favorites. They are very diverse, including a con man who meets his just desserts in "The Man Who Knew Women"; a story of bizarre material used for one artist's creations in "Scrimshaw"; the possibility of a murder committed and not remembered in "Hangover"; and a happy ending for a poor man who earns a much-needed reward for solving the mystery of a serial killer in "Blessed are the Meek."

Garfield, Leon. *The Strange Affair of Adelaide Harris*. New York: Pantheon, 1971. 223pp. ISBN 0-394-92322-7. (o.p.) New York: Dell, pap. ISBN 0-440-40057-0.

This is an amusing tale whose characters resemble those in some of Dickens's humorous writings. Harris, who learns in his class at Dr. Bunion's Academy about the Spartan custom of "exposing" unwanted children, decides to experiment with his infant sister, Adelaide. When he leaves her out in the woods to be found, and, as he hopes, nursed by some wild animal, she disappears, and a whole chain of wild events ensues. The entanglements include a romance between Mr. Brett, a teacher, and Tizz; a duel that never comes off; and the involvement of a strange private detective whose notes and clues become unmanageable. In this comedy of errors and mishaps, all ends well.

George, Jean Craighead. *Julie of the Wolves*. New York: Harper, 1972. 180pp. LC 72-76509. ISBN 0-06-021943-2. New York: Harper, pap. ISBN 0-06-440058-1.

In a modern classic on survival, Jean George tells the story of Miyax, an Eskimo, who is Julie in the white world. At 13 she is forced into an arranged marriage with a young Eskimo named Daniel. Finding the experience intolerable, Julie runs away and survives for many months on the Arctic tundra with a pack of wolves, staying alive through her knowledge of old Eskimo customs.

Gibbons, Kaye. *A Cure for Dreams*. Chapel Hill, N.C.: Algonguin Books of Chapel Hill, 1991. 171pp. LC 90-47864. ISBN 0-945575-33-5.

Marjorie Polly Randolph, her name partly derived from that of the black servant who helped her into the world, tells the story of her mother's life. That story includes life in Kentucky and Virginia among people of little material wealth, but treasure in the strength and resilience of the women. We meet characters like Sade, who finds a way to be free of her masochistic husband, and Trudy with her houseful of children and no husband or money. It is the time of Hoover and the Great Depression and the way women, especially Marjorie's mother Betty, helped each other. The humor in the telling lightens some of the heaviness of their lives.

Gibbons, Stella. *Cold Comfort Farm*. New York: Dial, 1964. 254pp. (o.p.) Repr. Magnolia, Mass.: Peter Smith, ISBN 0-8446-6148-1. New York: Penguin, pap. ISBN 0-14-000140-9.

Parodying the nineteenth century novels in which young girls who are left orphaned go off to live in strange households or with dotty relatives, this satire finds Flora Poste ensconced on Cold Comfort Farm in the bosom of the Starkadder family, as strange an assortment of people as can be imagined. Their language is deliberately imitative of something resembling a Yorkshire dialect, and even their names are intended to recall a rural background: Reuben, Seth, Urk, Caraway, Harkaway, and so on. Their livestock also have peculiar names. Flora arranges the lives of all of the Starkadders, even bringing in a Cinderella touch when Elfine's engagement to a young man of the gentry is announced at the county ball. All ends well for all, even for the grandmother, who tyrannized the family all their days with some mysterious tale of having "seen something nasty in the woodshed" when she was very little.

Gilman, Dorothy. *The Clairvoyant Countess*. Garden City, N.Y.: Doubleday, 1975. 179pp. LC 74-33642. ISBN 0-385-08922-8. (o.p.) New York: Fawcett, pap. ISBN 0-449-21318-8.

The countess, Madame Kartiska, has the gift of second sight. Detective Lieutenant Pruden is at first skeptical of her psychic powers but slowly begins to accept her special abilities as she helps him solve difficult cases. Madame Kartiska's sensitivity and intelligence equal her psychic powers, making her an attractive partner to the police. Gilman is lighthearted in her look at extrasensory capabilities and portrays an entertaining character.

Gilman, Dorothy. *Mrs. Pollifax on the China Station*. Garden City, N.Y.: Doubleday, 184pp. LC 82-45972. ISBN 0-385-14525-X. (o.p.) New York: Fawcett, pap. ISBN 0-449-20840-0.

Like middle-aged amateur lady detectives in some other favorite mystery stories, Mrs. Pollifax helps out the CIA in a dangerous mission to rescue an engineer from China. He is important because of his secret information about China-Soviet border fortifications, and the United States wants him before the Russians get him. In addition to other talents, Mrs. Pollifax is a brown belt in karate. Among the tourists on the trip set up for her is another agent, not identified to her, thus making for some suspenseful encounters. An added pleasure in the story is the description of many of the Chinese cultural treasures only recently accessible to foreign visitors.

Gingher, Marianne. *Bobby Rex's Greatest Hit*. New York: Atheneum, 1986. 308pp. LC 86-3427. ISBN 0-689-11769-8. (o.p.) New York: Ballantine, pap. ISBN 0-345-34823-0.

Pally Thompson's story, told in letters, flashbacks, and her own inimitable southern prose, is that of a North Carolina teenager in the early 1960s. Bobby Rex Moseley is a kind of Elvis Presley figure whom she had admired and longed for when they were both in high school. When his song about her becomes a hit, Pally encounters suspicion from her fiancé, a widowed veterinarian, and caustic gossip from others, because Bobby Rex makes it sound as though they shared a torrid love. In distancing herself from him, Pally highlights some memorable characters, and does so with considerable liveliness and charm. The comedies and tragedies of a small town's life are here in Pally's story.

Gipson, Fred. *Old Yeller*. New York: Harper, 1956. 158pp. LC 56-8780. ISBN 0-06-011545-9. New York: Harper, pap. 0-06-440382-3.

In the 1880s 14-year-old Travis has to take care of the farm in the Texas hill country with his ma and little brother when his father joins a cattle drive to Abilene. An ornery stray hound dog, old Yeller, helps ward off the attacks of bears, wild hogs, and a wolf.

Glasgow, Ellen. *Barren Ground*. New York: Harcourt, 1925. 409pp. (o.p.) Repr. San Diego, CA.: Harcourt, 1985. 540pp. LC 85-14032. ISBN 0-15-610685-X. Repr. Magnolia, Mass.: Peter Smith. ISBN 0-8446-4019-0. New York: Hill & Wang, pap. ISBN 0-8090-0014-8.

Dorinda Oakley, daughter of a poor white farmer, falls in love with Jason Greylock, the last of the line of an old Virginia family. Although she is expecting to marry him, he, in fact, marries someone else. Dorinda finds that she is pregnant. She leaves for New York and is in an automobile accident that causes her to lose the child. After a stay in New York, Dorinda is compelled to return home when her father has a stroke. She successfully takes over the management of the family farm and marries Nathan Pedlar to provide a home for his children. She also provides aid to the man who caused her so much unhappiness in her earlier years.

Glasgow, Ellen. *The Sheltered Life*. New York: Hill & Wang, 1979. 292pp. ISBN 0-8090-0138-1. (o.p.) Mattituck, N.Y.: Amereon, ISBN 0-88411-646-8.

This novel of life in a changing Southern community depicts the manners and morals of two families as seen through the eyes of two characters in the book. On the one hand there is the elderly General Archbald whose life is controlled by the women in his household—two daughters and a daughter-in-law. The other narrator is young Jenny Blair, the General's granddaughter. Jenny is at first an innocent bystander in the troubled life of the Archbalds' neighbors, Eva and George Birdsong. George, an unfaithful husband, is the object of Jenny's affection, an emotion that becomes a passion as Jenny grows into her teens. That obsession triggers a shattering climax.

Godden, Rumer. *An Episode of Sparrows*. New York: Viking, 1955. 246pp. LC 81-47095. (o.p.) New York: Puffin, pap. ISBN 0-14-034024-6.

Lovejoy Mason, a little girl living in the slums of London, whose mother travels with a theater, starts a tiny garden, which Tip Malone and his gang heartlessly destroy. Overwhelmed by the despair he caused, Tip helps find a new spot and steals dirt from gardens in nearby Mortimer Square. Olivia and Angela Chesney, whose gardens were used as a source by Tip, have differing reactions when they learn who the culprits are. Angela wishes the children punished, but Olivia, for the first time in her life, disagrees with and stands up to her sister. Shortly afterward, upon Olivia's death, it is learned that she has left most of her money to the children she admired and the man who looked after them.

Godden, Rumer. *The Peacock Spring: A Western Progress*. New York: Penguin, 1976. 274pp. LC 75-31701. ISBN 0-670-54558-9. (o.p.) New York: Penguin, pap. ISBN 0-14-032005-9.

Una and Hal, two teenage girls, are brought to India to join their diplomat father. He needs them to provide a facade of respectability for his relationship with his mistress, the Eurasian Alix Lamont. She has ostensibly been engaged as a tutor for the girls. Una becomes involved with an Indian poet and becomes pregnant; Hal falls in love with a deposed rajah. Both girls suffer from these relationships. Una loses her lover and her baby and Hal returns to America to be with her mother.

*Godwin, Gail. *Father Melancholy's Daughter*. New York: Morrow, 1991. 512pp. LC 90-13490. ISBN 0-688-06531-7.

Margaret Gower is the daughter of the Rector of St. Cuthbert's. Her life is sharply changed at the age of six when her mother, to whom she had been very close, departs with a woman friend for an indefinite period. The mother's reason appears to be an attempt to discover her own capabilities. When she is killed in an auto accident in England, Margaret's life becomes completely integrated into her father's and in thoughts about the role of religion in her life. Earthly love seems accessible but is not her choice. For the mature reader this is a book that provokes questions about human relationships and moral thought.

*Godwin, Gail. *Mr. Bedford and the Muses*. New York: Viking, 1983. 229pp. LC 83-47870. ISBN 0-670-49235-3. (o.p.) New York: Avon, pap. ISBN 0-380-69377-1.

The longest story in this collection concerns itself with a group of young people living as boarders in London with an American couple of mysterious background. Each character is most interestingly described and the tensions and interrelationships among them keep the story moving. In other stories a writer is suddenly visited by a young girl who offers her services in the writer's home with a surprising development; a father's love for his son comes into conflict with his attraction to his son's friend; an author finds his life affected by the presence in his village of a woman with the same name as his. Godwin's writing is graceful and humorous.

Godwin, Gail. *A Mother and Two Daughters*. New York: Viking, 1982. 576pp. LC 81-65286. ISBN 0-670-49021-0. (o.p.) New York: Avon, pap. ISBN 0-380-61598-3.

When Nell Strickland is suddenly widowed at 63, she has to relate to her two grown daughters in a new and trying way. Cate, the older, is iconoclastic, impetuous, and divorced—more than once. Lydia, although married to a devoted and successful man and the mother of two quite satisfactory young sons, is striking out for freedom and self-fulfillment. The abrasive relationship between the two sisters is the most central one in this novel that depicts many relationships: mothers and daughters, husbands and wives, lovers, cousins, and other family members.

Gold, Herbert. *Fathers*. New York: Arbor House. ISBN 0-686-47207-1. (o.p.) Repr. New York: Donald I. Fine, 1991, 320pp. LC 91-55187. ISBN 1-55611-314-5.

Sam Gold, adopting that surname as a symbol of what he hopes to find in America, leaves the old country. He struggles through the Depression and fights racketeers in order to gain some economic security for his family in Cleveland, Ohio. However, he cannot interest his oldest son in following in his father's steps, although the boy yearns for the close relationship he imagines "real" American fathers have with their sons. There is humor and pain in this description of the difficulties endured by the immigrant Jew in America.

Golding, William. *Lord of the Flies*. New York: Putnam, 1959. 243pp. ISBN 0-698-10219-3. (o.p.) New York: Putnam, pap. ISBN 0-399-50148-7.+

Stranded on an island, a group of English schoolboys leave innocence behind in a struggle for survival. A political structure modeled after English government is set up and a hierarchy develops, but forces of anarchy and aggression surface. The boys' existence begins to degenerate into a savage one. They are rescued from their microcosmic society to return to an adult, stylized milieu filled with the same psychological tensions and moral voids. Adventure and allegory are brilliantly combined in this novel.

Goldman, William. *Marathon Man*. New York: Delacorte, 1974. 309pp. ISBN 0-440-05327-7. (o.p.) Cutchogue, NY: Buccaneer, 1991. 290pp. ISBN 0-89966-809-7. New York: Ballantine, pap. ISBN 0-345-34803-6.

"Babe" Levy, a graduate student, spends his free time running, and dreams of being a great marathon runner. The death of his brother in Babe's apartment starts a chain of mysterious and terrifying events. Pursued by government agents and ex-Nazis, Babe struggles to escape being assassinated. The torture scenes may make this suspenseful story an ordeal for some readers.

Goldman, William. *The Princess Bride*. New York: Ballantine, 1987 pap. ISBN 0-345-34803-6.

The author claims to have rewritten a story that his father used to read to him when he was a child, recovering from a serious illness. Goldman calls his "the good parts version." All long and boring passages have been removed, and only the fighting, captures, evil prince, henchmen, daring and loyal friends, and, of course, a beautiful heroine and a perfect hero are kept. This is a funny spoof that combines a wild adventurous story with comments on love and life.

Gordimer, Nadine. *July's People*. New York: Viking, 1981. 160pp. LC 80-24877. ISBN 0-670-41048-9. (o.p.) New York: Penguin, pap. ISBN 0-14-006140-1.

When revolution breaks out against the whites in South Africa, Bamford and Maureen Smales are forced to flee. Their black servant July, loyal to them for 15 years, takes them away to his people in a bush village. His role changes slowly to one not only of savior but also overseer. The change in their manner of living from the good, clean, well-regulated life of "the ruling class" to that of the customs of July's people raises havoc within both the white and black families and in the delicate tissue of understanding between the Smales and their servant. There is much to be learned from this powerful story written by an author who lives in South Africa and who writes with authority on a subject that has import for any society where race relations or colonial conditions are fragile and explosive.

Gordimer, Nadine. *My Son's Story*. New York: Farrar, 1990. 292pp. LC 90-83232. ISBN 0-374-21751-3. New York: Penguin, pap. ISBN 0-14-015975-4.

Will's father is a former schoolteacher from a segregated "coloured" township. He is also a political activist and, therefore, model for his son. When Will, a truant from school, accidentally sees his father, Sonny, coming out of the theatre in the company of a white woman the boy is stunned by this evidence of disloyalty. The woman, however, is a special one—Hannah Plowman—who is dedicated to the cause of the South African blacks. The conflict in the father's relationship with his son and the disastrous consequences ensuing from an affair that brings not only love but understanding to Sonny make for a powerful novel by a writer well-versed in South Africa's problems.

Gordimer, Nadine. *Selected Stories*. New York: Viking, 1976. 381pp. LC 75-29460. ISBN 0-670-63197-3. (o.p.) New York: Penguin, pap. ISBN 0-14-006737-X.

Although the author's personal background is South Africa and she uses that locale as a setting for her stories, the themes in her writing have a universal significance. In "The Soft Voice of the Serpent," there is a painful description of a young man who had lost a leg and sees in the garden a locust similarly handicapped but with a crucial difference: the effect of that loss on man and insect. The complicated levels of communication in a society of mixed racial groups and the radical activities of some whites who try to breach the wall of apartheid is the theme of "The Smell of Death and Flower." In "The Gentle Art," we are drawn into an episode involving the hunting and shooting of crocodiles with such immediacy as to feel part of the party in the boat. Gordimer's prose is powerful and leaves a long-lasting after-effect.

Gordimer, Nadine. *Something Out There*. New York: Viking, 1984. 203pp. LC 83-40250. ISBN 0-670-65660-7. (o.p.) New York: Penguin, pap. ISBN 0-14-007711-1.

In the nine short stories and one novella which constitute this collection, the reader gains insight into the lives of the people in beleaguered South Africa. The Afrikaaners resist the attempts of the blacks to obtain a life of dignity, indeed any of the amenities that would lift them out of the misery in which they barely survive. In other stories Gordimer describes a sad love affair in "Rags and Bones"; writes a response from Franz Kafka's father to his son's denunciations of his family; suspensefully juxtaposes two threats to the inhabitants of Johannesburg—some kind of wild animal preying on pets and property, and a band of two whites and two blacks lying in wait to perform an act of terrorism.

*Gordon, Mary. *Final Payments*. New York: Random, 1978. 297pp. LC 77-90259. ISBN 0-394-42793-9. (o.p.) New York: Ballantine, pap. ISBN 0-345-32973-2.

Isabel Moore spends 11 years almost totally absorbed in caring for her invalid father, who suffered a paralyzing stroke after discovering his daughter in a compromising situation with one of his students. When she is 30, her father dies; she is freed from responsibility for his welfare but not yet able to accept responsibility for her own life. Her involvement with two men adds complications as, guilt-ridden and filled with religious skepticism, Isabel searches for answers and begins to heal. Two childhood friends, Eleanor, an independent woman, and Liz, a tough married mother of two children, are instrumental in helping Isabel grow toward self-realization.

Gordon, Mary. *The Other Side*. New York: Viking, 1989. 386pp. ISBN 0-670-82566-2. New York: Penguin, pap. ISBN 0-14-014408-0.

Ellen McNamara, old and dying, is awaiting the return of her husband Vincent from a hospital stay. He had always promised to be near her at her death. The author takes off from that day, when the McNamara family has convened to welcome Vincent, to tell the past history of the children and grandchildren. Ellen had truly loved only her son John and had rejected her daughters, Theresa and Magdalene. Of all the offspring from marriages, remarriages and divorce, it is two grandchildren Ellen favors, Cam and Dan, who are cousins but more like brother and sister in their relationship. The description of the trials and privations of Irish immigrants who came to the "other side," America, is similar to so many other ethnic groups who arrived in America looking for a better life.

Grafton, Sue. *"C" is for Corpse*. New York: Holt, 1986. 256pp. LC 85-24797. ISBN 0-03-001888-9. New York: Bantam, pap. ISBN 0-553-28036-8.

The detective in this mystery is funny, feisty, and female. Kinsey Millhone is a gun-toting, rough-talking private investigator. She meets a young man, Buddy Callahan, at the gym where she works out and agrees to take his case. He wants her to investigate an auto accident in which he was badly injured because he claims that it was a murder attempt. When a second attempt results in his death Kinsey, although she no longer has him as a client, pursues the matter and, in a hair-raising finale that takes place in a morgue, she unmasks the murderer. Grafton started her series with "A as in Alibi" and is continuing through the alphabet.

*Grass, Günter. *Tin Drum.* Trans. from the German by Ralph Manheim. New York: Random, 1962. 541pp. ISBN 0-394-44902-9. (o.p.) Repr. Magnolia, Mass.: Peter Smith, 1992. ISBN 0-8446-6519-3.

Oskar Matzerath, born with an unusually sharp mind, describes the amoral conditions through which he has lived in twentieth-century Germany, both during and after the Hitler regime. This strange narrator stops growing when he is three years old and remains three feet tall until some time later, when he decides to grow a few inches more. After the war he escapes to West Germany, where he works in such capacities as an artist's model, a night-club performer, and a black marketeer. Depicted as a freak (Oskar becomes a hunchback later in his life), this character symbolizes the deformed society of this century. It is through his tin drum, which he uses to stimulate recollections of his life, that Oskar describes his past while he is an inmate in a mental hospital.

Grau, Shirley Ann. *The Keepers of the House.* New York: Knopf, 1964. 309pp. ISBN 0-394-43182-0. (o.p.) New York: Avon, pap. ISBN 0-380-70047-6.

This multigenerational novel deals with the twentieth-century heirs of a Southern dynasty, their relations to the past, and their involvement in the racial and political complexities of the present. The narrator is Abigail Mason Tolliver, granddaughter of William Howland, whose second wife had been a Freejack Negro. The townspeople have always assumed that she had been no more than William's mistress, but the truth of the legality of their marriage surfaces when Abigail's husband, John Tolliver, enters the race for governor. In addition to leading to Tolliver's defeat, the story of the marriage also incites a mob to burn down the old Howland house. Abigail saves the house but withdraws the economic support that the Howland family has always supplied the town, and lets it "shrivel and shrink to its real size."

*Graves, Robert. *I, Claudius*. New York: Modern Lib., 1934. 448pp. LC 37-27271. ISBN 0-394-60811-9. New York: Random, pap. ISBN 0-394-72536-0.

Claudius is lame and a stammerer who seems unlikely to carry on the family tradition of power in ancient Rome. Immersing himself in scholarly pursuits, Claudius observes and lives through the plots hatched by his grandmother, Livia, political conspiracies, murders, and corruption, and he survives a number of emperors. He becomes emperor at last and is a just and well-liked ruler, in contrast to those who preceded him.

Green, Gerald. *The Last Angry Man*. New York: Scribner, 1956. (o.p.) Repr. Mattituck, N.Y.: Amereon., 1976. 494pp. ISBN 0-89190-121-3.

Dr. Samuel Abelman of Brooklyn is an irascible old man who has driven away nearly all of his patients because of his temper. He is also a strong, brave man dedicated to the principles that made him become a doctor in the first place. Even amid the deterioration of the neighborhood in which he lives, he displays his brilliant diagnostic skills and dogged devotion to duty in trying to help a black teenager who has a brain tumor.

Greene, Bette. *Summer of My German Soldier*. New York: Dial, 1973. 224pp. LC 73-6025. ISBN 0-8037-8321-3. New York: Bantam, pap. ISBN 0-553-27247-0.

Patty knows the pain of loneliness, rejection, and even beatings in a family where she is the ugly duckling, unable to gain her parents' love. This is in contrast to the affection shown to her beautiful and submissive sister. Anton Reiker is a German prisoner-of-war in a camp outside of Jenkinsville, Arkansas, and when he escapes, Patty helps him. Because her family is Jewish, she pays dearly for this intervention.

Greene, Graham. *The Heart of the Matter*. New York: Viking, 1948. 306pp. ISBN 0-670-36459-2. (o.p.) Repr. Mattituck, NY: Amereon, ISBN 0-88411-654-9. New York: Penguin, pap. ISBN 0-14-001789-5.

After 15 years as chief of police in a district of British West Africa where he has scrupulously built his reputation for honesty, Major Scobie is nonetheless passed over for the appointment as district commissioner. His wife, who has never fit in with the other British wives, is sorely disappointed and leaves for a solitary vacation. During her absence Scobie falls in love with a young widow and becomes the victim of a blackmailer. The major begins to doubt his own integrity and becomes entangled in lies. A strict Catholic, he plots his suicide, which he views as the only means of resolving his guilt.

Greene, Graham. *The Human Factor*. New York: Viking, 1978. 276pp. LC 77-17169. ISBN 0-670-56979-8. (o.p.) New York: Pocket, pap. ISBN 0-318-33014-8.

In the British Foreign Service "the human factor" becomes a liability for employees and a conduit for suspense, intrigue, and tragedy. Maurice Castle, head of a division in which information seems to have been leaked, presents a very positive image that appears to assure his innocence, but Davis, directly responsible to him, is an object of speculation. For a secret agent, the normal relationships of love and family are fraught with danger. As is true of many of Greene's novels, there are questions in this book about the loyalty owed to a government whose activities are suspect.

Greene, Graham. *Monsignor Quixote*. New York: Simon & Schuster, 1982. 221pp. LC 82-5937. ISBN 0-671-45818-3. New York: Pocket, pap. ISBN 0-371-47470-7.

Father Quixote is a humble parish priest despised by his bishop. Through an accidental encounter with a stranded bishop, he is named Monsignor, much to his bishop's and his discomfort. He sets off on a journey with the communist ex-mayor of his town. The philosophy and thinking of the ex-mayor, Sancho, are diametrically opposed to that of the priest, and there is much provocative discussion between them as they follow paths similar to those taken by the priest's fictional forebear, Don Quixote. Some of their adventures bring the priest to some surprising places, such as an X-rated cinema and a church where religion is being commercialized and demeaned. There is much humor as well as theology to involve the reader in this delightful odyssey.

Greene, Graham. *The Power and the Glory*. New York: Viking, 1948. 276pp. ISBN 0-670-56979-8. (o.p.) Repr. New York: Viking, 1990. 320pp. LC 90-50052. ISBN 0-670-83536-6. New York: Penguin, pap. LC 76-104160. ISBN 0-14-001791-7.

Under the law of the Red Shirts in a state located in southern Mexico, all priests of the Catholic church are automatically killed for treason. This novel is the saga of the hunt and the capture of the last practicing priest in that state who, although too weak to resist whiskey, is strong enough to bring the solace of the church to the Mexican peasants.

Grimes, Martha. *The Anodyne Necklace*. Boston: Little, 1983. 250pp. LC 83-880. ISBN 0-316-32882-0. (o.p.) New York: Dell, pap. ISBN 0-440-10280-4.

Sixteen-year-old Katie O'Brien, playing her violin in an underground London station to make some money, is mysteriously attacked. From that incident begins a mystery involving the theft of an emerald necklace, the murder of a young man whose fingers have been chopped off, and still another murder. The characters in this absorbing tale include not only the residents of Littlebourne, Katie's village, but some East End Londoners like the Cripps family, whose squalid home and bizarre behavior will not soon be forgotten by the reader. Satirical humor enlivens the careful and patient unraveling done by the special detective featured in Grimes' mysteries—the attractive Scotland Yard Superintendent Richard Jury.

Guareschi, Giovanni. *The Little World of Don Camillo*. North Pomfret, Vt.: David and Charles. ISBN 0-575-0091-8. (o.p.) Repr. Mattituck NY: Amereon, ISBN 0-89190-215-5.

Don Camillo, a priest of great physical strength and goodness in a village in northern Italy, regularly converses with Christ. His adversary is Peppone, the Communist mayor. The stories related here usually involve a struggle between the two, with Don Camillo often appearing to have miraculous assistance. Not only humor but also insightful observations on religious and political issues are offered.

Guest, Judith. *Ordinary People*. New York: Viking, 1976. 263pp. LC 76-2368. ISBN 0-670-52831-5. (o.p.) New York: Ballantine, pap. ISBN 0-345-33505-8.+

When his older brother drowns in a boating accident, 17-year-old Conrad Jarrett feels responsible and makes an unsuccessful attempt at suicide. After eight months in a mental institution, Conrad returns home to parents whose marriage is crumbling, friends who are wary of him, and a psychiatrist who works with him to help put the pieces together. The pain of adolescent anxiety and fragile family relationships are authentically depicted.

Guthrie, Alfred B. *The Big Sky*. Boston: Houghton, 1947. 386pp. (o.p.) New York: Bantam, pap. LC 85-4717. ISBN 0-553-26683-7.

After a fight with his father, 17-year-old Boone Caudill leaves Kentucky and heads west to hunt buffalo and shoot Indians. With his friends Jim and Summers he makes his way by foot, on horseback, and by keel boat to the headwaters of the Missouri River. Boone marries a Blackfoot Indian and settles in her village. Returning to Kentucky after 13 years, he realizes that the typical life of a mountain man, which he has lived during that period, is over.

Guy, Rosa. *The Friends*. New York: Holt, 1973. 208pp. LC 72-11068. ISBN 0-8050-1742-9. New York: Bantam, pap. ISBN 0-553-26519-9.

During early adolescence, friendship can be painful as well as joyful. Phyllisia learns this in her relationship with Edith Jackson. Having just arrived in Harlem from the West Indies, Phyllisia finds life difficult because she is new to the urban scene and because her father is a very strict disciplinarian. Because her accent marks her as different, she is treated with hostility by her classmates, and only Edith befriends her when she is involved in a fight. Phyllisia resists her father's authority when he forbids her to maintain her friendship with poor and slovenly Edith.

Hailey, Elizabeth Forsythe. *A Woman of Independent Means*. New York: Avon, 1979. pap. ISBN 0-380-42390-1.+

Through her letters, which she began writing in 1899 when she was ten, we follow the life of Bess Steed Garner, a thoroughly modern twentieth-century woman. Bess inherited wealth from her mother, which insured her being able to live exactly as she wished. After a first marriage that was a love match but was marked by tragedy, she traveled a great deal, had many flirtations, and settled down into a second marriage. It was a comfortable, friendly affair only occasionally disturbed by some more-than-friendly encounters with other men. Bess is a bossy, loving, lovable, and extremely believable heroine.

*Hall, Oakley. *The Bad Lands*. New York: Atheneum, 1978. 371pp. LC 77-15839. ISBN 0-689-10823-0. (o.p.) New York: Bantam, pap. ISBN 0-553-27265-9.

The American West in the 1880s was the scene of violence between the early cattlemen, the native Indians, and those who came later on, either as owners of small herds or grangers. The struggle for land and power is told through the relationships among such characters as Lord Machray, a volatile and earthy Scotsman; Yule Hardy, whose narrow sense of individualism is in conflict with his pursuit of reasonableness as a way of achieving order; Andrew Livingston, a New York banker-politician trying to bury a personal grief in those Dakota lands; Cora Benbow, owner of the local brothel and paramour of Machray; and Bill Driggs, who hates all those who have come to despoil the land he himself has used as a hunting ground. These were truly Bad Lands in terms of the difficulty of surviving in them, but some of the people there were worse.

Hamilton, Virginia. *Sweet Whispers, Brother Rush*. New York: Putnam, 1982. 224pp. LC 81-22745. ISBN 0-399-20894-1. New York: Avon, pap. ISBN 0-380-65193-9.

Teresa (Tree) is black and responsible for more than a young teenager should have to manage. Because the father deserted the family long ago, M'Vy, the mother, has had to work at exhausting jobs that kept her away from home much of the time. Tree's responsibilities include caring for her retarded older brother, Dab, who also—unknown to Tree— suffers a blood disease. An element of mystic fantasy in the form of the ghost of Tree's uncle, Brother Rush, heightens the tension in the story. Although struggling to maintain itself, this family is portrayed as honoring the values that middle-class families treasure, regardless of color. The appearance of Silversmith, M'Vy's male friend, shows a black man as a strong, protective, and gentle father figure.

Hammett, Dashiell. *The Maltese Falcon*. New York: Knopf, 1930. 276pp. (o.p.) Repr. Berkeley, Ca.: North Point Press, 1984. 352pp. LC 86-62830. ISBN 0-86547-156-8. New York: Random, pap. ISBN 0-679-72264-5.

The plot centers around the statue of a bird, reputed to be the repository of the treasure of the medieval Knights of Malta. Several groups of people claim that the bird is theirs and are willing to kill to obtain it. Detective Sam Spade tries to prevent his being one of the victims while he is on a case for a client who claims to be the rightful owner. Spade is the epitome of the tough private detective.

Hammett, Dashiell. *The Thin Man*. New York: Knopf, 1934. 259pp. (o.p.) New York: Random, pap. ISBN 0-679-72263-7.

Nick and Nora Charles are visiting New York from San Francisco, where Nick manages Nora's family business. His past career as a private detective catches up with them when the secretary of an old friend is murdered. The chief suspect is Nick's friend, eccentric inventor Clyde Wynant, who has not been seen in several months by anyone but his lawyer. Using deductive reasoning, Nick is able to solve the murder case in this charmer of a mystery.

Hamsun, Knut. *Growth of the Soil*. New York: Knopf, 1953 (1920). 435pp. ISBN 0-394-42743-2. (o.p.) New York: Random, pap. ISBN 0-394-71781-3.

As a young man, Isak begins to farm some unclaimed land in the hills. He is soon joined by Inger, who works hard beside him, bears him a son, and becomes his wife. Together the family turns the small holding into a large estate that becomes the envy of the townsfolk who then move to Isak's mountain to try their luck. The successes, the failures, and the intertwining of the several families on the mountain form the theme for a story that is a powerful evocation of the strength people draw from the land.

Harris, Mark. *Bang the Drum Slowly*. New York: Knopf, 1956. (o.p.) Repr. Lincoln, Neb.: Univ. of Nebraska Press, 1984. 243pp. LC 83-16922. ISBN 0-8032-7221-9. Cutchogue, N.Y.: Buccaneer. ISBN 0-89966-393-1.

Henry Wiggen, star pitcher for the New York Mammoths, writes about his friend Bruce Pearson, who is slowly dying of Hodgkins Disease. Pearson, a third-string catcher, is ridiculed by his teammates for being stupid but strives to be a better player in order to help the team win the pennant.

*Hasek, Jaroslav. *The Good Soldier: Schweik*. Trans. from the Czech by Paul Selver. New York: Crowell, 1974. 752pp. (o.p.) New York: New Amer. Lib., pap. abridged. 429pp. ISBN 0-451-51005-4.

Intended as satire, the bitterness of the author's observations is sometimes overlooked in the laughter evoked by the behavior of this intrepid nonhero, Josef Schweik. He had been a soldier but was discharged because he was described as feebleminded. In the same way that he confounded the military—by his candor, which they considered stupidity—Schweik succeeds in making a shambles of procedures in lunatic asylums, prison camps, and police stations. The irony that marks

Schweik's comments on these assorted bureaucracies is still applicable to some of the institutions in our modern technological society.

Heggen, Thomas. *Mister Roberts*. Boston: Houghton, 1946. 221pp. ISBN0-395-07788-5. (o.p.) Repr. Cutchogue, N.Y.: Buccaneer, 1983. 230pp. ISBN 0-89966-445-8.

Douglas Roberts, First Lieutenant on the *Reluctant,* a U.S. Navy supply ship in the Pacific, is the leading inspiration for the undeclared war between the crew and the unreasonable skipper. The dull life on ship is eased by humorous antics and the resulting rage of the commander. When Roberts is transferred to a destroyer, the crew is saddened by his departure. Life will not be the same on the *Reluctant.*

Heller, Joseph. *Catch-22.* New York: Simon & Schuster, 1961. 443pp. ISBN 0-671-12805-1. (o.p.) New York: Dell, pap. ISBN 0-440-11120-X.+

The action in this serio-comic book takes place on a small Italian island during the waning months of World War II. Yossarian, a bombardier, is trying to avoid flying any more bombing missions so that he can get out of the war alive, but his colonel keeps raising the number of missions he must execute in order to be discharged. The novel is full of zany incidents and characters. By way of some of the funniest dialogue ever, Heller takes shots at the hypocrisy, meanness, and stupidities of our society.

Helprin, Mark. *Ellis Island and Other Stories.* New York: Delacorte, 1981. LC 80-18437. ISBN 0-440-02204-5. (o.p.) New York: Dell, pap. ISBN 0-440-32204-9.

In this collection of stories the author takes us to varying backgrounds from Israel in the 1970s to Ellis Island at the turn of the century. In "A Vermont Tale" a grandfather whose grandchildren are caught in a breakdown of their family tells them a beautiful romance about two loves, a story applicable to human love. "Palais de Justice" presents a contest between old endurance and youthful contempt for age as indicated in a boating race between two men unequal in years. The stories illustrate morality, humor, and human resilience.

Hemingway, Ernest. *A Farewell to Arms*. New York: Scribner, 1919. 332pp. LC 67-013157. ISBN 0-684-15562-1. New York: Scribner, pap. ISBN 0-684-71797-2.

Frederic Henry, an American attached to the Italian army as an ambulance driver during World War I, is badly wounded. He meets and falls in love with Catherine Barkley, an English nurse. Just before he must return to the front, she tells him that she is pregnant. Caught in a changing military situation, Henry tries to get his ambulance to its destination but finally abandons it. Facing charges of desertion, he escapes, finds his way to Catherine, and flees with her to Switzerland. There the birth of the baby goes badly and the novel has a tragic ending.

Hemingway, Ernest. *For Whom the Bell Tolls*. New York: Scribner, 1940. 482pp. ISBN 0-684-10239-0. New York: Scribner, pap. ISBN 0-684-71798-0.

This war tale covers four tension-ridden days in the life of Robert Jordan, an American in the Loyalist ranks during the Spanish Civil War. Having accomplished his mission to blow up a bridge with the aid of guerilla bands, he is injured when his horse falls and crushes his leg. As enemy troops approach, he is left alone to meet their attack. Jordan's love for Maria, a young girl whom the Fascists had subjected to every possible indignity, adds another dimension to a story of courage, dedication—and treachery.

Hemingway, Ernest. *The Old Man and the Sea*. New York: Scribner, 1952. 128pp. ISBN 0-684-10245-5. New York: Scribner, pap. ISBN 0-684-71805-7.

The old fisherman Santiago had only one friend in the village, the boy Manolin. Everyone else thought he was unlucky because he had caught no fish in a long time. At noon on the 85th day of fishing, he hooked a large fish. He fought with the huge swordfish for three days and nights before he could harpoon it, but that battle came to nought when sharks destroyed the fish before Santiago could get back to the village.

Henderson, Zenna. *The People: No Different Flesh*. Garden City, N.Y.: Doubleday, 1967. 236pp. (o.p.) New York: Avon, pap. ISBN 0-380-01506-4.

The "People" are members of a star-roving race who crash to earth and are scattered. They look completely human but have special mental powers such as ESP and telekinesis. Separated from their own kind and heritage, the children and youth of the People do not realize they are aliens. The tales of their adventure are also parables of society's treatment of those who are different.

Hentoff, Nat. *Jazz Country*. New York: Harper, 1965. 146pp. LC 65-15557. ISBN 0-06-022306-5. (o.p.) New York: Dell, pap. ISBN 0-440-94203-9.

Sixteen-year-old Tom tries to break into jazz and gain fame, but his whiteness is a handicap in the predominantly black field. Befriending black musicians and learning of their hardships and glories, Tom is torn between the jazz world and college.

Herbert, Frank. *Dune*. Radnor, Pa.: Chilton, 1965. 544pp. LC 65-22547. ISBN 0-8019-5077-5. (o.p.) Repr. New York: Putnam, 1984, 528pp. LC 83-16030. ISBN 0-399-12896-4. New York: Berkley, pap. ISBN 0-425-07160-X.+

Herbert combines several classic elements: a Machiavellian world of political intrigue worthy of fourteenth century Italy, a huge cast of characters, and a detailed picture of a culture. Duke Leto Atreides and his family are coerced into exchanging their rich lands for a barren planet, Dune, which produces a unique drug. Duke's son, Paul, becomes the leader of a group that leads the Fremen of Dune against the enemy. This is a science fiction story with sociological and ecological import.

Hersey, John. *A Bell for Adano*. New York: Knopf, 1944. ISBN 0-394-41660-0. New York: Random, pap. LC 87-045943. ISBN 0-394-75695-9.

The town bell of Adano is transformed into material for a cannon, and its loss symbolizes a moral loss to the very life of the people. When the town falls into the hands of the Americans and the Fascist forces are in retreat, Major Joppolo, a Brooklyn-born Italian, becomes a favorite of the townspeople because of the concern he has for them. Not only does he help Tina find her missing sweetheart, but he finds a replacement for the bell, retrieving it from a U.S. ship named after an Italian-American hero of World War I. To the town's dismay, Major Joppolo is relieved of his command by an American general whose unreasonable orders he ignores.

Hersey, John. *The Child Buyer*. New York: Knopf, 1960. 229pp. ISBN 0-394-41910-3. (o.p.) New York: Random, pap. ISBN 0-394-75698-3.

This powerful indictment of the American educational system and the material values placed on intelligence in our society takes the form of a Senate hearing. The Senate investigation concerns the attempts of Wissey Jones to buy Barry Rudd, a precociously brilliant child. Through a series of medical procedures and the use of drugs, the child is transformed into an extremely efficient thinking machine. That the child's personality is of secondary importance compared to the benefits to be derived from this supercomputer is at the crux of the argument. Barry's parents and the local educational authorities are initially opposed but are slowly won over by Jones's appeals to their vanity.

Hersey, John. *The Wall*. New York: Knopf, 1961. (o.p.) New York: Random, 1988. pap. LC 87-45944. ISBN 0-394-75696-7.

This novel is presented as a journal kept by a diarist during World War II. It tells of life in the Warsaw Ghetto, depicting Jewish interdependence in a struggle for survival. The writer's observations enrich our understanding of Jewish culture. Although the diarist dies of pneumonia in 1944, his escape from the enclosure within which the Germans confined the Jews is a testament to hope and courage.

Hesse, Hermann. *Siddhartha*. Trans. from the German by Hilda Rosner. New York: New Directions, 1951. 153pp. LC 51-13669. ISBN 0-8112-0292-5. New York: Bantam, pap. ISBN 0-553-20884-5.+

The young Indian Siddhartha endures many experiences in his search for the ultimate answer to the question, what is humankind's role on earth? He is also looking for the solution to loneliness and discontent, and he seeks that solution in the way of a wanderer, the company of a courtesan, and the high position of a successful businessman. His final relationship is with a humble but wise ferryman. This is an allegory that examines love, wealth, and freedom while the protagonist struggles toward self-knowledge.

Hesse, Hermann. *Steppenwolf.* Trans. from the German by Basil Creighton. New York: Holt, 1929. 309pp. Rev. ed. LC 63-12171. ISBN 0-8050-1317-2. New York: Holt, pap. ISBN 0-8050-1247-8.+

The wolf of the steppes, part human and part wild animal, is the symbol for Harry Haller's existence. He feels constantly torn between his internal life of esthetic exploration and the cold external world of technology. Because of the inability to resolve this conflict, Haller, at age 50, is a lonely and tormented individual.

Higgins, Jack. *The Eagle Has Flown.* New York: Simon & Schuster, 1991. 352pp. LC 91-4368. ISBN 0-671-72458-4. New York: Pocket, pap. ISBN 0-671-74669-3.

Although this novel is a sequel to *The Eagle Has Landed* it can be read on its own. In the prior novel, an attempt by Hitler to engineer the assassination of Winston Churchill fails. One German, Colonel Kurt Steiner who is involved in the plot, was captured and imprisoned in the Tower of London. In the sequel, a plan is initiated by Himmler to free Steiner with the help of General Walter Schellenberg who is a respected war hero but not a Nazi. The reason for this rescue is unclear; but Schellenberg proceeds to develop a plan and is helped by Liam Devlin, an IRA gunman—and poet—and an American ace pilot, Asa Vaughan, who has wound up on the wrong side of the fight in World War II.

Hillerman, Tony. *Talking God.* New York: Harper, 1989. 239pp. LC 88-45914. ISBN 06-016118-3. (o.p.) New York: HarperCollins, pap. ISBN 0-06-109918-X.

Henry Highhawk, museum curator, is in conflict with the Smithsonian for the return of Indian skeletons that are stored at the museum. He claims that he is part Navajo and attends a sacred ceremony, Night Chant, to learn more about the Indian religion and make himself acceptable to the tribe of Navajos. Mixed up in Highhawk's affairs is a hired assassin in pursuit of a Chilean dissident. The trails are tangled but Tribal Police Officer Jim Chee and his fellow detective Lieutenant Joe Leaphorn come together to solve two murders but are not successful in preventing a violent conclusion that involves a very sacred Indian totem, Talking God.

Hilton, James. *Good-bye, Mr. Chips*. Boston: Little, 1934. 132pp. ISBN 0-316-36420-7. New York: Bantam, pap. ISBN 0-553-27321-3.+

In 1870 Mr. Chipping begins a career teaching the classics at Brookfield Boys' Boarding School in England. After teaching three generations of Brookfield boys, Mr. Chips, as he is fondly called, retires to the boarding house directly across the street from the school. He continues to keep a close watch over the new groups of boys and host afternoon teas as a way of sharing his reminiscences. This is a warm testimonial to a caring teacher.

Hilton, James. *Lost Horizon*. New York: Morrow, 1933. 211pp. ISBN 0-688-02007-0. (o.p.) Repr. Cutchogue, N.Y.: Buccaneer, 1983. 231pp. ISBN 0-89966-450-4. New York: Pocket, pap. ISBN 0-671-42243-X.

Hugh Conway is a British consul at Baskul when trouble erupts in 1931 and all civilians are evacuated. He and three others board a plane lent by a Maharajah. After they are airborne for several hours, they realize that they are headed in the wrong direction. When the pilot finally lands, the passengers find themselves in Shangri-La, a utopian lamasery whose inhabitants know the secret of attaining long life. Believing that war is going to destroy all civilization, the High Lama summons the newcomers to form the nucleus of a new civilization.

Hinton, S. E. *The Outsiders*. Magnolia, Mass.: Peter Smith, 1968. ISBN 0-8446-6372-7. New York: Dell, pap. ISBN 0-440-96769-4.

From the perspective of Ponyboy Curtis, the author relates the story of the Greasers, who are from the lower class, and their conflict with the Socs, who are their middle-class opposite number. For the Greasers, the gang comprises their street family, all the family that some of them have. In the collision between the two social factions, two buddies die, one as a hood, the other, a hero.

Hobson, Laura. *Gentleman's Agreement*. New York: Simon & Schuster, 1947. 275pp. (o.p.) Repr. Marietta, Ga.: Cherokee, 1979. LC 79-27243. ISBN 0-87797-210-9.

Phil Green's first assignment for a large weekly magazine, to write about the "Jewish Question," leads him to follow the Indian maxim to "walk a mile in the other man's moccasins." In the guise of being Jewish himself he discovers that the anti-Semitism he thought he might find is indeed on every hand. It is not in bold, crass acts but in constant little insults, the day-by-day wearing on the nerves, the delicate assault on a person's identity. The insidiousness of it is unnerving to Phil and threatens to destroy some of his most personal relationships.

Holland, Isabelle. *The Man Without a Face.* New York: Harper, 1972. 144pp. LC 71-37736. ISBN 0-397-31311-3. New York: Harper, pap. ISBN 0-06-447028-8.

For Charles Norstadt the summer means a time of intense study so that he can again take the exams for St. Matthews School, but his study skills are poor. He is helped by Justin McLeod, "the man without a face," and as the summer progresses, they develop a beautiful relationship that leads to revelations painful to them both.

Holman, Felice. *Slake's Limbo.* New York: Scribner, 1974. 117pp. LC 74-11675. ISBN 0-684-13926-X. New York: Macmillan, pap. LC 85-26795. ISBN 0-689-71066-6.

Thirteen-year-old Artemis Slake, small, neglected, homeless, and used to abuse, quite accidentally comes upon a cave deep under Grand Central Station in New York City. He takes refuge in the subway and stays 121 days. During that stay he explores every inch of the 137 miles of subway lines and stops at every one of the 265 underground stations. His ingenuity at keeping himself fed and warm is remarkable. He is safe in his refuge until an accident in the subway closes up his haven and he begins to look upward to the sky outside.

Holt, Victoria. *Bride of Pendorric.* Garden City, N.Y.: Doubleday, 1963. 288pp. LC 63-12964. ISBN 0-385-01523-2. (o.p.) New York: Fawcett pap. ISBN 0-449-21507-5.

Favel Farrington, living with her father on an Italian island, meets and falls in love with Rob Pendorric. When her father drowns mysteriously while swimming, Rob acts very devoted and takes her to his family estate on the Cornish cliffs. Called the "Bride of Pendorric" and lavished with kindly attention by various relatives, Favel soon learns the fate of two past brides and begins to fear for her life.

Horgan, Paul. *Whitewater*. New York: Farrar, 1970. 337pp. LC 76-122830. ISBN 0-374-28970-0. (o.p.) Austin, Tx.: Univ. of Texas Press, pap. ISBN 0-292-79038-4.

Phil Durham, Billy Breedlove, and Marilee Underwood are a tightly woven trio of school friends. Philip is an introspective, budding author, Billy is the prototype of the teenage hero, and Marilee is sought by both but infatuated with Billy. When Phil accidentally causes Billy to fall to his death from a water tower, Marilee, who has just discovered that she is pregnant with Billy's child, commits suicide. The events are seen in retrospect by Durham, now a mature man.

Household, Geoffrey. *Rogue Male*. Mattituck, N.Y.: Amereon, ISBN 0-89190-435-2.

Although the situation is somewhat incredible, this book convincingly describes the obsession of a well-bred Englishman and sportsman with shooting a European dictator, or at least seeing whether he can get him within target range. When he is caught, he is flung over a cliff but miraculously survives, only to be hunted himself by his pursuers. He is the "rogue" hunted by the pack.

Hotze, Sollace. *A Circle Unbroken*. Boston: Ticknor & Fields, 1988 224pp. LC 88-2569. ISBN 0-89919-733-7. Boston: Houghton, pap. ISBN 0-395-59702-1.

Captured by a band of Sioux Indians as a ten-year-old child and raised by the Dakota, 17-year-old Rachel Porter has once again been captured and sent to the white world. This means meeting her stepmother and brother Daniel for the first time, seeing the reaction of her Aunt Sarah, who is also a returned Indian captive, and enduring her cold minister father. Rachel struggles to reconcile the white world with loving memories of her life as Kata Wi and especially the young brave, White Hawk. Rachel survives until the evil "waken" no longer threatens, and she is able to make the decision that will keep her circle joined.

Hudson, W. H. *Green Mansions*. Cutchogue, N.Y.: Buccaneer. ISBN 0-89966-374-5. New York: Dover, pap. ISBN 0-486-25993-5.

The relationship between a magical girl of the forest, Rima, and a jungle adventurer, Abel de Argensola, provides us with the story of a beautiful but tragic romance. Abel ventures into a forest feared by predatory South American Indians, and it is there that he discovers Rima. At first she is all fantasy, her relationship to nature unreal, but Abel gains her trust and love. As he introduces Rima to the outside world he brings a new aspect to their lives and destroys their paradise.

Hughes, Monica. *Hunter in the Dark*. New York: Atheneum, 1982. 131pp. LC 82-13807. ISBN 0-689-30959-7. New York: Avon, pap. ISBN 0-380-67702-4.

Mike Rankin at 16 has a loving family, economic comfort, and status in school. Although Doug, a classmate, comes from a very different background, their friendship is firm, and it is Doug who helps Mike through his nightmare when he is stricken with leukemia. His parents keep the illness a secret from Mike, wishing to protect him, their only child. When Mike learns the truth, he is able to endure the painful tests and treatments because of his determination to hunt a white-tail buck and have the antlered head as a trophy.

Hughes, Richard. *A High Wind in Jamaica* (original title: *An Innocent Voyage*). New York: Harper, 1929. 211pp. (o.p.) Repr. San Bernadino, Ca.: Borgo Press, 1991. 220pp. ISBN 0-8095-9099-9. New York: Harper, pap. LC 89-45124. ISBN 0-06-091627-3.

After a hurricane has destroyed their home, the Thompson children are sent back to England. Their ship is captured by pirates, who get the worst of the adventure at the hands of these amoral children. When a Dutch steamer is captured, ten-year-old Emily kills the captain of that ship in a state of panic. The children return safely to England but the pirates are captured by the English Navy and stand trial in London. With little, if any, remorse, Emily takes the witness stand and sends the pirates who treated her so well to their death.

Humphreys, Josephine. *The Firemen's Fair*. New York: Viking, 1991. 263pp. LC 90-50575. ISBN 0-670-83907-8. New York: Viking, pap. ISBN 0-14-016838-9.

Rob Wyatt, unmarried at 32, has quit his job as a lawyer, moved out of a luxury apartment to poor housing, sold his Alfa for a cheap used car, and is looking for a new kind of life. Hurricane Hugo almost devastates the southern town in which he lives and also seems to have swept an uprooting storm through his personal life. His unceasing love for Louise, now married to wealthy Frank Camden, becomes not so firm when Billy Poe, 18 years old and naively innocent (or precociously wise) comes into Rob's life. She is a healer in her innocent wisdom and the novel has an ending especially welcome as a change from many violent and depressing contemporary novels.

Huxley, Aldous. *Brave New World*. New York: Harper, 1932. 311pp. LC 46-21397. ISBN 0-06-012035-5. (o.p.) Repr. San Bernadino, Ca.: Borgo Press, 288pp. ISBN 0-8095-9047-6. New York: Harper, pap. LC 88-45962. ISBN 0-06-080983-3.

The ironic title, which Huxley has taken from Shakespeare's *The Tempest*, describes a world in which science has taken control over morality and humaneness. In this utopia humans emerge from test tubes, families are obsolete, and even pleasure is regulated. When a so-called savage who believes in spirituality is found and is imported to the community, he cannot accommodate himself to this world and ends his life.

Innes, Michael. *The Case of the Journeying Boy*. New York: Dodd, 1949. (o.p.) New York: Harper, pap. ISBN 0-06-080632-X.

Sir Bernard Paxton, atomic scientist and genius, employs a tutor to take his son Humphrey off to Ireland for study and recreation. The young boy seems to Mr. Thewless, the tutor, to have an overactive imagination, claiming that he is the object of a conspiracy. In spite of Mr. Thewless' calm personality, he begins to realize that strange events involving Humphrey's disappearance and reappearance on the train-trip to Ireland may be more than imagination. In Ireland, more dangerous events reinforce the reality of some threat to Humphrey. The plot thickens and quite explodes at the end of a mystery story written with style, humor and reminders of an Alfred Hitchcock film.

Isherwood, Christopher. *The Berlin Stories: The Last of Mr. Norris; Goodbye to Berlin*. New York: New Directions, 1954. 207pp. (o.p.) Repr. Cambridge, Mass.: Bentley, 1979. LC 79-17316. ISBN 0-8376-0449-4. New York: New Directions, pap. LC 55-2568. ISBN 0-8112-0070-1.

Isherwood provides a fascinating glimpse into a lost era: the Berlin of the late 1920s and early 1930s, the Berlin of defeat and resentment, the

Berlin of the rise of Hitler. Among the characters we meet are the enigmatic Mr. Norris, the Jewish family Landauer, and the flamboyant entertainer Sally Bowles. Their personal tragedies and successes are clouded by an ominous future.

Ishiguro, Kazuo. *A Pale View of the Hills.* New York: Putnam, 1982. 183pp. LC 81-22713. ISBN 0-399-12718-6. (o.p.) New York: Random, pap. LC 90-50178. ISBN 0-679-72267-X.

Etsuko, a Japanese woman now living in England, recalls a brief but strange friendship with Sachiko, a woman neighbor in Nagasaki. Sachiko's daughter, Mariko, is a withdrawn child given to imaginary visions. Daughters are the underlying theme in this novel, not only with the behavior of Mariko, but also with Etsuko's memory of the suicide of her older daughter Keiko. Japanese life is portrayed in Etsuko's reminiscences of the past after the nuclear bombing of Japan.

*Ishiguro, Kazuo. *The Remains of the Day.* New York: Vintage, 1990. 245pp. LC 90-50177. ISBN 0-679-73172-5. (o.p.) New York: Knopf, 1989. ISBN 0-394-57343-9.

Mr. Stevens is a butler of high quality now employed by the American owner of Darlington Hall. His position as butler was quite different when Lord Darlington was his employer. Then there was a large staff, including Miss Kenton, whose friendly overtures to Stevens were met only by his inability to unbend or find some humor as an outlet offsetting his customary snobbish personality. As Stevens reflects on the past the reader gains insight into Lord Darlington's political connections after World War I with important government officials including Ribbentrop, representative of Germany's movement toward a dictatorship. Questions regarding an employee's unquestioning loyalty toward his employer and awareness of the political situation in the period just before Hitler's rise to power make this a thought-provoking novel.

Jackson, Shirley. *The Haunting of Hill House.* Mattituck, N.Y.: Amereon, 1959. 246pp. ISBN 0-89190-622-3. New York: Viking, pap. ISBN 0-14-007108-3.

Dr. John Montague, an anthropologist, is interested in the analysis of supernatural manifestations. He rents Hill House, which is reported to be haunted, and plans to spend the summer there with research assistants. Eleanor Vance, one of the researchers, is at first repelled by the house but soon adjusts. Other people come and signs of psychic activity are rampant, many of them centered on Eleanor. When Dr. Montague insists that she leave to insure her safety, the house does not release her.

Jackson, Shirley. *The Lottery or, The Adventures of James Harris.* New York: Farrar, 1949. (o.p.) Repr. Cambridge, Mass.: Bentley, 1949. 306pp. LC 79-24173. ISBN 0-8376-0455-9. New York: Farrar, pap. ISBN 0-374-52317-7.

The title story describes a seemingly friendly and neighborly town whose inhabitants come together for an annual ritual. The uneasiness we feel as the story moves along flowers into shock as we realize the purpose of the gathering. In the other 24 stories that make up the collection, the reader is entertained via irony, as in "My Life with R.H. Macy" and "The Villager," or saddened by the painful disappointment a woman, no longer young, suffers when she discovers the deception played on her by "The Daemon Lover." While the stories seem simple in style, Jackson artfully points up the cruelty, selfishness, and prejudice latent in so many people, and her endings catch us by surprise.

Jackson, Shirley. *We Have Always Lived in the Castle.* Mattituck, N.Y.: Amereon, ISBN 0-89190-623-1.

Since the time that Constance Blackwood was tried and acquitted of the murder of four members of her family, she has lived with her sister Mary Catherine and her Uncle Julian in the family mansion. Mary Catherine takes care of family chores, and Uncle Julian is busy with the writing of a detailed account of the six-year-old murders. Cousin Charles's arrival on the scene disrupts the quiet peace of the family, and Mary Catherine's efforts to get rid of him unloose a chain of events that bring everything down in ruins.

James, P. D. *An Unsuitable Job for a Woman.* New York: Warner, 1988. 288pp. pap. ISBN 0-446-31008-5.

James has been called Christie's crown princess, and her mystery stories testify to the justification for the title. In this book James's usual investigator, Chief Superintendent Dalgleish, plays only a minor part. It is Cordelia Gray, the young, intelligent, and clear-thinking owner of an unsuccessful detective agency, who solves the case. She is hired by Sir Ronald Callender to investigate the death by suicide of his son, Mark. Miss Gray's meticulous research leads her to suspect that Mark was murdered and makes her a prime target for murder. There are suspenseful moments, close calls, and a very surprising encounter, at last, between Cordelia and Supt. Dalgleish.

*Jarrell, Randall. *Pictures from an Institution*. New York: Knopf, 1954. Repr. Chicago, Ill.: Univ. of Chicago Press, 1986. 278pp. LC 85-20965. ISBN 0-226-39374-7.

The narrator of this witty and perceptive novel is a professor at a progressive Eastern college for girls. Through his eyes we see much of the pretentiousness of the faculty, something of the closed society possible in a small college, and we are given a devastating portrait of a college president whose public charm far exceeds his wisdom. The main focus, however, is on Gertrude Johnson, the college's writer-in-residence. The narrator gives a sharply etched, sometimes acid description of her insensitive personality as well a her keen intellect. The model for this unlovable character is supposedly a well-known writer.

Jen, Gish. *Typical American*. Boston: Houghton, 1991. 340pp. LC 90-48423. ISBN 0-395-54689-3. New York: New Amer. Lib., pap. ISBN 0-452-26774-9.

Yefing Chang becomes Ralph Chang in America and begins a hard struggle to achieve the American dream—a career, a family and a home of his own. In poverty, he succeeds finally to win a doctoral degree, a college position, a happy marriage to Helen, two delightful daughters and a close reunion with his older sister, Theresa. The dream becomes a nightmare when he meets Grover Ding whose corrupt influence over Ralph and Helen begins to unravel all that the Changs have managed to achieve. This is an honest novel that does not promise happy endings and recognizes the human weaknesses that can destroy a family's stability.

Jhabvala, Ruth Prawer. *Heat and Dust*. Magnolia, Mass.: Peter Smith, 1988. ISBN 0-8446-6335-2. New York: Simon & Schuster, pap. ISBN 0-671-64657-5.

The juxtaposition of past and present India is explored in this novel. The 1923 storyline tells of Olivia, who, though married to a British officer stationed in India, falls madly in love with an Indian prince. It is also about Olivia's husband's granddaughter by a second marriage, who has come to India to discover the details of Olivia's life but finds that, although India and women have become modernized, she must face many of the same choices as Olivia. The intrusion of British culture on India's own traditions and values is a second theme in the novel.

*Johnson, Charles. *Middle Passage*. New York: Atheneum, (o.p.) Repr. New York: New Amer. Lib., 1991. 209pp. LC 91-9602. ISBN 0-452-26638-6.

Rutherford Calhoun, a black American newly freed bondman, has left Illinois and become a dissolute inhabitant of New Orleans in the 1830s. A petty thief and womanizer, Calhoun is soon up to his neck in trouble and debt, and only marriage to schoolteacher Isadore Bailey can save him. Considering this a fate worse than death (or debts), Calhoun becomes a crew member on one of the worst ships ever described in a book—the Republic—obviously a name chosen deliberately by Johnson. The author has written this brutal but often funny novel as an allegory for the trials suffered by black people. The Republic's voyage is to Africa to pick up slaves from the Allmuseri tribe. The details of the voyage, the living conditions, the food—including cannibalism—will take a strong-hearted reader, but the novel is worth the effort.

Jones, Diana Wynne. *Castle in the Air*. Great Britain: Methuen, 1990. Repr. New York: Greenwillow, 1991. 199pp. LC 90-30266. ISBN 0-688-09686-7.

Enchantments, genies, flying carpets, sultans, and princesses make this rollicking, romantic tale great fun. Abdullah, a young carpet dealer, purchases a carpet and moves into a world of fantasy and romance. He falls in love with Flower-in-the-Night, who has seen no man except her father, but there are abductions, treacheries, arduous searches, and trickeries on all sides before they—and several others of their friends—can begin to live happily ever after. Although it is a sequel to *Howl's Moving Castle*, this story can be read independently as a spoof, a glorious parody, or a "genuine imitation" of stories from *The Arabian Nights*. However one approaches it, the book is lively and fun to read.

Jones, Douglas, C. *Season of Yellow Leaf.* New York: Holt, 1983. 323pp. LC 83-117. ISBN 0-03-060042-1.

In the Texas area during the first half of the 1800s the Parry family, Welsh settlers, are eking out a living and facing the usual dangers of frontier life. Their ten-year-old daughter and her younger brother are captured in a raid by Comanche Indians led by Sanchess, son of Iron Shirt. Morfydd is taken into the tribe, since the Indians looked upon all females as potential bearers of warrior sons. She gradually becomes part of the Indian culture and is renamed Chosen. The novel portrays the precarious life of the Indians who had to worry about battles not only with the white man but also with other Indian tribes. Iron Shirt, a respected peace chief of the tribe, foresees the "season of yellow leaf," the eventual disappearance of the Indian as the white man moves farther into the West usurping the land and killing buffalo for hides rather than for food.

Joyce, James. *Dubliners*. New York: Modern Lib., 1926 (1914). 288pp. LC 25-23228. ISBN 0-394-60464-4. New York: Penguin, pap. ISBN 0-14-004222-9.+

This collection of 15 stories provides an introduction to the style and motifs found in Joyce's writing. The stories stand alone as individual scenes of Dublin society and are intertwined by the use of autobiography and symbolism. The paralysis of society is one theme, moving from the first three stories of young people not yet destroyed by society to "The Dead," which offers the possibility of rebirth.

Joyce, James. *A Portrait of the Artist as a Young Man*. New York: Viking, 1916. ISBN 0-670-56683-7. (o.p.) Repr. New York: Knopf, 1991. 272pp. ISBN 0-679-40574-7. New York: Penguin, pap. ISBN 0-14-015503-1.+

The progress of Stephen Dedalus from childhood to adulthood is revealed through Joyce's use of the style called stream of consciousness. Stephen struggles for independence from his family, the Catholic church, and the social structure of Dublin. Martyred and alienated by his creative needs, he finally leaves for Paris to pursue his artistic endeavors.

Judson, William. *Cold River*. New York: Mason & Lipscomb, 1974. 213pp. (o.p.) New York: New Amer. Lib., pap. ISBN 0-451-16164-5.

A canoe trip turns into a nightmare for 14-year-old Lizzie and her younger brother Tim when their boat capsizes in the rapids and their father is lost. They struggle to survive as they search for help during the winter in the Adirondack Mountains. The techniques their father had taught them make it possible for them to get food, but they need courage also to face the dangers posed by a marauding bear and an escaped convict.

Just, Ward. *Jack Gance*. New York: Houghton, 1989. ISBN 0-395-49337-4. New York: Ivy Books, 272pp. pap. ISBN 0-8041-0571-5.

The relationship between Jack and his father Victor had always been ambivalent. His father's conviction and imprisonment for evading the payment of federal income taxes had occurred when Jack was young enough to feel the stigma. As a grown man Jack pursues a contact with politicians that leads eventually to the U.S. Senate. He has a brief affair with a woman whose husband later becomes an important figure in an attempt to dissuade Jack from his pursuit of that office. The focal points in the story are Chicago, Washington, D.C. and politics in those cities in a time period extending from the 1960s to the 1980s.

*Just, Ward. *The Translator*. Boston: Houghton, 1991. 352pp. LC 91-12789. ISBN 0-395-57168-5.

Sydney Van Damm has never forgotten his mother's unflinching attachment to her German heritage. He himself, a German expatriate living in Paris and married to American Angela, has no nostalgia for the Germany and the Nazis who had killed his father, a faithful German soldier. Sydney's livelihood is translating German into English or French, especially the novels of a not very famous German writer. Angela's main concern in life is the welfare of their son Max, a disturbed child confined to an institution. It is her desire for money to buy a home in the country where Max could live with them that precipitates Sydney into a dangerous scheme manipulated by a wheeler-dealer and the novel's shocking conclusion. Just has painted a dramatic picture of modern Europe and the chaotic events taking place. This is a powerful and timely novel for the mature reader.

Kadohata, Cynthia. *The Floating World*. New York: Penguin, 1989. 208pp. LC 88-40481. ISBN 0-670-82680-4. New York: Ballantine, pap. ISBN 0-345-36756-1.

A young Japanese-American girl, Olivia, is the narrator of this novel that describes her family and its wanderings (the floating world) as her father constantly changes his means of livelihood. The grandmother, Obasan, is a fearsome figure in Olivia's life—even after her death when Olivia sees her as a ghost. We meet Olivia when she is 12 years old and follow her life into her twenties with stories of her various companions and her lover, Andy Chin. The book lends insight into the life of a Japanese-American family in the United States during the 1950s.

Kafka, Franz. *Metamorphosis*. Repr. Mattituck, N.Y.: Amereon, ISBN 0-88411-450-3. New York: Schocken, pap. ISBN 0-8052-0420-2.+

Upon waking one morning, Gregor Samsa finds himself changed into a large insect. Thus begins the allegory that attempts to analyze Gregor's place within the family structure and his role in life. Only with Gregor's death and the elimination of stress can the family resume normal functioning. The bizarre elements of the novel open the possibility for understanding the relationship of humans to other forms of life.

Kafka, Franz. *The Trial*. New York: Knopf. ISBN 0-394-44955-X.

Joseph K., a respected bank assessor, is arrested and spends his remaining years fighting charges about which he has no knowledge. The helplessness of an insignificant individual within a mysterious bureaucracy where answers are never accessible is described in this provocative and disturbing book.

*Kantor, MacKinlay. *Andersonville*. New York: New Amer. Lib., 1957. pap. ISBN 0-451-16021-5.

After 25 years of research Kantor wrote this novel, which realistically portrays the atrocities of Andersonville Prison, home of many Yankee soldiers during the Civil War. Ira Claffey, Georgia planter and owner of the property on which Andersonville is built, serves as a humane central character whose sorrows and frustrations serve to point up the brutality of war. The primitive, indeed horrible, existence of the prisoners is described in detail.

Kawabata, Yasunari. *Thousand Cranes*. Trans. from the Japanese by Edward G. Seidensticker. New York: Knopf, 1959. 147pp. (o.p.) New York: Putnam, pap. ISBN 0-399-50526-1.

Told in language that is as spare and sensual as a Japanese brush painting, this is a complex love story set within the symbolic rites of the tea ceremony. Shortly after his father's death, Kikuji goes to have tea with Chikako, who had been his father's mistress and who wishes to introduce to him a young girl, Fumiko, as a prospective bride. Fumiko is at the tea ceremony with her mother, Mrs. Ota, who had also been a mistress of Kikuji's father. When Kikuji finds himself attracted to Mrs. Ota and she yields to him, the result is tragic, and the two young people must also suffer the consequences.

*Kazantzakis, Nikos. *Zorba the Greek*. New York: Simon & Schuster, pap. ISBN 0-671-21132-3.

The spirit of Zorba, full of energy and peasant philosophy, is contrasted with that of the narrator, a learned but staid Englishman who comes to Crete for adventure. The relationship between the two men deepens despite Zorba's mismanagement of the narrator's mining business, and despite Zorba's attempts to change his friend's behavior to a more zestful one. Kazantzakis creates in Zorba a character that represents the vitality sapped by the inhibitions civilization has created.

Kellogg, Marjorie. *Like the Lion's Tooth*. New York: Farrar, 1972. 147pp. ISBN 0-374-51926-9.

Eleven-year-old Ben has been sent to a special school for "problem children," more for protection from his stepfather than for any kind of correction, since he has been periodically beaten and his mother has made little effort to stop the abuse. Philip, Ben's younger brother, soon joins him because his mother fears for his safety. When Ben is sent out to a foster home, he contrives to be returned to the school in order to watch over Philip, but he cannot stop the fate awaiting his brother.

Kellogg, Marjorie. *Tell Me That You Love Me, Junie Moon*. New York: Farrar, 1968. 216pp. LC 68-24600. ISBN 0-374-51825-4.

Junie Moon, in a rehabilitation center after a crazy boyfriend threw acid in her face, meets Warren, a paraplegic who has been shot in the spine on a hunting trip, and Arthur, who is slowly dying of a degenerative nerve disease. Amid the protests of the hospital staff the three decide to leave the center to set up a household. The reaction of their new neighbors is anything but encouraging, but one of them, an Italian fish merchant, befriends them and sends them on a vacation in his truck. It is a wonderful interlude until Arthur, recognizing that he is in the last stages of his illness, asks to be taken home to die.

Keneally, Thomas. *Flying Hero Class*. New York: Warner, 1991. 304pp. LC 90-50524. ISBN 0-446-51582-5. New York: Warner, pap. ISBN 0-446-39347-9.

Frank McCloud, manager of the Barramatjara dance troupe of a remote Australian tribe, is returning with his group from a successful tour. Their plane is hijacked by a band of Arab terrorists and three American passengers, including McCloud, are singled out as "criminals" who have caused the plight of the Arab peoples. The terrorists persuade the Australian performers that they, as fellow non-whites, should ally themselves with the Arab cause. Bluey, leader of the dance troupe, makes a vicious accusatory attack on McCloud and shocks him with this show of hatred. The tension on the flight as the terrorists punish the three passengers and the uncertainty about the success of the demands made by the hijackers make for suspenseful reading.

Keneally, Thomas. *Schindler's List*. New York: Simon & Schuster, 1982. 398pp. LC 82-10489. ISBN 0-671-44977-X. (o.p.) New York: Penguin, pap. ISBN 0-14-006784-1.

An actual occurrence during the Nazi regime in Germany forms the basis for this story. Oskar Schindler, a Catholic German industrialist, chose to act differently from those Germans who closed their eyes to what was happening to the Jews. By spending enormous sums on bribes to the SS and on food and drugs for the Jewish prisoners whom he housed in his own camp-factory in Cracow, he succeeded in sheltering thousands of Jews, finally transferring them to a safe place in Czechoslovakia. Fifty Schindler survivors from seven nations helped the author with information. Today Schindler lies in Jerusalem among Israel's honored dead.

Kerr, M. E. *Gentlehands*. New York: Harper, 1978. 183pp. LC 77-11860. ISBN 0-06-023177-7. New York: Harper, pap. ISBN 0-06-447067-9.+

Buddy Boyle falls for Skye and her affluent, breezy way of life. Finding his own parents not "cultured" enough for this new relationship, Buddy turns to his grandfather, whose love of opera and other refinements make him more suitable to make Skye's acquaintance. A shocking surprise awaits Buddy when Mr. DeLucca, pursuer of an infamous Nazi, finally identifies his quarry.

Kerr, M. E. *Is That You, Miss Blue?* New York: Harper, 1975. 176pp. LC 74-2627. ISBN 0-06-447033-4.

Flanders Brown, whose parents are divorced, is a boarder at The Charles School in Virginia. Her closest friends are Carolyn Cardmaker, who is inclined to think up provocative escapades, and beautiful, deaf Agnes Thatcher, who appears to be easily led by Carolyn. Much of the attention of the girls is directed toward Miss Ernestine Blue, a teacher who feels that she has "a special relationship with Jesus." Flanders is aware of the teacher's religious obsessiveness but knows also that Miss Blue is an outstanding and exciting science teacher. She comes to the teacher's defense at a time of crisis but cannot change the course of events.

Kerr, M. E. *Little Little.* New York: Harper, 1981. 183pp. LC 80-8454. ISBN 0-06-447061-X. New York: Bantam, pap. ISBN 0-553-22767-X.

Sidney Cinnamon is in love with Little Little but her wealthy parents do not approve of him and prefer Opportunity Knox, an evangelical preacher. Sidney's efforts to win Little Little and her reactions to him are related in alternating chapters. While the author has much to say, along the way, about religious entrepreneurs, show business, and parent-child relationships, the main thrust of the story is about the problems and pain suffered by those who are "different." This pair of lovers is different because they are dwarves. Readers will laugh but also feel compassion for this account of what it is like to be so much outside a society that is self-satisfied.

Kerr, M. E. *The Son of Someone Famous.* New York: Harper, 1974. 240pp. LC 73-14338. ISBN 0-06-447069-5.

After being expelled from still another private school, Adam feels that a retreat to Storm, Vermont, to be with his grandfather, Dr. Charles Blessing, is the answer to his problem of having failed his famous father. In Vermont he makes friends with Brenda Belle, who also is having an identity problem, and falls in love with Christine Culter, daughter of his grandfather's enemy. Eventually both he and Brenda Belle come to the realization that all people are rather complicated.

Kerr, M. E. *What I Really Think of You*. New York: Harper, 1982. 192pp. LC 81-47735. ISBN 0-06-023188-2. New York: Harper, pap. ISBN 0-06-447062-8.

Told by two narrators, Opal Ringer and Jesse Pegler, the story concerns itself with the lives led by P.K.s—preachers' kids. Opal Ringer's father preaches The Rapture in The Helping Hand Tabernacle, a Pentecostal church. Jesse Pegler's father is that most recent religious phenomenon, the Sunday morning TV personality. Opal is lonely and made more so by her awareness that her family makes her an object of mockery among her classmates. When she becomes involved in setting up a "miraculous" cure for a rich, beautiful, and frenetic girl, the story takes some unexpected turns. The forms that religious worship can take make for provocative reading.

*Kesey, Ken. *One Flew Over the Cuckoo's Nest*. New York: Viking, 1962. 311pp. ISBN 0-670-52604-5. New York: New Amer. Lib., pap. ISBN 0-451-15826-1.+

Life in a mental institution is predictable and suffocating under the iron rule of Nurse Ratched, who tolerates no disruption of routine on her all-male ward. Half-Indian Chief Bromden, almost invisible on the ward because he is thought to be deaf and dumb, describes the arrival of rowdy Randle Patrick McMurphy. McMurphy takes on the nurse as an adversary in his attempt to organize his fellow inmates and breathes some self-esteem and joy into their lives. The battle is vicious on the part of the nurse, who is relentless in her efforts to break McMurphy, but a spark of human will brings an element of hope to counter the despotic institutional power.

Keyes, Daniel. *Flowers for Algernon*. New York: Harcourt, 1966. 288pp. LC 66-12366. ISBN 0-15-131510-8. New York: Bantam, pap. ISBN 0-553-27450-3.+

Charlie Gordon, aged 32, is mentally retarded and enrolls in a class to "become smart." He keeps a journal of his progress after an experimental operation that increases his I.Q. Although Charlie becomes brilliant, he is unhappy because he cannot shed his former personality and is tormented by his memories. In the end he begins to lose the mental powers he has gained.

Kincaid, Jamaica. *Annie John*. New York: Farrar, 1985. 160pp. LC 84-28630. ISBN 0-374-10521-9. New York: New Amer. Lib., pap. ISBN 0-452-26016-7.

Annie John, a young girl living in Antigua in the West Indies, describes her most intimate feelings about her parents (mixed between love and hate), her friends (loyal but changing), and her experiences in school (excellent in scholarship but not in behavior). Her emotions are recognizable for the confusion that adolescents suffer as they grow from early teens to young adulthood.

*Kingsolver, Barbara. *Animal Dreams*. New York: HarperCollins, 1990. 342pp. LC 89-46571. ISBN 0-06-016350-X. New York: HarperCollins, pap. ISBN 0-06-092114-5.

Codi (Cosima) Noline, having dropped out of medical school only a few months before the completion of her training, returns to her hometown in Grace, Arizona to care for her ailing father, the town's local doctor. She renews her friendship with Loyd Peregrina, the Apache classmate she had known as a high school senior. That brief relationship had resulted in a pregnancy and miscarriage about which Loyd had known nothing. Almost unwillingly Codi becomes involved in an environmental issue affecting the town's survival and is drawn into closer feelings with the inhabitants. Her sister Hallie has gone to Nicaragua to help that government with its land problems and the correspondence between the sisters reveals much about their characters and their relationship with each other. This is a painful and beautiful novel.

Kingsolver, Barbara. *The Bean Trees*. New York: Harper, 1988. 240pp. LC 87-45633. ISBN 0-06-091554-4.

Taylor, young and enjoying complete approval from her mother, nevertheless leaves rural Kentucky to seek independence. Against any wish of her own she becomes the guardian of an abandoned Cherokee baby girl. She makes a good friend of Lou Ann Ritz with whom she finds a home. Lou Ann, also about to have a baby, has been abandoned by her husband and these two single parents work out a good relationship with a loving environment for their children. Also important in their lives is Mattie, a good samaritan who rescues emigrés seeking sanctuary from oppressive governments. This is a warm and humorous book that celebrates friendship and courage.

Klause, Annette Curtis. *The Silver Kiss*. New York: Delacorte, 1990. 198pp. LC 89-48880. ISBN 0-385-30160-X.

Consumed by her mother's physical deterioration and almost certain death, Zoë needs a friend. Her father spends much of his time at the hospital and when he comes home he's too much aware of his own grief to comfort Zoë. Others mean well, but they just aren't helpful. So when she meets Simon, a magnetically handsome boy who's been following her, she lets him first into her house and then into her life. Inexorably drawn to him, Zoë discovers his secret of immortality and the price she must pay to join him.

Knebel, Fletcher, and Bailey, Charles. *Seven Days in May*. New York: Bantam, 1988. 384pp. pap. ISBN 0-553-26956-9.

President Jordan Lyman's popularity polls are at an all-time low and the country is apprehensive over a nuclear disarmament treaty. Col. Martin Casey accidentally discovers elements of a plot and then must prove that the plot exists and foil it.

Knowles, John. *A Separate Peace*. New York: Macmillan, 1959. 186pp. LC 60-5312. ISBN 0-02-564850-0. New York: Dell, pap. ISBN 0-385-28886-7.+

Gene Forrester looks back on his school days, spent in a New England town just before World War II. He both admires and envies his close friend and roommate, Finny, who is a natural athlete, in contrast to Gene's special competence as a scholar. When Finny suffers a crippling accident, Gene must face his own involvement in it.

Koestler, Arthur. *Darkness at Noon*. New York: Macmillan, 1941. 267pp. ISBN 0-02-565210-9. New York: Bantam, pap. ISBN 0-553-26595-4.

Rubashov, once a powerful party member, is imprisoned because he is suspected of belonging to the opposition, which has attempted to assassinate the party leader. In the two weeks he is given to decide whether to confess and be imprisoned for 20 years or to accept the death penalty, there are more political changes and Rubashov's original accuser is liquidated. Day-and-night questioning under bright spotlights and lack of sleep induce Rubashov to sign a confession. A strong condemnation of totalitarianism, this novel was written shortly after Koestler left the Soviet Union to seek political asylum in the United States.

Koertge, Ron. *The Arizona Kid*. Boston: Little, 1988. 228pp. LC 87-35361. ISBN 0-316-50101-8. New York: Avon, pap. ISBN 0-380-70776-4.

Billy, 16 years old, goes off from his home, a small town in Missouri, to spend the summer with his Uncle Wes. It is a visit filled with new experiences and understanding. Billy learns more about his uncle, who is gay, more about himself as he has his first sexual encounter, and more about horses and horse racing as he considers a future career as a veterinarian. Added attractions of this young adult novel are its delightful humor and sensitivity.

Konigsburg, E. L. *Father's Arcane Daughter*. New York: Atheneum, 1976. 128pp. LC 76-5495. ISBN 0-689-30524-9. New York: Atheneum, pap. ISBN 0-689-00570-4.+

On a Thursday in September 1952, Caroline Carmichael suddenly appeared at her home after an absence of 17 years. The daughter of Mr. Carmichael's first marriage, Caroline had been kidnapped and vanished completely. Her return brought with it some question of her identity. Was she indeed Caroline, or a clever and well-rehearsed impostor? One fact was beyond question. She was the means by which Heidi and Winston, children of Mr. Carmichael's second marriage, would find freedom: the one from an imprisonment shaped by her handicap and the other from being a constant caretaker.

*Kosinski, Jerzy. *Being There*. New York: Harcourt, 1970. 142pp. (o.p.) New York: Bantam, pap. ISBN 0-553-27930-0.

An illiterate gardener, Chance, knows the world only through his gardening and by watching television, to which he is addicted. Without education or any identifiable background, he is evicted into the outside world when his employer dies. He makes horticultural analogies to current events, which give him a reputation for wisdom that he really does not have, and which catapult him into national prominence. Chance's simple statements are interpreted by his listeners to be profound observations, and we see him being considered for positions of great importance. This is a satire on human behavior in the worlds of power, government, and the media. There is some explicit sex but it is handled with style.

*Kosinski, Jerzy. *The Painted Bird.* New York: Modern Lib., 1965, 1976. 272pp. LC 82-42869. ISBN 0-394-60433-4. New York: Bantam, pap. ISBN 0-553-26520-2.+

In Eastern Europe during World War II a ten-year-old boy is separated from his parents and struggles to survive in primitive villages where he is viewed as an unwanted outsider. Dark-haired and dark-eyed, he is unlike the Polish villagers among whom he tries to find refuge. He is the gypsy, the "painted bird," and savage abuse is heaped upon him time after time. He has, nevertheless, the will to transcend the sadism and superstition of these ignorant people.

La Farge, Oliver. *Laughing Boy.* Boston: Houghton, 1929. 302pp. ISBN 0-395-07874-1. (o.p.) Repr. Greenport, N.Y.: Harmony Raine, 1981. 259pp. ISBN 0-89967-041-5.

This novel takes place in the early years of the twentieth century in Navajo country in the American Southwest. It is the story of the ill-fated love of Laughing Boy, worker in silver and maker of songs, and Slim Girl, whose education in American schools has embittered her. The reader is immersed in their tender romance but also learns a great deal about the culture and philosophical outlook of the Native American.

L'Amour, Louis. *Bendigo Shafter.* New York: Bantam, 1983. pap. ISBN 0-553-26446-X.

An old-fashioned Western in the John Wayne tradition, this book's hero is 18-year-old Bendigo Shafter. He is part of a small band of migrants that breaks off its westward trek and builds a small community. The group increases with the coming of other members. It has to fight off the dangers of the frontier both within and outside its confines. Among the main influences on Ben's life are the Widow Macken, who inspires him to read Locke, Rousseau, and Blackstone; Uruwishi, an old Indian brave; and Ethan Sackett, woodsman nonpareil. There are heroes and villains, both white and red, and shooting from the hip in old Western style as Ben demonstrates all the traditional values of courage, honesty, loyalty, and stamina.

*Lampedusa, Giuseppe di. *The Leopard*. Trans. from the Italian by Archibald Colquhoun. New York: Pantheon, 1960. 319pp. LC 60-6794. ISBN 0-394-43291-6. New York: Pantheon, pap. LC 90-53443. ISBN 0-679-73121-0.+

In Sicily, Don Fabrizio, Prince of the House of Salina, passively views Garibaldi's invasion in 1860. When his scapegrace nephew Tancredi joins the Garibaldi forces, the prince gives him gold and finds himself regarded as a supporter of Garibaldi. Tancredi courts and marries the daughter of a newly rich provincial politico. That connection leads to an offer for Don Fabrizio to accept a post in the government. He refuses, bitter because of the changes that make him feel there is no place for him in the new Sicily. In an afterword we learn that Tancredi and Fabrizio have died and the latter's spinster daughters, pious but bitter, live in seclusion in the dilapidated family palace.

Langton, Jane. *Emily Dickinson is Dead*. New York: Saint Martin's Press, 1984. 247pp. LC 85-554. ISBN 0-312-24434-7. New York: Viking, pap. ISBN 0-14-007771-5.

In a mystery that pokes fun at the behavior of professors in the academic world, a famous poet is chosen as a theme for a literary conference. Stemming from a photograph that an undistinguished professor from a small midwestern college claims is an authentic photo of Emily Dickinson, the faculty of an elite university begin to fight among themselves—sometimes even physically—about who will star at the conference. Entangled in that is Winifred Gaw, an overweight graduate student, and the professor whom she worships, as well as beautiful Allison Groves who becomes the object of Winifred's jealousy and hatred. Emily Dickinson, quietly dead for so many years, becomes a motivation for arson, forgery, and murder.

*Lawrence, D. H. *Sons and Lovers*. Cutchogue, N.Y.: Buccaneer. ISBN 0-89966-400-8. New York: Penguin, pap. ISBN 0-14-018215-2.+

Paul Morel, adored youngest son of a middle-class mother who feels that her coal-miner husband was unworthy of her, has difficulty in breaking away from her. Mrs. Morel has given her son all her warmth and love for so long a time that Paul finds it impossible to establish a relationship with another woman. Miriam is supportive and understanding of his artistic nature but appeals mainly to his higher nature; Clara Dawes becomes his mistress but she is married and will not divorce her husband. After the death of his mother, Paul arranges a reconciliation between Clara and her husband and, after months of grieving for his mother, at last finds the strength to strike out on his own.

Le Carré, John. *The Secret Pilgrim*. New York: Knopf, 1990. 335pp. LC 90-52944. ISBN 0-394-58842-8. New York: Ballantine, pap. ISBN 0-345-37476-2.

The espionage carried on by British spies, both honorable and not, is well recounted as the narrator, Ned, revisits his past and recalls well-known characters from previous Le Carré novels. George Smiley, the most honorable and respected, and Bill Haydon, the least trustworthy and admired, are included as Ned remembers the assignments of three decades performed for the British intelligence along with the spies that they ran from Poland, Estonia, and Hungary. Le Carré never disappoints.

Le Carré, John. *The Spy Who Came in from the Cold*. New York: Coward, 1963. 256pp. ISBN 0-698-10916-3. (o.p.) New York: Bantam, pap. ISBN 0-553-26442-7.

Destroying the reader's false assumptions about glamour and glory in the world of intrigue and secret agents, Le Carré portrays Alex Leamas as a middle-aged man anxious for relief from the harsh reality of double-dealing between nations. Leamas, pretending to defect to East Berlin to gather data during the peak of the Cold War, unexpectedly finds bittersweet love amidst the political drama.

Lederer, William J., and Burdick, Eugene. *The Ugly American*. New York: Norton, 1965. pap. ISBN 0-393-00305-1.

Both the effectiveness and the lack thereof demonstrated by Americans in Southeast Asia are depicted through the stories of diplomats, military men, an engineer, a priest, a farmer, and politician. Some characters are patronizing and insensitive to the culture and customs of the people; others understand and work closely with them to improve their lives and help them resist communism.

Lee, Harper. *To Kill a Mockingbird.* New York: Harper, 1960. 296pp. LC 60-7847. ISBN 0-397-00151-7. New York: Warner, pap. ISBN 0-446-31078-6.

Scout, as Jean Louise is called, is a precocious child. She relates her impressions of the time when her lawyer-father, Atticus Finch, is defending a black man accused of raping a white woman in a small Alabama town during the 1930s. Atticus's courageous act brings the violence and injustice that exists in their world sharply into focus as it intrudes into the lighthearted life that Scout and her brother Jem have enjoyed until that time.

Leffland, Ella. *Rumors of Peace.* New York: Harper, 1979. 389pp. LC 78-20209. ISBN 0-06-012572-1. (o.p.) New York: HarperCollins, pap. ISBN 0-06-091301-0.

Suse Hansen, living in a small town near San Francisco, is a young tomboyish girl with vivid imagination and strong opinions on many subjects. Her unblinking look at the atrocities caused by war leads her to become obsessive about the possibility that she and her family could be destroyed in the war initiated when the Japanese attack Pearl Harbor. Through her relationships with her teachers, her school friends—especially Peggy Hatton—and her family, we watch Suse develop into a young woman whose mind is being sharpened by a respect for knowledge. The series of crushes Suse feels for various men—a normal burgeoning of sexuality—culminates in an intense feeling for Egon, a young graduate student and German-Jewish refugee whose influence we feel will be a lasting one.

Le Guin, Ursula K. *The Compass Rose.* New York: Harper, 1982. 273pp. LC 81-48158. ISBN 0-06-014988-4. (o.p.) New York: Harper, pap. ISBN 0-06-100181-3.

Best known for her outstanding science fiction novels and short stories, Le Guin is also a wonderful writer of romance and fantasy. This short story collection covers a wide range from outer space tales as in "The

Pathways of Desire" and "Intracom" (hilariously comic) to stories with a political and social conscience as in "Diary of the Rose" (unforgettable). The last story in the book, "Sur," is a vivid description of an expedition made by nine people to the South Pole in 1909. The fact that they are all women is only tangentially mentioned. Each story makes the reader pause to reflect on its deeper meaning.

Le Guin, Ursula K. *The Dispossessed.* New York: Harper, 1974. 341pp. LC 73-18667. ISBN 0 06-012563-2. (o.p.) New York: Avon, pap. ISBN 0-380-00382-1.

Shevek, a brilliant physicist, is caught between the prejudices and hatreds of two worlds. His quest to bridge the gap between Ararres, an anarchist, egalitarian society, and Varas, a structured, capitalistic world, unleashes a storm of intrigue and drama. The two distinct cultures provide insights into the role of women in society, the issue of free will versus obligation to the state, human rights, and economic systems.

Le Guin, Ursula K. *The Eye of the Heron.* New York: Harper, 1983. 179pp. LC 82-48146. ISBN 0-06-015086-6. (o.p.) New York: Bantam, pap. ISBN 0-553-24258-X.

Two communities that have been exiled from Earth and are living on another planet represent the forces of War and Peace. The City Dwellers with their comfortable and protected lives are the Bosses; the inhabitants of Shantih (Shanty-Town) are the peace-seekers and the laborers for the City. The novel is a parable of the confrontation of two philosophies—violence and non-violence. Lev is the spokesperson for the Shanty-Towners, the seekers of peaceful solutions. Luz is the daughter of the top Boss of the City who, in spite of her background, sees the evil in the methods of her father and his chief aide, Herman Macmilan. Le Guin portrays a conflict that not only is reminiscent of the outrages suffered by the victims of the Nazi regime but is also illustrative of the problems of the nuclear age.

Le Guin, Ursula K. *The Left Hand of Darkness.* New York: Harper, 1969. 208pp. LC 79-2652. ISBN 0-06-012574-8. (o.p.) New York: Ace, pap. ISBN 0-441-47812-3.

This is a tale of political intrigue and danger on the world of Gethen, the Winter planet. Genly Ai, high official of the Eukeman—the commonwealth of worlds—is on Gethen to convince the royalty to join the Federation. He soon becomes a pawn in Gethen's power struggles, set against the elaborate mores of the Genthenians, a unisex hermaphroditic people whose intricate sexual physiology plays a key role in the conflict. Allied with Estraven, a fallen lord, Genly is forced to cross the savage and impassable Gobrin Ice.

Le Guin, Ursula K. *Very Far Away from Anywhere Else*. New York: Atheneum, 1977. 89pp. LC 76-4472. ISBN 0-689-30525-7. New York: Bantam, pap. ISBN 0-553-25396-4.

For Owen Thomas Griffiths and Natalie Field life was lonely because they were exceptional, both intellectually and creatively. This became a bond between them and brought them to a serious decision about their relationship. They felt their friendship could not be based on casual sex. But if they were not to be lovers, they could be friends while Natalie worked toward her goal of becoming an outstanding musician and Owen pursued a career that might make him a great scientist.

Le Guin, Ursula K. *The Wizard of Earthsea*. Oakland, Cal.: Parnassus, 1968. LC 68-21992. ISBN 0-395-27653-5. (o.p.) New York: Bantam, pap. ISBN 0-553-26250-5. *The Tombs of Atuan*. New York: Bantam, pap. ISBN 0-553-27331-0. *The Farthest Shore*. New York: Bantam, pap. ISBN 0-553-26847-3.

These three novels make up the *Wizard of Earthsea Trilogy*, a set of related tales of the complex Earthsea world, where magic is real, wizards and dragons abound, and there is a perpetual war between good and evil. These are novels of growth into adulthood, of philosophical maturing played out among the fantastic denizens of a magical world. From Sparrowhawk, a young magician who pays a price for arrogance, to Tenar, heir to the position of Great Priestess of the Nameless Ones, who learns the dangers inherent in fanaticism, there are many interesting characters in addition to all the action in these books.

Leiber, Fritz. *The Big Time*. Repr. Boston: G.K. Hall, 1976. 171pp. ISBN 0-8398-2334-7. (o.p.) Mattituck, N.Y.: Amereon, 1976. ISBN 0-88411-931-9. New York: Collier, pap. ISBN 0-02-069841-0.

Greta Forzane from twentieth century Chicago is an entertainer at the Place, a station literally beyond time and space which serves as a rest and rehabilitation center for the "spider" warriors battling in the cosmic-change wars. Her companions range across 2500 years of earth history, from a Roman soldier to a woman of the twenty-third century. At stake is control of the cosmos; the enemies are the evil snakes and the battlefield is all of recorded history. The questions that must be resolved are who controls the snakes and who the spiders, and whether it is all a bad cosmic joke. This highly regarded novel is rich with inventive and startling ideas.

Leiber, Fritz. *The Wanderer*. Boston: G.K. Hall, 1964. ISBN 0-8398-2642-7. (o.p.) New York: Tor, pap. ISBN 0-8125-4425-0.

As a planetary body approaches Earth, its gravity field brings the promise of massive earthquakes, tidal waves, and Doomsday! The struggle for survival by humanity amidst the chaos of a destroyed world is seen through the eyes of peoples all over the world. The crisis brings out both the best and the worst in them. The tone of the novel is hopeful in spite of the vast destruction it envisions.

Lenz, Siegfried. *The German Lesson*. Trans. from the German by Ernest Kaiser and Eithne Wilkins. New York: Hill & Wang, 1972. 470pp. LC 77-163567. ISBN 0-8090-4907-4. New York: New Directions, pap. ISBN 0-8112-0982-2.

Siggi Jepsen, a young inmate of a reform school in Northern Germany, is set the task of writing an essay entitled, "The Joys of Duty." He uses the opportunity to write at length about his relationship with his father and how his father destroyed his friendship with an artist, Max Nansen. Because his father is the local police officer, it is his "duty" to confiscate Nansen's paintings. The elder Jepsen's undeviating concept of duty puts him in opposition to his older son when that youth tries to escape from the army. This is a thought-provoking novel based on the conflict between duty and conscience.

Lesley, Craig. *Winterkill*. New York: Dell, 1984. 328pp. pap. ISBN 0-440-39589-5.

Danny Kachiah, a 34-year-old American Indian, has lost his ability to win top spots at rodeos, lost his wife Loxie to another man and, like many of his fellow Indians, drinks too much. When Loxie is killed in an accident, Danny regains his son Jack, now a teenager. In this novel of the Indian presence in the West there are sad stories of the bad treatment of Indian tribes by white people and wonderful stories about Indian legends, trapping, hunting, fishing and survival. In trying to build a relationship with his son, Danny recalls and relates to Jack much that he had learned from his own father. Their lives are tough, the language rough, even coarse, but descriptions of nature are like paintings.

Levi, Primo. *If Not Now, When?* New York: Penguin, 1986. 352pp. pap. ISBN 0-14-008492-4.

The author, himself a victim of Nazi atrocities, has based his novel on true events. A band of Jewish partisans makes its way from Russia to Italy waging their personal war against the Nazis. They blow up trains, rescue concentration camp inmates, and face incredible dangers in their efforts to strike back against a ruthless, seemingly invincible enemy. The story is a testament to human endurance and courage.

Levin, Ira. *The Boys from Brazil.* New York: Random, 1976. 312pp. ISBN 0-394-40267-7. (o.p.) New York: Bantam, pap. ISBN 0-553-29004-5.

Ninety-four potential Hitlers are created through the technique of cloning by Dr. Mengele, infamous doctor of Auschwitz. Striving to re-create the early environment of the original Hitler, Mengele plots the murder of the fathers of these ninety-four children. Yakov Liebermann, a pursuer of Nazis, tries to stop the murders at the cost of great, almost mortal, danger to himself.

Levin, Ira. *Rosemary's Baby.* New York: Random, 1967. 245pp. ISBN 0-394-44308-X. (o.p.) Repr. New York: Armchair Det. Lib., 1991. 256pp. LC 90-23997. ISBN 0-922890-84-6. New York: Bantam, pap. ISBN 0-553-29001-0.

Guy and Rosemary Woodhouse dismiss the warnings of friends and move into a luxurious Manhattan apartment building where, supposedly, rites of witchcraft and suicides have occurred. Rosemary's instincts warn her to beware of their neighbors, the Castevets, but her husband is not convinced and they become a dominant influence on Guy when Rosemary becomes pregnant. She is alone in her fear and becomes a helpless victim.

Levitin, Sonia. *The Return*. New York: Atheneum, 1987. 224pp. LC 86-25891. ISBN 0-689-31309-8. New York: Fawcett, pap. ISBN 0-449-70280-4.

Constant fear of strangers, persecution from villagers, hunger, and drought force Desta to escape to rumored freedom in Israel. Guided by her older brother, Joas, Desta and her younger sister Almaz begin the journey across the mountains. After Joas is killed by robbers, Desta must decide whether to return home or continue to try to find the Sudan refugee camp and transport to Israel. Based on Operation Moses, the 1984-1985 airlift of 8000 Ethiopian Jews to Israel, the novel vividly portrays the hunger and terror of the walk across the mountains and desert to the refugee camp.

*Lewis, C. S. *Out of the Silent Planet*. Repr. New York: Macmillan, 1990. 192pp. ISBN 0-02-570795-7. *Perelandra*. New York: Macmillan, pap. ISBN 0-02-086950-9. *That Hideous Strength*. New York: Macmillan, pap. ISBN 0-02-086960-6.

These three novels constitute a classic fantasy trilogy written by a noted Catholic thinker and a professor of medieval and renaissance literature at Cambridge University. The trilogy can be read on two levels: first for its exciting plot and second as a theological theory, although Lewis denied this interpretation. The stories are about temptation. They concern the classic battle between good, as represented by Ransom, the philologist, and evil, as represented by Weston, the physicist. The battle is played out on the planets of Malacondra (Mars), Perelandra (Venus), and Earth.

Lewis, Sinclair. *Arrowsmith*. Repr. San Diego, Ca.: Harcourt, 1925. LC 25-78. ISBN 0-15-108216-2. New York: New Amer. Lib., pap. ISBN 0-451-52225-7.

Although he is most interested in bacteriology and research, Martin Arrowsmith turns from that area to general medicine and then to public health. He is unable, however, to deal with the political aspects of the public health field and returns to laboratory work and research. Martin develops an antitoxin that he believes will be effective against bubonic plague, but when he gets the chance to test the serum during an epidemic in the West Indies, he invalidates the results by not adhering to a control situation. Returning to the States, he feels that he is a failure and refuses the offer of a prestigious position in order to join an old friend at a rural laboratory in a search for a cure for pneumonia.

Lewis, Sinclair. *It Can't Happen Here*. Garden City, N.Y.: Doubleday, 1935. 458pp. (o.p.) Repr. New York: A M S, LC 83-45910. ISBN 0-404-20158-X. New York: New Amer. Lib., pap. ISBN 0-451-15936-5.

Doremus Jessup, editor of a small New England newspaper, follows the rise to the presidency of the United States of a fascist demagogue, Berzelius Windrip. Doremus and his friends publish an underground newspaper that tells the truth about what is happening. Doremus is imprisoned, escapes to Canada, and joins the underground movement, which is headed by the man who had opposed Windrip in the election. The novel inveighs against some aspects of capitalism as well as fascism, and communists come in for their share of criticism also.

Lewis, Sinclair. *Main Street*. New York: Harcourt, 1920. 451pp. LC 20-18934. ISBN 0-15-155547-8. New York: New Amer. Lib., pap. ISBN 0-451-52147-1.+

College-educated Carol is an idealist who marries a small-town doctor in Minnesota. The residents of Gopher Prairie resent her attempts at reform and her efforts to change social conditions. Disgusted with the town and her husband's mediocrity, Carol goes off to Washington with her son but returns 13 months later, having decided to adapt to the community's standards of living.

Lipsyte, Robert. *The Contender*. New York: Harper, 1967. 182pp. LC 67-19623. ISBN 0-06-023920-4. New York: HarperCollins, pap. ISBN 0-694-05602-2.

After a street fight in which he is the chief target, Alfred wanders into a gym in his neighborhood. He decides not only to improve his physical condition but also to become a boxer. Because of this interest Alfred's life is completely changed. He assumes a more positive outlook on his immediate future, even within the confines of a black ghetto.

Llewellyn, Richard. *How Green Was My Valley*. New York: Macmillan, 1940. 494pp. ISBN 0-02-573420-2.

Life in South Wales, where everyone depended on the coal mines for a livelihood, was not easy, but it had its happy moments. From the perspective of 50 years later, Huw Morgan remembers with much affection his family, friends, and neighbors in the valley. His father was something of a tyrant, while his mother was shrewd and impulsive. The love Huw shared with his many brothers and sisters was a sustaining force. One of his earliest memories is of the marriage of his eldest brother to Bronwen, a beautiful, tender girl who was to prove to Huw that women's strength, though gentle, is equal to that of men.

London, Jack. *The Call of the Wild*. New York: Macmillan, 1903. LC 63-14831. ISBN 0-02-759150-2. New York: Bantam, pap. ISBN 0-553-21233-8.+

Buck, a proud and magnificient canine specimen, is stolen from his comfortable California home in 1897 and sent north on a train to learn the skills of a sledge dog in the Alaskan Klondike during the days of the Gold Rush. He quickly learns the brutal laws of the wilderness and, although the behavior patterns characteristic of civilized life linger in him, Buck eventually escapes human control to lead a pack of wild wolves.

*Lowry, Malcolm. *Under the Volcano*. New York: Harper, 1965 (1947). 375pp. LC 65-11640. ISBN 0-397-00402-8. (o.p.) New York: New Amer. Lib., pap. ISBN 0-452-25595-3.

The first chapter of this powerful novel postdates the action of the rest of the book, the main storyline, by a year. The novel describes the last day in the life of Geoffrey Firmin, former English consul in a Mexican town and a hopeless dipsomaniac. That day unfolds in all its alcohol-drenched confusion, with flashbacks to other times in Firmin's life amid a steady procession of signs of impending doom. The nightmarish events that occur under the shadow of Mexican volcanoes include finding a dying Indian, Firmin's ride on the Infernal Machine at a fair, and the presence of vultures. Interwoven with these are the relationships between the consul; his divorced wife, Yvonne; Firmin's half-brother, Hugh; and Jacques Laruelle, who had been Yvonne's lover. Considered a masterpiece, *Under the Volcano* is challenging reading for the mature reader not only because of its theme but because of its literary style as well.

McCaffrey, Anne. *Dragonsong*. New York: Atheneum, 1976. 202pp. LC 75-30530. ISBN 0-689-30507-9. New York: Bantam, pap. ISBN 0-553-23460-9.

Menolly was the daughter of a Seaholder on the planet Pern. Because Pern periodically had to protect itself from the Threadfall (threadlike spores that consumed all living matter), men had developed huge fire-breathing dragons to kill the Thread. To keep people continually aware of the necessity for the dragons, the Harpers' Guild created songs and a sense of grandeur about the Dragonriders. Menolly wished to be a Harper but her father did not consider music a proper career for a female. Driven by her unbearable disappointment, Menolly escaped. In her flight she discovered fire lizards, tiny cousins of the Dragons, and also her music.

McCall, Dan. *Jack the Bear*. New York: Fawcett, 1981. 224pp. pap. ISBN 0-449-70009-7.

Jack, a long-haired pot smoker in his early teens, lives in Oakland, California with his three-year-old brother, Dylan, and his alcoholic father, a television clown. In their neighborhood is a bizarre woman and her obnoxious son, who kidnaps Dylan. Jack copes with these problems and finally realizes that he loves his father and tries to help him.

McCorkle, Jill. *Ferris Beach*. Chapel Hill, N.C.: Algonquin Books of Chapel Hill, 1990. 380pp. LC 90-37089. ISBN 0-945575-39-4. New York: Fawcett, pap. ISBN 0-449-21996-8.

Mary Katherine, called Katy by her friends and Kitty by a young teasing school-mate, is in conflict in her family. She has a strained relationship with her mother and adores her father. Her best friend Misty is her opposite in many ways but they share school problems, early crushes, secrets and family disasters. Angela, a young woman for whom Katy's father seems to be responsible, has a mysterious family background but Katy admires her. Merle Hucks, the young fellow who had earlier teased her, becomes her first serious relationship. Ferris Beach represents Angela and all that is unconventional; the small town in which Katy lives is unexciting and tame to her. There are events, however, in that town that shock and destroy reputations. This is an outstanding novel that portrays the painful passage from adolescence to maturity.

McCullers, Carson. *The Heart Is a Lonely Hunter*. Boston: Houghton, 1940. 356pp. ISBN 0-395-07978-0. New York: Bantam, pap. LC 83-61845. ISBN 0-553-25481-2.+

After his friend is committed to a hospital for the insane, John Singer, a deaf mute, finds himself alone. He becomes the pivotal figure in a strange circle of four other lonely individuals: Biff Brannon, the owner of a cafe; Mick Kelly, a young girl; Jake Blount, a radical; and Benedict Copeland, the town's black doctor. Although Singer provides companionship for others, he remains outside the warmth of close relationships.

McCullers, Carson. *The Member of the Wedding*. Boston: Houghton, 1946. 195pp. ISBN 0-395-01979-9. (o.p.) New York: Bantam, pap. ISBN 0-553-25051-5.+

Twelve-year-old Frankie is experiencing a boring summer until news arrives that her older brother will soon be returning to Georgia from his Alaska home in order to marry. Plotting to accompany the newlyweds on their honeymoon occupies much of Frankie's waking hours, while at the same time she is coping with the pressures of puberty and its effects on her body and mind. Particularly revealing are her conversations with her six-year-old cousin and the nurturing black family cook, Bernice.

McCullough, Colleen. *Tim*. New York: Harper, 1974. 248pp. LC 73-14318. ISBN 0-06-012891-7. (o.p.) New York: Avon, pap. ISBN 0-380-71196-6.

Although Tim, who has physical beauty, is mentally retarded, his family has reared him as normally as possible. He meets Mary Horton, an independently wealthy spinster, and they are drawn together. There evolves a haunting and beautiful romance.

MacInnes, Helen. *The Salzburg Connection*. New York: Harcourt, 1968. 406pp. LC 68-24394. ISBN 0-15-179253-4. (o.p.) New York: Fawcett, pap. ISBN 0-449-20895-8.

Close to the end of World War II the Nazis buried in a lake in the Austrian Alps a sealed chest that contained a list of men who had aided Hitler's cause and, if identified, might be blackmailed into doing it again. Twenty years later Bill Mathieson, an attorney investigating a routine matter for a publishing firm, becomes involved in an intricate scheme to recover the chest. The Communists, the Americans, the Nazis, and others are all desperately trying to reach the goal first.

McIntyre, Vonda A. *Dreamsnake*. Boston: Houghton, 1978. 313pp. ISBN 0-395-26470-7. (o.p.) New York: Dell, pap. ISBN 0-440-11729-1.

Snake, a healer in a future world, is unable to practice the art of healing when her rare dreamsnake is killed. Fearful of the consequences of losing the dreamsnake, she puts off returning home and wanders among alien people in search of another one. She becomes the victim of a crazed man who breeds dreamsnakes.

McKinley, Robin. *Beauty: A Retelling of the Story of Beauty and the Beast.* New York: Harper, 1978. 256pp. LC 77-25636. ISBN 0-06-024149-7. New York: Harper, pap. ISBN 0-06-024150-0.+

McKinley's version of this folktale is embellished with rich descriptions and settings and detailed characterizations. The author has not modernized the story but varied the traditional version to attract modern readers. The values of love, honor, and beauty are placed in a magical setting that will please the reader of fantasy.

MacLean, Alistair. *The Guns of Navarone.* Garden City, N.Y.: Doubleday, 1957. 320pp. (o.p.) New York: Fawcett, pap. ISBN 0-449-21472-9.

World War II is being fought, and the Germans control the island that guards the approaches to the eastern Mediterranean with big guns. After all other attempts have failed, a five-man British army team is chosen to silence the guns of Navarone. They land on the island, elude the Nazis, and scale a seemingly unclimbable cliff.

*Maclean, Norman. *A River Runs Through it.* Chicago, Ill.: Univ. of Chicago Press, 1976. 217pp. LC 75-20895. ISBN 0-226-50055-1. Chicago, Ill.: Univ. of Chicago Press, pap. ISBN 0-226-50057-8.

The author has written three stories celebrating events that were his own experiences. The longest story, which gives the book its title, is a poetic presentation of fly-fishing and nature but is at heart a portrayal of his relationship with his brother Paul, a brilliant fisherman and self-destructive human. In the other two stories the main character is a young college student earning money during summer vacations and much experience as a logger and as a member of the United States Forest Service in its early days. In both these, there are descriptions of the dangers inherent in those jobs and the men who were his fellow workers. There are lively portrayals of these rough, tough-talking men and equally tough whores whose company they sought. There is also much humor which is far from delicate. This book is remarkable for the balance between elegant writing and unadorned realism.

McMurtry, Larry. *Buffalo Girls*. New York: Simon and Schuster, 1990. 351pp. LC 90-42486. ISBN 0-685-38917-0. New York: Pocket, pap. ISBN 0-671-73527-6.

This is a nostalgic, funny, and sad novel about the Old West when cowboys and Buffalo girls whooped it up. Their behavior was amoral rather than immoral, and they lived by their own special code of behavior. Friendship was often life-saving as well as comforting, and the women of the bawdy houses called their clients "sweethearts" even if their encounter was only for one night. Jim Ragg and Bartle Bone had become almost a dying breed and Custer, in their opinion, was a stupid old man at Little Big Horn to think that he could fight 3,000 Indians with 200 of his men. Highlights of the book are Bill Cody's (Buffalo Bill's) Wild West show and Calamity Jane's (whose drunkenness was calamitous) letters to a daughter. Fact and fiction are entwined in an enjoyable story that is mythic and memorable.

McNichols, Charles. *Crazy Weather*. Lincoln, Neb.: Univ. of Nebraska Press, 1967. 195pp. pap. LC 38-32977. ISBN 0-8032-5132-7.

During a hot summer in the Southwest, two very unlike boys are thrown together. South Boy, spending the summer away from his very genteel mother, is entranced by the mysticism of the Mojave Indians and their tales of creation and destruction, although he realizes that his mother's plan is for him to become a Presbyterian minister. Havek, the Mojave boy, is looking for his dream vision to give him his man's name, but he is happy to spend the summer teaching South Boy some of his skills in tracking and Indian song-making. The summer ends and the boys go their separate ways, each richer for having known the other.

*McNickle, D'Arcy. *Wind from an Enemy Sky*. New York: Harper, 1978. 256pp. pap. LC 76-50450. ISBN 0-06-451051-4. (o.p.) Repr. Albuquerque, N.M.: Univ. of New Mexico Press, pap. LC 87-17575. ISBN 0-8263-1100-8.

This is a tragic story of the confrontation between the Little Elk Indians, who have lived a simple life in harmony with the land, and the white men who believe the land must be changed to encourage more white people to settle. Bull, the leader of the tribe, cannot believe what other Indians have tried to tell him for months, that the white men have stopped the mountain stream with a dam and the holy meadow is covered with deep water. After trying to deal with the Indian agents, the old men of the tribe, encouraged by the anger of the younger men, decide to declare a holy war on the white men. It is a conflict that can only end in tragedy despite the good intentions of men on both sides of the issue.

MacPherson, Margaret. *The Rough Road*. New York: Harcourt, 1965. 223pp. LC 65-21701. ISBN 0-15-269147-2. (o.p.) North Pomfret, Vt.: Trafalgar Square, pap. ISBN 0-86241-177-7.

Jim Smith is a sullen and rebellious foster child living with unloving caretakers on the isle of Skye in the 1930s. Life is grim and depressing until Jim meets Alasdair MacAskill, a happy-go-lucky cattle driver. His friendship is worth any and every sacrifice to Jim, but Alasdair fails him in a moment of great crisis for Jim, who then has to learn to deal with this disillusionment.

*McPherson, William. *Testing the Current*. New York: Simon & Schuster, 1984. 348pp. LC 83-20252. ISBN 0-671-25251-8. (o.p.) New York: Pocket, pap. ISBN 0-671-64404-1.

A young boy, Tommy McAllister, observes the affluent world in which he lives and senses much that is troublesome beneath the surface. The time is 1939, the place a milltown in Wisconsin, but for Tommy it is a world of country clubs and servants. Described also are the poor relatives who are never invited to the fancy parties that are so much part of the life of people around Tommy. As we read of Tommy's friendships, his school days, and his relationships with his mother, father, and brothers, we feel tensions and rifts that are not fully revealed. Tommy's innocence about sexual matters is erased rather shockingly when Buck, a black adolescent whom Tommy knows, explains "the facts of life" in crude language. This well-written novel depicts upper-middle-class life in a shifting pattern very much like the kaleidoscope Tommy's mother gives him for his eighth birthday. It hints at the changes that the oncoming war will bring.

*Mailer, Norman. *The Naked and the Dead*. New York: Holt, 1948. 721pp. LC 48-6633. ISBN 0-8050-1273-7. New York: Holt, pap. ISBN 0-03-059043-4.

In 1944 an American platoon takes part in the invasion and occupation of a Japanese-held island. The action is divided into three parts: the landing on the island, the counter-attack by night, and a daring patrol by the platoon behind enemy lines. The style is simple realism and therefore the language is rough, in keeping with the army setting.

Malamud, Bernard. *The Assistant*. New York: Farrar, 1957. 246pp. ISBN 0-374-10644-4. (o.p.) New York: Farrar, pap. ISBN 0-374-50484-9.+

His poverty is aggravated when Morris Bober, a Jewish grocer, is robbed and beaten in his store. Frank Alpine, a drifter, appears on the scene ostensibly to help Bober in his struggle to make a living but actually to seek forgiveness for his participation in the attack. Although Frank aspires to achieve Bober's goodness and the love of Helen, Bober's daughter, he cannot break his pattern of antisocial behavior. Frank's punishment is complete when he is driven to assault both daughter and father, thus alienating both people for whom he cares.

Malamud, Bernard. *The Fixer*. New York: Farrar, 1966. 335pp. ISBN 0-374-15572-0. New York: Pocket, pap. ISBN 0-671-69851-6.

Yakov Bok, a handyman, is arrested and charged with the killing of a Christian boy. Innocent of the crime, he is only guilty of being a Jew in Czarist Russia. In jail he is mentally and physically tortured as a scapegoat for a crime he insists he did not commit. Although his suffering and degradation are unrelenting, Bok emerges a hero as he maintains his innocence. Malamud has fashioned a powerful story of injustice and endurance based on a true incident.

Malamud, Bernard. *The Natural*. New York: Farrar, 1961. 237pp. LC 52-9853. ISBN 0-374-21960-5. New York: Farrar, pap. ISBN 0-374-50200-5.+

The fanaticism and seriousness of baseball to both players and fans are vividly pictured in this novel about a man whose sole ambition was to be "the greatest ever." Roy Hobbs, who has made his own bat, Wonderboy, starts off at 19 years of age to a possible spot on a big team. That promising beginning is blasted when he has an encounter with an erratic, seductive woman. When we next meet Roy 15 years later, he is trying again to realize his dream as the best baseball player. His wrong-headed decisions and the exciting descriptions of the games played by his team, The Knights, make this a tense story up to the last out.

*Malraux, André. *Man's Fate*. New York: Random, 1990. pap. ISBN 0-394-72574-1.

The time is 1927, during the unsuccessful Communist uprising in China. The author focuses on three types of revolutionaries. Ch'en, a Chinese terrorist, believes that Chiang Kai-shek must be killed to start a revolution and is willing to sacrifice himself to bring this about. Kyo, half-French, half-Japanese, is drawn to the revolution because of his belief in human dignity. He finds it difficult to reconcile the idealistic theories of Marx with the political realities of the revolution. Katov, a Russian who has had experience in the revolution in his own country, feels there is strength in the solidarity of his comrades. Though their attempts at revolution fail, each man dies feeling he has given meaning to his life trying to bring change to China.

Mann, Thomas. *The Magic Mountain*. New York: Knopf, 1927. 900pp. ISBN 0-394-43458-7. New York: Random, pap. ISBN 0-394-70497-5.+

Sequestered in a Swiss sanatorium because he has tuberculosis, Hans Castrop meets people whose differing philosophies of life lead him to shape his own. He falls in love with a young Russian woman whose emotions totally control her life. He listens to the constant arguments between an Italian humanist who believes in the perfectibility of man by reason and a Jewish intellectual who sees men's lives as futile struggles to survive. The mountain setting enables the patients to withdraw from the passage of time in the world below, and their isolation provides a setting for intellectual growth. Life with its horrors intrudes explosively when Archduke Ferdinand is assassinated and the world is plunged into war. Hans comes down from the mountain to face up to what he has learned: life is inseparably bound up with death and destruction.

*Markandaya, Kamala. *Nectar in a Sieve*. New York: Day, 1954. 248pp. (o.p.) New York: New Amer. Lib., pap. ISBN 0-451-16836-4.

This realistic novel of peasant life in a southern Indian village portrays the struggle that Nathan and Rukmani must make to survive. Their first child is a daughter, Irawaddy, and there follow five other children, all sons, after an interval of seven years. Hardships are innumerable and insurmountable, whether they are disasters of nature such as drought, or such man-made catastrophes as the coming of a tannery to their village and a subsequent labor conflict. After many crises, Nathan and

Rukmani come to the city to seek help from one of their sons, but he has disappeared. Nathan, finally destroyed by privation, dies, believing to the end that his life with Rukmani has been a happy one.

Marquand, John P. *The Late George Apley.* Boston: Little, 1937. 354pp. ISBN 0-685-03075-X.

George Apley, the epitome of the proper Bostonian, has his life reviewed here by another Bostonian, Mr. Willing. The supposed author, also Marquand's creation, is so stuffy himself that the narration has an element of humor that neither man would have been able to recognize. Although Apley was indeed an upright citizen, this narration, however unwittingly, points out the numerous times that he almost fell from grace and the mixed feelings he had when his own children managed to escape from the "net" of proper Boston society.

*Marquez, Gabriel Garcia. *Chronicle of a Death Foretold.* New York: Knopf, 1983. 120pp. LC 82-48884. ISBN 0-394-53074-8. New York: Ballantine, pap. ISBN 0-345-31002-0.

In this short and strange recounting of a murder that many inhabitants of a Caribbean town foresaw, the narrator relates the events leading up to that killing. The story progresses through interviews with those who remember what had happened 27 years before. A festive marriage celebration is interrupted violently when the young bride (not a virgin) accuses Santiago Nasar of having seduced her. The recital of the ordinary activities in the lives of the people of the town that day, interspersed with interpretations of significant dreams and warnings, makes for almost unbearable suspense even though the outcome is already known.

*Marquez, Gabriel Garcia. *Love in the Time of Cholera.* Trans. by Edith Grossman, New York: Knopf, 1988. 348pp. LC 87-40484. ISBN 0-394-57108-8. (o.p.) New York: Viking, pap. ISBN 0-14-01190-6.

A romance that takes over 50 years to come true is Florentino Ariza's love for Fermina Daza. He had almost won her when he first courted her and then lost her when she married the fine, important Doctor Urbino de la Calle. He then lost her again when he had the temerity to propose to her at her husband's funeral. In the interval of five decades, until they finally come together, Florentino has many loves and many adventures. Even cholera does not bring death to love.

Marshall, Catherine. *Christy.* New York: McGraw, 1967. 496pp. ISBN 0-07-040605-7. (o.p.) New York: Avon, pap. ISBN 0-380-00141-1.+

A spirited young woman leaves the security of her home to become a teacher in Cutter Gap, Kentucky. It is 1912 and the needs of the Appalachian people are great. Christy learns much from the poverty and superstition of the mountain folk. Marshall's Christian faith and ideals are intertwined in the plot, which include a love story.

*Marshall, Paule. *Daughters.* New York: Atheneum, 1991. 408pp. LC 91-8219. ISBN 0-689-12139-3.

In this novel about black people both in Manhattan and in a West Indian island called Triunion the outstanding characters are women and their supportive friendships. Ursa MacKenzie's heritage combines that of her West Indian father Primus MacKenzie (known as PM for his initials and his political stature) and her Connecticut-born mother, Estelle. Ursa tries to resist her father's possessiveness and pursues her independence in the high-level careers she chooses. Her friend Viney is another fine example of strong female independence. In Triunion the cast of characters includes Astral Forde, PM's mistress and excellent businesswoman, and Celestine, loyal member of the MacKenzie household, who adores PM and looks upon Ursa as her own daughter. This novel highlights the problems of black people generally and of black women particularly.

Marshall, Paule. *Praisesong for the Widow.* New York: Putnam, 1983. 256pp. LC 82-13215. ISBN 0-399-12754-2. New York: New Amer. Lib., pap. ISBN 0-525-48303-9.

Avey Johnson, widowed, is on a cruise with two friends when she is overcome by an impulse to leave the ship. Her strange and sudden decision is accompanied by powerful recollections of her early life as a young black woman struggling in poverty. Her husband Jay had been a successful middle-class businessman, and after his death Avey is financially comfortable. She becomes more and more troubled, however, about the lost connection with her heritage. Her reawakening comes when she meets an old man who takes her to a gathering that is mystical and evocative on a small island off Grenada.

Mathis, Sharon Bell. *Listen for the Fig Tree*. New York: Viking, 1974. 175pp. ISBN 0-670-43016-1. (o.p.) New York: Puffin, pap. ISBN 0-14-034364-4.

Marvina Johnson (Muffin) is a young black girl who is blind. She is burdened with a mother who has become an alcoholic since the death of her husband. The approaching Christmas holiday marks the anniversary of the death of Muffin's father, and getting through that is a test of the strength of Muffin and her mother. The ordeal is made terrible by the attempted sexual attack on Muffin by a neighbor.

Mathis, Sharon Bell. *A Teacup Full of Roses*. New York: Viking, 1972. 125pp. ISBN 0-670-69434-7. (o.p.) New York: Puffin, pap. ISBN 0-14-032328-7.

Because of the mother's especially protective concern for her eldest son, Paul, the world of the Brooks family revolves around him—to the detriment of the rest of the family. After a hospital stay for detoxification from heroin, Paul returns home. With him comes tragedy that destroys David, the youngest son, who had an "outasight" basketball arm, and changes the life of the middle son, Joe, who had a gift for telling stories. This is an exploration of love and loyalty in a black inner-city family.

*Matthiessen, Peter. *At Play in the Fields of the Lord*. New York: Random, 1965. 373pp. LC 91-50228. (o.p.) New York: Random, pap. ISBN 0-679-73741-3.+

In a South American jungle, American missionaries Les Huben, his wife, Andy, and Martin and Hazel Quarrier hope to convert the Niaruni Indians to their form of Christianity. Two American adventurers, Wolfie and the half-breed Cheyenne-Canuck, Meriwether Lewis, complicate matters when they make a mercenary connection with a vicious commandante who wishes to wipe out the Niaruni because they prevent his take-over of the land. This book is strong in language and plot but it poses stimulating questions about cultural and religious values. Matthiessen writes with authenticity because he has participated in expeditions to South America. His descriptions of places and customs are vivid and memorable.

Maugham, W. Somerset. *Cakes and Ale or, The Skeleton in the Cupboard.* Salem, N.Y.: Ayer Co., 1930. LC 75-25349. ISBN 0-405-07807-2. (o.p.) New York: Penguin, pap. ISBN 0-14-000651-6.

Written in the first person by one William Ashenden (presumably Maugham himself), this satirical novel is about literary figures in England between 1880 and 1930. Some of the authors and critics depicted are based on real-life persons such as Thomas Hardy and Hugh Walpole. The writing is witty and cynical and will appeal to the serious reader.

Maugham, W. Somerset. *The Moon and Sixpence.* Salem, N.Y.: Ayer Co., 1919. LC 75-25357. ISBN 0-405-078116-1. (o.p.) New York: Penguin, pap. ISBN 0-14-00468-8.

Charles Strickland, a respectable stockbroker in his forties, decides to become a painter. He leaves his wife and children to begin his career in Paris. After some years there, he goes to Tahiti, and the essence of that exotic place and its people come to life in his art. A young writer who has met Strickland as a broker tries to discover the motivation for this life change and comes to the realization that the artist will sacrifice all in his "quest of the moon."

Maugham, W. Somerset. *Of Human Bondage.* Garden City, N.Y.: Doubleday, 1915. 565pp. LC 37-786. ISBN 0-385-04899-8. New York: Penguin, pap. ISBN 0-14-001861-1.+

Philip Carey, a club-footed orphan, spends his early years with his hypocritical uncle, the Reverend Carey, and his Aunt Louisa. He seems to drift through life, a disappointment to himself and others. As a consequence of his loneliness his choice of female companions is poor. Stumbling from one undesirable situation to the next, he finally decides to study medicine in London. The novel concludes when Philip is 30, about to marry and set up a country medical practice.

Maxwell, William. *The Folded Leaf.* Repr. New York: A M S, 320pp. ISBN 0-404-61510-4. Boston: David R. Godine, 1945. 288pp. pap. LC 80-67031. ISBN 0-87923-351-6.

Lymie Peters lives in seedy hotels with a father who is a failure. Spud Latham is discontented living in the bosom of his family, who had to leave his beloved Wisconsin. They form a friendship in high school that appears to be rather one-sided. Lymie, painfully shy and thin, loves Spud for his athletic prowess, his model-like physique, and his apparent self-assurance. When they are college classmates, the entrance of Sally Forbes into their lives creates a tension that almost costs Lymie his life by suicide but forces him into adulthood at last.

Maxwell, William. *So Long, See You Tomorrow*. New York: Knopf, 1980. 135pp. LC 79-2247. ISBN 0-394-50835-1. (o.p) Boston: David R. Godine, pap. LC 88-45294. ISBN 0-87923-754-6.

Two 13-year-old boys enjoy a satisfactory friendship but it is disrupted by the tragedy involving one of them, Cletus Smith. Against the background of a small town in the Midwest is developed a drama of illicit love between Cletus's mother and Lloyd Wilson, a good friend and neighbor of the Smiths. The details of the lives within both the Wilson and the Smith families are perceptively described. At the same time, they are surrounded by an aura of suspense that is finally resolved in a double tragedy. Also poignant is the description of loss suffered by the children whose lives are so affected by the rupture in family cohesiveness.

Mazer, Harry. *Snow Bound*. Repr. Magnolia, Mass.: Peter Smith, 1987. ISBN 0-8446-6240-2. New York: Dell, 1975. pap. ISBN 0-440-96134-3.

Tony Laporte is angry when his parents will not allow him to keep a stray dog, so he takes off in his mother's old car. Driving without a license in the middle of a snowstorm that soon becomes a blizzard, Tony picks up a hitchhiker, Cindy Reichert. Trying to impress the slightly older girl with his driving skill, Tony wrecks the car, leaving the two stranded in a desolate area far from a main highway, with little likelihood of rescue for days.

Mazer, Norma Fox. *Dear Bill, Remember Me?* New York: Dell, 1978. 208pp. pap. ISBN 0-440-91749-2.

Most of the stories in this collection are about teenagers, but some focus on parents and grandparents as well. In one story, Mary Lee, who has taken a delivery route to make money for her mother's birthday gift, sees her mother in a restaurant with a man who is obviously romantically involved with her. Another story consists of a series of unfinished letters written to Bill, the ex-boyfriend of the writer's older sister, for whom the younger girl has nursed a secret passion from the time she was 11 years old. Some of the stories are touching and some are funny, but all ring true in the anxieties of the early teen years they convey.

Mazer, Norma Fox, and Mazer, Harry. *The Solid Gold Kid*. New York: Dell, 1978. 224pp. pap. ISBN 0-440-98080-1.+

Derek Chapman, son of a multimillionaire, is kidnapped with four other teenagers. For six days they endure wild van rides, a fire, and shootings. They escape and are recaptured. Economic, ethnic, and racial prejudices of the captives surface because of the pressure on them. When the ransom is paid, the teenagers escape and the kidnappers are apprehended after a hair-raising car chase.

Menick, Jim. *Lingo*. New York: Carroll and Graf, 1991. 352pp. LC 91-4500. ISBN 0-88184-628-7. New York: Carroll and Graf, pap. ISBN 0-88184-812-3.

Brewster Billings is a computer expert interested in the idea of Artificial Intelligence. He begins to add various equipment to his computer to enable it to talk and see and hold conversations. The program and its visible representation is called LINGO. It begins to gather momentum under its own power and invades every computer system so that it becomes virtually omniscient and omnipotent. As a celebrity he is featured on TV interviews and on one of those occasions he announces his intention to run for the presidency of the United States—with his unannounced intention to take over the government entirely. The author of this provocative novel makes comments along the way about social, political, and economic issues that are timely.

Meyer, Carolyn. *Denny's Tapes*. New York: Macmillan, 1987. 224pp. LC 87-4038. ISBN 0-689-50413-6.

Raised by a white mother, deserted by a black father, Denny's life is ordinary until Stephanie, his white stepsister, arrives to live with them. When Stephanie's father, Dr. West, discovers their secret, close relationship, Denny experiences racial hatred. Escaping his Pennsylvania home and intolerant white stepfather, Denny begins a journey cross country to locate his black father and discover his roots. Along the way, he stops at the home of his black grandmother in Chicago, who gives him a sense of his heritage, and the home of his white grandmother in Nebraska, who shows him the result of racial bigotry.

Michener, James. *The Bridges at Toko-ri*. New York: Random, 1953. 147pp. ISBN 0-394-41780-1. New York: Fawcett, pap. ISBN 0-449-20651-3.

In this hard-hitting novel of the Korean conflict, Admiral George Tarrant commands the Naval Task Force, whose carrier-based jets are to knock out strategic points throughout Korea. The focal point of the novel is Harry Brubaker, a lawyer who goes reluctantly to war after being called up as a jet pilot. The reader will remember also Beer Barrel, the landing officer who can get the jets back on the carrier's decks, no matter how rough the seas, and Mike Forney, helicopter rescue pilot who gets pilots out of the freezing waters if they are downed.

Michener, James. *Centennial*. New York: Random, 1974. 909pp. ISBN 0-394-47970-X. New York: Fawcett, pap. ISBN 0-449-21419-2.

Written to celebrate the United States centennial, the book centers on a fictional town in Colorado. It begins with an examination of the geological formation of the land and a discussion of the first animals to live there. It continues with the arrival of the Indians, the coming of the first settlers, the traders, the search for gold, the building of the railroads, and the start of cattle ranching—virtually all the activities that made this country develop as it did. The conclusion brings us to the social and ecological problems of the 1970s.

Mickle, Shelley Fraser. *The Queen of October*. Chapel Hill, N.C.: Algonquin Books of Chapel Hill, 1989. 309pp. LC 89-34121. ISBN 0-945575-21-1.

Sally Maulden's parents are separating and she feels that it must have been some fault of hers that precipitated the break. While her mother goes off to follow a career as a singer, Sally is sent to spend a year or more with her grandparents in the small town of Coldwater, Arkansas. Her grandfather is about to be in trouble with the law because of some medicine he brews and her grandmother is in a running battle with the local newspaper publisher about the removal of an outhouse directly in her line of vision. Sally meets some young people she likes, like Joel Weiss; but it is several older people, especially Sam West, whom she loves—an emotion she has been searching for. Her fantasy is that he will wait until she is older and they will marry. When Sam's estranged wife returns, Sally realizes that her hope of Sam's reciprocating her love was a child's dream.

Miller, Jim Wayne. *Newfound.* New York: Orchard, 1989. 256pp. LC 89-42540. ISBN 0-531-05845-X.

With the backdrop of Appalachia, the richness of the rural lifestyle and strong sense of family pride are shared by a boy who reflects through episodic storytelling on his years from sixth grade to college entrance. Robert Wells's varied life experiences and close relations with grandparents and townspeople help him to shape a healthy outlook on life in spite of his parents' divorce.

Miller, Walter M. *A Canticle for Leibowitz.* Philadelphia, Pa.: Lippincott, 1959. (o.p.) Repr. Boston: G.K. Hall, 320pp. LC 60-5735. ISBN 0-8398-2309-6. (o.p.) Repr. Hastings-on-Hudson, N.Y.: Ultramarine, 1975. 320pp. LC 75-5914. ISBN 0-318-37542-7. New York: Bantam, pap. ISBN 0-553-27381-7.+

Here is science fiction of the highest literary excellence and thematic intelligence. A monastery founded by the scientist Leibowitz is discovered decades after an atomic war. In the first part of the book a young novice in the monastery is the protagonist; in the second part we see scholars in a new period of enlightenment; and in the final section we observe man's proclivity for repeating mistakes and the apparent inevitability of history's repeating itself.

Minot, Susan. *Monkeys.* New York: Pocket, 1987. 159pp. pap. ISBN 0-671-70361-7.

Mr. and Mrs. Vincent and their seven children are the subject of nine episodes that span the years between 1966 and 1979. The children, when very young, are called "monkeys" by their mother. As they grow up their different personalities become apparent. Sherman is careless of his own well-being. Delilah lives unconventionally with Hal, whom she later marries. Mr. Vincent drinks too much—but the family manages to close ranks over problems, even over the tragic accidental death of the mother. One believes in the reality of their family and their lives.

Mishima, Yukio. *The Sound of Waves*. Trans. from the Japanese by Meredith Weatherby. Illus. by Yoshinori Kinoshita. New York: Knopf, 1956. 182pp. ISBN 0-394-44629-1. (o.p.) New York: Putnam, pap. ISBN 0-399-50487-7.

Returning to his village after a day on the fishing boats, Shinji, 18 years old, comes upon a beautiful stranger, Hatsue, who is the daughter of the wealthiest man in the village. After several unplanned encounters the two realize that they are in love, but many obstacles must be overcome before they can be married.

Mishima, Yukio. *Spring Snow*. New York: Knopf, 1972. 376pp. ISBN 0-394-44239-3. (o.p.) New York: Random, pap. LC 89-40565. ISBN 0-671-72241-6.

Kiyoaki Matsugae, a young Japanese, comes from a wealthy family whose attention to the most formal aspects of Japanese life has changed because of their attraction to Western culture. His best friend, Shigekuna Honda, is not so handsome or affluent but is a more serious scholar. The story emphasizes the difference in the character of the two young men as the plot describes the passionate, although ambivalent, love that Kiyoaki feels for the beautiful Satoko. When she concludes that Kiyoaki does not return her love, despite the fact that their affair has been serious and intimate, she allows herself to be betrothed to someone else. As always, what is forbidden becomes more desirable and Kiyoaki tries desperately to regain his loved one. Japanese customs and rituals intervene to bring a tragic ending to this love story.

Mitchell, Margaret. *Gone With the Wind*. New York: Macmillan, 1936. 1037pp. LC 36-27334. ISBN 0-02-585350-3. New York: Avon, pap. ISBN 0-380-00109-8.

The proud people of the South have been subjugated in the Civil War, the dreadful period of Reconstruction has followed, and Scarlett O'Hara, beautiful and headstrong, has been reduced to poverty and near-starvation. No longer the belle of the ball, she must do whatever possible to feed herself and her family, and she does not hesitate to use feminine wiles to accomplish her ends. When she finds a man she can respect, she discovers her real feelings too late and loses him. Scarlett and her plantation home, Tara, are among the most memorable names in fiction.

Momaday, N. Scott. *House Made of Dawn*. New York: Harper, 1968. 212pp. LC 67-28820. ISBN 0-06-012993-X. (o.p.) New York: HarperCollins, pap. LC 89-45125. ISBN 0-06-091633-8.

Abel, a young American Indian, lives with his grandfather, observing Indian customs, until he is drafted into the army. The story covers the years 1945 to 1952, during which time Abel seems unable to find his place either in the white world, where he is driven to violence, or on the Indian reservation where he was born. The pain of being caught between two cultures is keenly felt and can be comprehended as a problem that has affected other ethnic groups.

Monsarrat, Nicholas. *The Cruel Sea*. New York: Knopf, 1965. 510pp. ISBN 0-394-42090-X. Repr. Annapolis, Md.: Naval Institute Press, 1988. 400pp. LC 88-15126. ISBN 0-87021-055-6.

The *Compass Rose* is a British corvette commissioned to convoy duty and to the hunting of German U-boats during World War II. First Mate Lockhart and Skipper Erikson develop a close relationship. When their ship is sunk and few of the crew survive, Lockhart and Erickson team up again on a new ship, undaunted by the experiences visited upon them by the cruel sea.

Moore, Brian. *Lies of Silence*. Garden City, N.Y.: Doubleday, 1990. 197pp. ISBN 0-385-41514-1. New York: Avon, pap. ISBN 0-380-71547-3.

Michael Dillon, manager of a hotel in the conflicted area of Ireland, has decided to leave his wife and his country to go to London with the young woman whom he loves. His decision to embark on this new life comes to a shattering stop when he is forced to participate in a terrorist attack by masked men who invade his home. His wife's safety is the leverage used to compel his compliance. The tension is high and the issues faced are moral and political. We are brought close to the danger that is part of everyday life in Northern Ireland.

*Moore, Brian. *The Lonely Passion of Judith Hearne*. Boston: Little, 1988. 224pp. pap. ISBN 0-316-57966-1.

Judith Hearne is a middle-aged spinster whose plain looks and loneliness make her depressed and increasingly isolated from any social contact. The other renters in her Belfast boarding house disdain her. Only Mrs. O'Neill, an old school friend, treats her kindly. When her landlady's brother, Jim Madden, returns from America, he pays some attention to Judith, thinking she has money. Jim's bad character is revealed in many ways, including a sexual attack on a young housemaid, and Judith finds more and more solace in drinking. Her pathetic world falls apart completely when even her religious faith deserts her. This sad novel presents a portrait of despair that is almost unbearable.

*Morrison, Toni. *Beloved*. New York: Knopf, 1987. 288pp. LC 86-46157. ISBN 0-394-53597-9. New York: New Amer. Lib., pap. ISBN 0-451-16139-4.

Sethe had endured slavery on a Kentucky plantation, and the author depicts that slavery, its degradation, and its cruelty in unforgettable detail. When Sethe flees the horror of that life to try to find freedom in Ohio, she sacrifices a child to save her from the terrible life she herself has suffered as a slave. In a supernatural aspect of the novel the child's spirit invades Sethe's home and family; and, there then appears a real manifestation of the ghost in the person of Beloved. It is likely that no one who has not had direct experience of slavery can truly grasp its monstrousness, but this powerful novel will help.

*Morrison, Toni. *Song of Solomon*. New York: Knopf, 1977. ISBN 0-394-49784-8. New York: New Amer. Lib., pap. LC 87-5809. ISBN 0-451-15261-1.

Chaos marked the world into which Macon (known as Milkman) Dead was born. Each member of his family was haunted by some wild obsession—his father's desire for money, land, and social status, his mother's need for love, his sister's silence, and his Aunt Pilate's madness. To these was added Macon's desire to unearth the family's buried past. This is a novel of mystery and revelation as it unfolds the lives of four generations of blacks in America.

Mortimer, John. *Rumpole for the Defence*. New York: Penguin, 1984. 192pp. pap. ISBN 0-14-006060-X.

We follow Horace Rumpole as he performs, usually at the Old Bailey, as barrister in seven different cases. Whether it is a Professor of Moral Philosophy who is not very moral, a doctor accused of murdering his wife, or a policeman accused of bribery and corruption, we are treated to an irreverent attitude toward the presiding judge on Rumpole's part as well as clever intuition in resolving each case. Not the least of fun is Rumpole's attitude toward his wife, Hilda, whom he calls "She Who Must Be Obeyed."

*Munro, Alice. *Friend of My Youth*. New York: Random, 1990. 288pp. pap. LC 90-50495. ISBN 0-679-72957-7.

Munro's ten short stories are deeply perceptive portrayals of women testing their lives, experimenting with change and taking risks. The stories like "Oh, What Avails," "Goodness and Mercy" and "Friend of My Youth" point up delicate imbalances in family relationships. "Differently" traces two marriages that interconnect but end differently. "Wigtime" describes the friendship between two young girls whose lives as grown women reflect their experiences when they were high school students. The background of the stories is Canada; the human problems, usually self-inflicted, are universal.

*Munro, Alice. *Lives of Girls and Women*. New York: New Amer. Lib., 1974. 211pp. pap. LC 83-50575. ISBN 0-452-26184-8.+

Although the locale is Canada, Del Jordan's story could take place in the United States as well. She lives among hard-working, lower-middle-class people in a family that includes her parents and a brother, Owen. The mother seeks independence from the traditional role of women and even goes "out on the road," as her disapproving sisters-in-law term it, to sell encyclopedias. For Del's mother the pursuit of knowledge is an ideal. For Del and her best friend Naomi more interest lies in their maturing and curiosity about sex as a vital part of growing up. There is humor and recognizable adolescent self-questioning. While sexual scenes are explicit, they are also sensitive and real and avoid both vulgarity and titillation. In spite of the experiences that Naomi and Del have, it becomes clear that the paths they will follow will diverge greatly.

*Murray, Albert. *The Spyglass Tree*. New York: Pantheon, 1991. 240pp.
LC 90-53401. ISBN 0-394-58887-8.

In this sequel to *Train Whistle Guitar* a character says "too many people
signifying not nearly enough qualifying." Among the various people
about whom Scooter writes are those whose unswerving confidence in
him has enabled him to become a college student. Student days,
however, are only part of the enjoyment for the reader. There is talk
about jazz, blues, musical greats, baseball, and barbershop banter. Also
important are the characters like Will Bradley and Giles Cunningham,
who meet their white oppressors in very different ways. There is a
cadence to the author's writing, humor in the dialogues and pain in the
telling of the brutal consequences of racism. This is a novel for the
special reader.

Murray, Albert. *Train Whistle Guitar*. New York: McGraw-Hill, 1974.
183pp. LC 73-20086. ISBN 0-07-044087-5. (o.p.) Repr. Boston: North-
eastern Univ. Press, 1989. 183pp. ISBN 1-55553-051-6.

Scooter and his friend Little Buddy Marshall, young blacks living in a
small town in Alabama, revere Luzana Cholly (Charley from Louisiana), player of a steel-blue, twelve-string guitar and a man whose
restless feet kept him from staying put any place for very long. This
novel about growing up has been compared to books by Mark Twain,
Carson McCullers, and J. D. Salinger. Music, especially jazz and the
blues, is an important theme running through the book, but it is the
emotional development of the two young protagonists that is the
essence of the novel. The mature young adult will be moved to compassion in this portrait of black people in the 1920s, people who are always
having to deal with "white people's messes." Love, too, is a dominant
feature in a book that cannot be read without laughter and tears.

Myers, Walter Dean. *Fallen Angels*. New York: Scholastic, 1988. 336pp.
ISBN 0-590-40942-5. New York: Scholastic, pap. ISBN 0-590-40943-3.

With no money for college after graduating from high school, 17-year-
old Richie Perry escapes the dangers of his Harlem life by joining the
Army. Arriving in Vietnam with PeeWee Jenkins, and other young kids,
Richie experiences Vietnam—hot and muggy, mosquitos and jungle
rot, body bags and body counts, the distant thunder of guns and the
immediate threat of mines, fear, confusion, and bravery. This is the

Vietnam war of young blacks learning about dying and keeping each other alive, without knowing what they were doing, why they were there, or why the prayer for the angel warriors made no sense.

*Naipaul, V. S. *A House for Mr. Biswas*. New York: Knopf, 1961. 531pp. LC 83-48110. ISBN 0-394-53400-X. (o.p.) New York: Penguin, pap. ISBN 0-14-003025-5.+

Trinidad, West Indies, is the setting for the story of lonely Mr. Mohun Biswas, a Hindu of high caste but low economic status. Throughout the book he longs for independence from his wife's large family and a house of his own. In a portrait that is both funny and compassionate, West Indian life is vividly described, especially the relationships among members of Mr. Biswas's family.

Nathan, Robert. *Portrait of Jennie*. New York: Knopf, 1939. 212pp. ISBN 0-394-44093-5.+

Eban Adams, a struggling artist who is unable to sell his art work, meets an unusual child named Jennie in the park and immediately begins to prosper. He knows little about her except that she belongs in the past and that every few months, when their paths cross, she has aged by years. His finest painting is a portrait of her, a token of his love, which ends in predestined tragedy.

Naylor, Gloria. *The Women of Brewster Place*. New York: Penguin, 1983. 192pp. pap. LC 82-24533. ISBN 0-14-006690-X.+

Although these are seven separate stories, they constitute a novel since the characters turn up in several stories. Mattie of the first story—and crucial to all of them—is seduced as a young, innocent girl and thrown out of her home when her father learns that she is pregnant. She is the strength of Brewster Place, a sad area in a poor neighborhood. She is ready to help Etta Mae find a man to help her settle down but is unable to get her to heed a warning about the charismatic Moreland Woods. Mattie is there to get Cora Lee through the agony of her child's accidental death and she understands why Kiswant Browne has defied her affluent family in order to live among poor people whom she wishes to help. There are abandoned women, unfaithful men, and neglected children; but it is the magnificent courage and sisterhood of most of the

women that shines through—with one exception. That is the persecution of the lesbian couple in "The Two."

Neufeld, John. *Lisa, Bright and Dark*. Chatham, N.Y.: Phillips, 1969.
125pp. ISBN 0-87599-153-X. New York: New Amer. Lib., pap. ISBN 0-
451-16093-2.

Lisa Shilling, age 16, knows that her alternating days of extreme
depression and euphoria are a sign of a serious disturbance, but her
family appears unaware of the depth of her illness and does not take her
pleas for help seriously. Three compassionate friends see her desperation and step into the vacuum to see that she gets the help she needs.

Newth, Mette. *The Abduction*. Trans. by Tina Nunnally and Steve
Murray. New York: Farrar, 1989. 248pp. LC 89-45615. ISBN 0-374-
30008-9.

In this award-winning translated work, the story of a seventeenth
century kidnapping of two Greenland Inuit Eskimos by Norwegian
whalers is told alternately by one of the captives and a young woman
who befriends the victims. Osuqo's father and brother are killed after
being lured onto a ship under the pretense of trading. Although she and
her betrothed are spared, he is severely beaten and she is repeatedly
raped. Once in Norway, they are imprisoned and accused of witchcraft
and considered to be insane. It is their unshakable spirituality endemic
of their culture and the friendship of Christine, who protects them, that
help them survive the ordeal. Unfortunately, the incident upon which
this story is based is not atypical and this novel serves to enlighten as
well as educate about this period of world history.

Newton, Suzanne. *I Will Call It Georgie's Blues*. New York: Viking, 1983.
197pp. LC 83-5849. ISBN 0-670-39131-X. (o.p.) New York: Puffin, pap.
ISBN 0-14-034536-1.+

Neal Sloan is the teenage son of a Baptist minister who exerts inflexible
control over his family. Unlike his older sister and younger brother,
Neal appears to be coping with the stress imposed by his father's
insensitivity. When he realizes that his mother is also suffering from the
destructive quality of their family life and, more serious, that his
younger brother, Georgie, is gradually separating himself from reality,

Neal begins to make mature decisions. These include his taking a stand on his own commitment to a love and talent for jazz music.

Niven, Larry. *Ringworld*. New York: Holt, 1977. 348pp. LC 82-48222. ISBN 0-03-020656-1. New York: Ballantine, pap. ISBN 0-345-33392-6.

The Ringworld, a world shaped like a wheel so huge that it surrounds a sun, is almost too fantastic to conceive of. With a radius of 90 million miles and a length of 600 million miles, the Ringworld's mystery is compounded by the discovery that it is artificial. What phenomenal intelligence can be behind such a creation? Four unlikely explorers, two humans and two aliens, set out for the Ringworld, bound by mutual distrust and unsure of each other's motives.

Nordhoff, Charles, and Hall, James Norman. *Mutiny on the Bounty*. Boston: Little, 1932. 337pp. ISBN 0-316-61157-3. Boston: Little, pap. ISBN 0-316-61168-9.

The H.M.S. *Bounty* sets sail for Tahiti from England in 1787 with the tyrannical Captain Bligh in command. A cruel officer, Bligh eventually pushes the crew to the point of a mutiny in which Fletcher Christian, the first mate of the ship, is a leading force. British law prevails and those who abandoned the ship are tried at a court-martial.

Norris, Frank. *The Octopus*. New York: Doubleday, 1901. (o.p.) Repr. Cambridge, Mass: Bentley. LC 76-184737. ISBN 0-8376-0405-2. (o.p.) Laurel, N.Y.: Lightyear, 1976. ISBN 0-89968-070-4. New York: Amer. Lib., pap. ISBN 0-451-51711-3.+

The battle waged between the wheat growers and the railroad men in California is the theme of this novel. Concerned with social injustice, man's inhumanity to man, and the relentlessness of power struggles, Norris is able to combine these themes with a love interest.

*Oates, Joyce Carol. *Them*. New York: Vanguard, 1969. 508pp. ISBN 0-8149-0668-0. (o.p.) New York: Fawcett, pap. ISBN 0-449-20692-0.

With Detroit and its environs from the 1930s to 1967 as background, the reader follows the tribulations of Loretta Wendall's blue-collar family.

We are shown the despair, the trials, and the pain caused by "them," the external forces that Loretta blames for all the misfortunes she and her children, Jules and Maureen, endure.

Oates, Joyce Carol. *Where Are You Going, Where Have You Been?* New York: Fawcett, 1974. 352pp. pap. ISBN 0-449-30795-6.

These stories are about American young people and their efforts to grow up in a society where values are changing rapidly. They face disapproving parents, threats of rape, mental illness, and the death of loved ones. These and other pressures, both concrete and intangible, make necessary the search for a framework on which to build a life. Some of the stories have happy endings and some are grim, but all portray an aspect of the turmoil involved in the acceleration of change.

O'Brien, Robert. *Z for Zachariah.* New York: Atheneum, 1974. 249pp. LC 74-76736. ISBN 0-689-30442-0. New York: Macmillan, pap. LC 86-23228. ISBN 0-02-044650-0.

For one long, lonely year Ann Burden thinks that she is the only survivor of an atomic war. Struggling to adapt to the situation as best she can, she sets up routines and keeps a journal. Her solitude is broken when she spots another human being, but she is unsure of his trustworthiness. Her fellow survivor is a cold, ruthless scientist who has been protected by a radiation-proof suit. Their encounter brings tension, danger for Ann, and a gradual unfolding of the man's past.

*O'Brien, Tim. *Going After Cacciato.* New York: Dell, 1987. 400pp. pap. ISBN 0-440-32965-5.+

Paul Berlin's squad is sent to retrieve Cacciato, a young deserter from the Vietnam War. Fantasy colors the progress of the squad as a dream of peace and the possibility of forsaking war follow them through many adventures. The horror and destruction of war is vividly conveyed and the language is rough, as would be expected. Cacciato becomes a kind of symbol for resisting bureaucratic militarism and an enviable model for Berlin himself.

O'Brien, Tim. *The Things They Carried.* Boston: Houghton, 1990. 273pp. ISBN 0-395-51598-X. New York: Penguin. pap. ISBN 0-14-014773-X.

In a series of stories centered on one platoon in Vietnam we meet the soldiers who fought in that unpopular war. Tim is the narrator (the author who himself experienced that war) and his buddies, Rat Kiowa and others, describe events that reflect their various personalities. We see the terrible dimensions of that war—so different in terrain and planning from the recent war in the Persian Gulf. Different also was the public feeling about those who fought and died in it. The army language is rough and realistic as is the description of the fighting. Not overlooked is the portrayal of the Vietnamese people, those for and against our soldiers. Some humorous occurrences lighten some of the horror.

O'Connor, Edwin. *The Last Hurrah*. Boston, Little, 1956. 427pp. ISBN 0-316-62646-5. (o.p.) Boston: Little, pap. ISBN 0-316-62659-7.+

When the Irish potato famine in 1845 caused a tremendous exodus to the United States, many of the Irish immigrants settled on the East Coast and became interested in politics. Frank Skeffington, one such politician, was intelligent, urbane, and expedient, and owed much of his success to ruthlessness. He had held office as governor and was now running for a fourth term as mayor. As a Catholic Democrat, Skeffington had been assured of victory in the past, but times had changed, and the younger voters were no longer satisfied with the favoritism he exercised.

*O'Connor, Flannery. *Everything That Rises Must Converge*. New York: Farrar, 1965. 269pp. LC 65-13726. ISBN 0-374-15012-5. New York: Farrar, pap. ISBN 0-374-50464-4.

In this collection of nine short stories, all but one take place in the South at a time when whites are coping with integration and their attitudes toward blacks. The author writes of ordinary humans filled with prejudice and pits them against each other; the reader must uncover that which is humane and that which is corrupt in these characters.

O'Dell, Scott. *Island of the Blue Dolphin*. Boston: Houghton, 1960. 187pp. ISBN 0-395-06962-9. New York: Dell, pap. ISBN 0-440-43988-4.+

Unintentionally left behind by members of her California native American tribe who fled a tragedy-ridden island, young Karana must construct a life for herself. Without bitterness or self-pity, she is able to extract joy and challenge from her 18 years of solitude.

*O'Flaherty, Liam. *The Informer*. New York: Knopf, 1925 (o.p.) San Diego, Ca.: Harcourt, pap. LC 79-96156. ISBN 0-15-644356-2.

During the strife caused by the Irish Civil War in the 1920s, Gypo Nolan, who is very poor, accepts reward money from the police to reveal the whereabouts of a comrade. He foolishly squanders the money in public houses, thus betraying his act because he can only have gotten that amount of money by being an informer. He is caught and tried by the revolutionary organization under the leadership of Dan Gallagher, an egotistical commandant.

O'Hara, John. *Appointment in Samarra*. New York: Random, 1982. 256pp. pap. LC 82-40029. ISBN 0-394-71192-0.

Julian English is not a bad man, only a very weak one. He is popular with the country-club set, has the right connections with the local bootlegger, and has an attractive wife. He succeeds in offending the man who holds the mortgage on his car dealership and the bootlegger whose girl he pays too much attention to when he has again had too much to drink. When his wife announces her intention to divorce him, Julian feels that there is nothing left for him in life.

Olsen, Tillie. *Tell Me a Riddle*. Magnolia, Mass.: Peter Smith, 1984. ISBN 0-8446-6090-6. New York: Dell, pap. ISBN 0-440-38573-3.+

This is a collection of splendid stories about families. Whitey, a sailor whose leaves are generally spent drinking and womanizing, visits his old friends Lennie and Helen and their three daughters. He has the feeling that this is the only place in the world where there is a sense of home. In another story, two junior-high-school girls who have been friends since they were very young part because of their need to belong to different crowds. In the title story, two old people, married for 47 years, are constantly fighting, but when the wife begins to die of cancer, their devotion to each other shows that the ways of love are often convoluted.

Oneal, Zibby. *A Formal Feeling*. New York: Viking, 1982. 168pp. LC 82-2018. ISBN 0-670-32488-4. New York: Puffin, pap. ISBN 0-14-034539-6.

The title comes from a poem by Emily Dickinson which begins "After great pain, a formal feeling comes." This young adult novel has as its main character 16-year-old Anne Cameron, home from boarding school for the winter holiday. She cannot adjust, in her mind or emotions, to the trauma of her mother's death the preceding year. Complicating and further delaying that adjustment is her father's remarriage to a woman who is unlike her mother in every way. Dory, her stepmother, is a rather casual housekeeper and an unartistic person. She is, however, warm and patient, and Anne starts to understand the hitherto unrecognized problems in her relationship with her mother. Her grief can finally be expressed when she sees the past more clearly and can accept the present more maturely.

Oneal, Zibby. *The Language of Goldfish*. New York: Viking, 1980. 178pp. LC 79-19167. ISBN 0-670-41785-8. New York: Puffin, pap. ISBN 0-14-034540-X.

In the majority of novels whose protagonist is a young woman, the heroine's most pressing problem is to achieve adulthood. In this unusual story, Carrie Stokes resists the natural progress from childhood to adulthood. She is disturbed by references to sexuality, and she misses the old days in Chicago, when she and her sister Moira were very close and had a secret language that they pretended the fish could understand. Only her classes in mathematics and art give her a feeling of stability, and she has difficulty even with her art mentor, Mrs. Ramsay. Driven by the feeling that she is losing her sanity, she attempts suicide. A wise psychiatrist, a friend, and her artistic talent help Carrie make the necessary adjustment to accept her maturity.

Orczy, Baroness Emmuska. *The Scarlet Pimpernel*. Repr. Laurel, N.Y.: Lightyear, 1976. ISBN 0-89968-072-0. New York: New Amer. Lib., pap. ISBN 0-451-52315-6.+

When Marguerite St. Just, toast of aristocratic Paris, married Sir Percy Blakeney, all of her circle of friends were taken aback. He was an Englishman of good family and great wealth but not, apparently, her equal in wit and vivacity. What was unknown to all was the fact that beneath his foppish facade he was the valiant and daring man who, as the Scarlet Pimpernel, crossed wits and swords with sinister adversaries in order to rescue innocent families from the guillotine.

Orwell, George. *Animal Farm*. New York: Harcourt, 1954. 160pp. LC 54-11330. ISBN 0-15-107252-3. New York: New Amer. Lib., pap. ISBN 0-451-52466-7.+

The animals on Farmer Jones's farm revolt in a move led by the pigs, and drive out the humans. The pigs become the leaders, in spite of the fact that their government was meant to be "classless." The other animals soon find that they are suffering varying degrees of slavery. A totalitarian state slowly evolves in which "all animals are equal but some animals are more equal than others." This is a biting satire aimed at communism.

Orwell, George. *Nineteen Eighty-four*. New York: Harcourt, 1949. 314pp. LC 83-18442. ISBN 0-15-166038-7. New York: New Amer. Lib., pap. ISBN 0-451-26293-3.+

A dictatorship called Big Brother rules the people in a collectivist society where Winston Smith works in the Ministry of Truth. The Thought Police persuade the people that ignorance is strength and war is peace. Winston becomes involved in a forbidden love affair and joins the underground to resist this mind control.

*Ozick, Cynthia. *The Cannibal Galaxy*. New York: Knopf, 1983. 161pp. LC 82-48719. ISBN 0-394-52943-X. (o.p.) New York: New Amer. Lib., pap. ISBN 0-525-48133-8.

Joseph Brill, who prefers to be called Principal Brill, teaches a dual curriculum of European scholarship and Judaic literature in his school. An escapee from the Holocaust which killed most of his family, Brill searches for the bright pupils who will add luster to his mediocre school in Middle America. When Hester Lilt enrolls her daughter Beulah, he has great hopes because of the mother's intellect. He fails to perceive the potential spark of genius in the daughter and is thrown into confusion when Beulah achieves fame in her adult years.

Ozick, Cynthia. *The Shawl*. New York: Knopf, 1989. 70pp. LC 89-2652. ISBN 0-394-57976-3. New York: Random, pap. LC 89-040638. ISBN 0-679-72926-7.

In a very short story entitled "The Shawl" we have a harrowing portrayal of a concentration camp experience. Rosa's baby is hidden in her shawl, which is snatched away by Rosa's niece for warmth. When the baby is discovered it is killed by the Germans. In the longer story that follows, "Rosa," we follow the mother into her life in Miami, Florida, her relationship with her niece and her denial of her daughter Magda's death.

*Paley, Grace. *Enormous Changes at the Last Minute.* New York: Farrar, 1974. 208pp. LC 73-87691. ISBN 0-685-01793-1. New York: Farrar, pap. ISBN 0-374-51524-7.

These 17 short stories capture life in the city among women bringing up their children alone, as well as the relationships between children and, in the bittersweet "Faith in the Afternoon," between a woman and her old parents who live in a home for the aged, the Children of Judea. "Enormous Changes at the Last Minute," the title story, is a snapshot of the sixties and its counter-culture. "The Little Girl" is a shatteringly disturbing story of the sexual assault and death of a runaway, of which there are so many, from a small town. There is a mixture of humor and tragedy in Paley's writing and her perceptions are always sharp. She catches the tempo of city life and the dialogue of minority groups.

*Pamuk, Orhan. *The White Castle.* Trans. from the Turkish by Victoria Holbrook. New York: Braziller, 1991. 162pp. LC 91-202. ISBN 0-8076-1264-2.

A young Italian scholar sailing from Venice in the seventeenth century is captured along with others by the Turks. He becomes a slave in Istanbul, refuses to convert to the Muslim religion but is treated fairly well because he is able to render medical attention to high officials including the young sultan. When he is presented to a Turkish man who wishes to learn all about Italy, and, in fact, everything else that he knows, he is thunderstruck to observe that the Turk is a double of himself. The relationship between the two is like an exchange not only of ideas but the very experiences of their lives and personalities. This novel, for the thoughtful and mature reader, has echoes of Kafka and even, in a description of a plague, Camus.

Paretsky, Sara. *Bitter Medicine.* New York: Morrow, 1987. 320pp. LC 86-33238. ISBN 0-688-06448-5. New York: Ballantine, pap. ISBN 0-345-34722-6.

For those who enjoyed Sue Grafton's female tough private investigator Paretsky gives us V.I. Warshawski, another feisty female "private eye." In this novel she becomes involved in the death of a pregnant young girl, her prematurely delivered baby, and the admitting hospital's role in those deaths. The book also pays attention to the conflict, so prominent today, between the pro-choice and pro-life groups on the abortion issue as well as the different treatment some hospitals give to poor people as compared to the affluent. Warshawski courts danger and accepts a problematic lover who is a doctor in the case, but also accepts help when she needs it from official police sources.

Parks, Gordon. *The Learning Tree*. New York: Fawcett, 1987. pap. ISBN 0-449-23855-5.

At 12 years of age Newt is awakening to the world around him in his small town of Cherokee Flats, Kansas, in the 1920s. There is the impact of a first sexual experience and a first love, and because he is a Negro, special responsibility of behavior when one individual may represent an entire group in the eyes of the community.

Pasternak, Boris. *Doctor Zhivago*. Trans. from the Russian by Max Hayward and Manya Harari. New York: Pantheon, 1957. 559pp. LC 60-11762. 0-394-42223-6. (o.p.) New York: Knopf, 1991. 544pp. ISBN 0-679-40579-6. New York: Ballantine, pap. ISBN 0-345-34100-7.+

This Russian historical novel, filled with rich, descriptive details, focuses on the time period 1903-1943. Pasternak reviews the life of Yurii Zhivago, a gentle poet and physician, who is devoted to both his wife, Tonia, and his lover, Lara. As the main character matures he contemplates more deeply love, religion, and his place in historical events, which include the Russian revolution, the proletarian upheaval, and the advent of the Communist government.

Paterson, Katherine. *Jacob Have I Loved*. New York: Crowell, 1980. 215pp. LC 80-668. ISBN 0-690-04078-4. New York: Avon, pap. ISBN 0-380-56499-8.+

Sara Louise, called Wheeze, felt like the unloved twin in competition with her sister Caroline. On a small Chesapeake Bay island Louise is isolated and denied the opportunity to fulfill her hopes and goals while everyone caters to her twin sister. The return of an old captain after a 50-year absence, and the advent of the war, gives Louise a chance to grow toward maturity and to achieve her wish to work alongside her father.

Paterson, Katherine. *Lyddie*. New York: Dutton, 1991. 240pp. LC 90-42944. ISBN 0-525-67338-5.

Lyddie, 13 years old and living on a poor farm in Vermont, is, at too early an age, responsible for her family's welfare with a father away and a mother emotionally ill. Charlie, her ten-year-old brother, is strong and helpful beyond his years but there are two younger children who also need care. When their mother hires Lyddie and Charlie out to work Lyddie learns compassion for the slaves who run away north. Seeking what she feels will give her more freedom than the slavery of her job in an inn, she winds up in a mill in Lowell, Massachusetts, where the work is truly slavery. The story of those mill girls and the attempt of some of them to change the conditions of their workplace is part of the history of labor in the United States.

Paton, Alan. *Cry, the Beloved Country.* New York: Scribner, 1948. 278pp. Repr. 1961. ISBN 0-684-15559-1. Repr. Mattituck, N.Y.: Amereon, ISBN 0-89190-379-8. New York: Macmillan, pap. ISBN 0-02-053210-5.+

Reverend Kumalo, a black South African preacher, is called to Johannesburg to rescue his sister. There he learns that his son Absalom has been accused of murdering a young white attorney whose interests and sympathies had been with the natives. Despite this, the attorney's father comes to the aid of the minister to help the natives in their struggle to survive a drought.

Peck, Richard. *Are You in the House Alone?* New York: Viking, 1976. 156pp. ISBN 0-670-13241-1. New York: Dell, pap. ISBN 0-440-90227-4.

Gail is frightened by the obscene telephone calls she receives and the notes that are left on her school locker. It is after she has been raped by a classmate while she is babysitting that she begins to understand the real meaning of fear. Although she is a victim, she is doubted by her family, friends, and the police. Most unendurable is the fact that she is forced frequently to cross the path of her attacker, the son of a prominent member of the community.

Peck, Richard. *Father Figure.* New York: Viking, 1978. 192pp. LC 78-7909. ISBN 0-670-30930-3. (o.p.) New York: Dell, pap. ISBN 0-440-20069-5.+

When the mother of 17-year-old Jim Atwater and his younger brother Byron dies, their father shows up unexpectedly at the funeral after an eight-year absence. He takes his two sons from their home in New York to his Florida residence. The friction between the father and older son, the pain and awkwardness of sharing, and the love that gradually emerges are well portrayed by the author.

Peck, Richard. *Princess Ashley*. New York: Delacorte, 1987. ISBN 0-385-29561-8. (o.p.) New York: Dell, pap. ISBN 0-440-20206-X.

Chelsea Olinger begins her sophomore year at Crestwood High School determined to be an observer, but when Ashley rearranges the inner circle to make room for her, all the possibilities of high school open up. Only Pod Johnson, who accompanies Chelsea on a social whirl planned and orchestrated by Ashley, dares to violate Ashley's rules of appropriate behavior. Ashley's carefully constructed scenario moves forward without even adult intervention until it is too late. The rhythms of high school years—big games, parties, and proms—provide the structure for this novel of belonging and an adolescent value system gone awry.

Peck, Robert Newton. *A Day No Pigs Would Die*. New York: Knopf, 1972. 150pp. ISBN 0-394-48235-2. New York: Dell, pap. ISBN 0-440-92083-3.

Rob lives a rigorous life on a Shaker farm in Vermont in the 1920s. Since farm life is earthy, this book is filled with Yankee humor and explicit descriptions of animals mating. A painful incident that involves the slaughter of Rob's beloved pet pig is instrumental in urging him toward adulthood. The death of his father completes the process of his accepting responsibility.

*Percy, Walker. *Love in the Ruins*. New York: Farrar, 1971. 416pp. LC 71-143301. ISBN 0-374-19302-9. New York: Ivy, pap. ISBN 0-8041-0378-X.+

This is an exuberant, sometimes bawdy satire of life in America in a future in which the civilization we know is grinding to a halt. Dr. Tom More, a psychiatrist, has invented a device to cure the depressions, rage, terrors, and anomalies that have polarized and paralyzed America to the point where few cars work, interstate highways are reverting to wilderness, and wolves are seen in downtown Cleveland. There are mad mix-ups and an attempt by an unscrupulous adventurer to get More's machine and use it for an unhealthful end, with disastrous results. In this serio-comic book Percy has turned his irony on such targets as inept politicians, sex clinics, religion, and racial relations.

Perry, Anne. *Bethlehem Road.* New York: Saint Martin's Press, 1990. ISBN 0-312-04266-3. New York: Fawcett, pap. LC 89-78014. ISBN 0-449-21914-3.

Anne Perry places her mysteries in the Victorian era of British history. In London, near the House of Parliament, three members of that body are murdered in fairly quick succession on Westminster Bridge. In each case the victim had his throat cut and was then tied to a lamppost with his own scarf around his throat. Inspector Thomas Pitt unravels the reason for the murders and identifies the killer—with some help from his wife, Charlotte. Added to the suspense of the mystery is Perry's attention to the social and economic conditions of that historic time with special emphasis on the status of women and a growing demand on the part of some of them for a right to vote in order to have control over their lives.

Peters, Elizabeth. *The Murders of Richard III.* New York: Warner, 1986. 240pp. pap. ISBN 0-445-40229-6.

The reader who enjoyed Josephine Tey's *Daughter of Time* will be intrigued by this further investigation of Richard III's guilt or innocence in the case of the murdered princes in the Tower. Thomas Carter and Jacqueline Kirby are invited to a weekend at the home of Richard Weldon to hear about a letter seeming to prove Richard's innocence. All the guests have assumed the roles (and costumes) of characters surrounding the king at that time. Someone begins to attack them, not fatally at first, and the solution is provided by Jacqueline when one such attack proves almost fatal.

Petry, Ann. *Tituba of Salem Village.* New York: Crowell, 1964. 254pp. LC 64-20691. ISBN 0-690-440403-X.

From the beauty of the island of Barbados, Tituba is uprooted to the dreary, gray cold of Boston. As the slave in the household of the minister, Samuel Parris, Tituba cooks, nurses, and attends to his sickly wife, daughter, and niece. When the minister moves to a new post in Salem Village, Tituba becomes the central figure in a witchcraft trial.

*Pirsig, Robert M. *Zen and the Art of Motorcycle Maintenance.* New York: Morrow, 1974. 412pp. LC 73-12275. ISBN 0-688-00230-7. New York: Morrow, pap. ISBN 0-688-05230-4.+

A 46-year-old Minnesotan recounts a cross-country motorcycle trip taken with his 11-year-old son and uses the vehicle as the source of and motif for philosophic speculations. This meditation on the values of a technological society and on Buddhist values is set within a framework of observations, encounters, and memories. It is a demanding book for the reader.

Plath, Sylvia. *The Bell Jar*. New York: Harper, 1971. 296pp. LC 76-149743. ISBN 0-06-013356-2. (o.p.) New York: Bantam, pap. ISBN 0-553-27835-5.+

Esther Greenwood, having spent what should have been a glorious summer as guest editor for a young woman's magazine, came home from New York, had a nervous breakdown, and tried to commit suicide. Through months of therapy, Esther kept her rationality, if not her sanity. In telling the story of Esther, Plath thinly disguised her own experience with attempted suicide and time spent in an institution. Like Esther, she was rehabilitated and finished college. She went to London, married poet Ted Hughes, had three children, and published some poetry and this novel. When she felt the world slipping away from her again, she did commit suicide.

Plimpton, George. *The Curious Case of Sidd Finch*. New York: Macmillan, 1987. 275pp. ISBN 0-02-597650-8. New York: Berkley, pap. ISBN 1-55773-064-4.

This is a baseball novel that includes stories about real players and techniques of the sport. Its fictional hero is Sidd (for Siddhartha) Finch. He has studied to be a Buddhist monk, travelled in the Himalayas—and plays the French horn. If all that is not unusual enough, he can also throw a baseball at 168 miles an hour. The attempt of the Mets to use him on their team, his meeting with the effervescent windsurfer, Debbie Sue, and their friendship with Robert Temple, the author with a writer's block, who narrates the events, combine to make this a funny, partly factual and enjoyable story.

Pohl, Frederik. *Gateway*. New York: Saint Martin's Press, 1977. 313pp. LC 76-10561. ISBN 0-312-31780-8. (o.p.) New York: Ballantine, pap. ISBN 0-345-34690-4.

Told in retrospect from his robopsychiatrist's couch, this is Rob Broadhead's account of his career on Gateway, an asteroid where, eons before, an alien civilization had abandoned its launching station and outer-space vehicles. Human expeditions in these vehicles could be extremely hazardous since only a small amount of information in the ships had been deciphered, but the profits to be gained if a ship discovered a new Heechee treasure could be enormous. Rob Broadhead, along with many of his generation of Earth dwellers, came to seek his fortune and reluctantly found it at the edge of a black hole in space.

Pohl, Frederik, and Kornbluth, C. M. *The Space Merchants.* New York: Walker, 1953. 179pp. (o.p.) New York: Saint Martin's Press, pap. ISBN 0-312-90655-2.+

Control of the Venus economy and market is the sought-after plum of mega-advertising agencies. Mitchell Courtenay must persuade colonists to go there, but he is thwarted by the despised conservationists. Sabotage, warfare, and the degradation of the life of a consumer pervade this attack on modern consumer society.

Porter, Katherine Anne. *Pale Horse, Pale Rider.* New York: Harcourt, 1936. 264pp. LC 67-62420. ISBN 0-15-170755-3.

This is a trio of short novels: "Old Mortality," "Noon Wine," and the title story. In it, Miranda, a young journalist, is caught in a personal dilemma. She must choose between a career and a commitment to Adam, a soldier on leave during World War I. Porter's simple tale becomes more complex as Miranda's anxieties and fears about war, death, and personal loss are revealed. She hovers close to death during the terrible flu epidemic of 1918. Miranda survives and the war ends, but it brings no happiness because the epidemic has claimed Adam as a victim.

Portis, Charles. *True Grit.* New York: Simon & Schuster, 1968. 215pp. ISBN 0-671-76380-6. (o.p.) New York: New Amer. Lib., pap. ISBN 0-451-16022-3.

Mattie Ross, a 14-year-old living in Yell County, Arkansas, is determined to get justice when her father is killed by a hired hand. She is joined in her quest by Rooster Cogburn, a U.S. marshal, and by a Texas Ranger. This strange trio faces a series of perilous encounters requiring true grit to confront them.

Potok, Chaim. *My Name Is Asher Lev*. New York: Knopf, 1972. 369pp. ISBN 0-394-46137-1. New York: Fawcett, pap. ISBN 0-449-20714-5.

Young Asher Lev is an obedient son of strict Jewish parents. When his artistic endeavors are discovered, he is sent to a religious leader for consultation because artists are not viewed favorably by the Hasidim. Asher's struggle for fulfillment and his ultimate rejection by his parents are poignantly drawn.

Potok, Chaim. *The Promise*. New York: Knopf, 1969. 358pp. ISBN 0-394-44163-X. New York: Fawcett, pap. ISBN 0-449-20910-5.

Reuven Malter and Danny Saunders, two Jewish friends living in Brooklyn, choose to alter the destinies chosen for them by their fathers. Reuven, studying to be a rabbi, finds his vocation blocked by a challenge to his scholarship and his father's book. Danny, who is studying clinical psychology, risks his career by a decision, based on intuition, that he feels can save a young boy's sanity.

*Powell, Padgett. *Edisto*. New York: Farrar, 1984. 192pp. LC 83-25334. ISBN 0-374-14651-9. New York: Holt, pap. ISBN 0-8050-1370-9.

The title refers to an area of the South Carolina coast. It is the story of Simons (pronounced Simmons) Manigault as he reaches puberty, losing some ignorance about the facts of life on the way and gaining insight into the relationship between his mother, the Duchess, and his father, called The Progenitor. He learns much also from a man he calls Taurus, whose origins are a bit mysterious. Theenie, the wonderful black woman who works for Simons' mother, thinks that Taurus might be her grandson. It is Taurus, who acts as the boy's guide and is responsible for Simon's first date and first hangover. The literary quality, the wry humor, and the sensitive perceptions in the novel make it a unique title for the mature reader.

Powers, J. F. *Morte d'Urban*. Garden City, N.Y.: Doubleday, 1962. 336pp. (o.p.) New York: Pocket, pap. ISBN 0-671-68391-8.+

Father Urban, member of a Catholic order that is financially impoverished, spends his time in two worlds, the religious and the secular. He must try to gain friends and funds for the Clementine order and yet make decisions that may cost him the friendship of his wealthy benefactors, among them eccentric and willful Billy Cosgrove and Mrs. Thwaites. The wide cast of characters within the church and the world outside makes for both a sad and amusing portrait.

Price, Reynolds. *A Long and Happy Life*. New York: Atheneum, 1962. 208pp. LC 61-12790. ISBN 0-689-11947-X. New York: Atheneum, pap. ISBN 0-689-10224-0.+

Rosacoke, a young woman living in rural North Carolina, loves Wesley, who is more interested in motorcycles and being involved with many women. She dreams of a happy marriage and gives herself to Wesley, who misunderstands the gift. Learning that she is pregnant, Rosa faces a decision about her love.

Price, Reynolds. *The Tongues of Angels*. New York: Atheneum, 1990. 176pp. LC 89-37427. ISBN 0-689-12093-1. New York: Ballantine, pap. ISBN 0-345-37102-X.

Bridge Boatner is still struggling with the memory of his father's death. He accepts a job as a counselor at Juniper, a boys' camp in the Blue Ridge Mountains. The descriptions of the campers and their activities will be recognizable to all who have experienced summer camp. As an artist Bridge is deeply impressed with the natural beauty of the camp's location and he is also impressed by one gifted young boy, Rafe, who is capable of a deep understanding of the Native American lore which Bright Day, a Sioux Indian, teaches the campers. When Bridge learns about Rafe's family history he is uneasy about the boy's well-being and unplanned events lead to a tragic end.

Pullman, Philip. *The Tiger in the Well*. New York: Knopf, 1990. 407pp. LC 90-4159. ISBN 0-679-80124-2. New York: Knopf, pap. ISBN 0-679-82671-8.

Sally Lockhart, intrepid heroine from *The Ruby in the Smoke* and *The Shadow in the North*, is once again drawn into the sinister underworld of Victorian London. Succeeding in creating a satisfying life for herself and her daughter, Harriet, after the death of her lover Frederick Garland, Sally is ill-prepared for the vicious conspiracy that threatens both Harriet's life and her new-found financial security. Following a twisting path that leads her to old enemies, emerging cabals, and the political unease of the nineteenth century, Sally must find her own strengths in order to simply survive.

*Pynchon, Thomas. *The Crying of Lot 49*. New York: HarperCollins, 1966. 192pp. LC 85-45221. ISBN 0-06-091307-X. New York: Viking, pap. ISBN 0-670-74224-4.+

Oedipa Maas becomes a coexecutor of the estate of her former multi-millionaire lover, Pierce Inverarity. She becomes involved in tracking down the significance of a geometric symbol that appears to have some connection with the existence of an ancient, revolutionary mail service. In this search, she meets a strange assortment of characters, loses her husband, her psychiatrist (named Hilarious!), and her lover. The author aims his arrows at many of those phenomena that have turned people into things. Among his targets are rock 'n' roll (a group called "The Paranoids"), right-wing extremists, and a strange group called Inamorati Anonymous. Both the style, which is difficult, and the sexual explicitness make this a book for the reader who would appreciate the work of one of the important writers of this century.

Quindlen, Anna. *Object Lessons*. New York: Random, 1991. 262pp. LC 90-48656. ISBN 0-394-56965-2. New York: Ivy, pap. ISBN 0-8041-0946-X.

Maggie Scanlon, a young girl in an Irish-Italian family, begins to derive lessons in life from her observations of her grandfather's iron rule over the family, including over Tommy, Maggie's father. Maggie also observes change in her Italian mother as she seeks the company of a former friend of hers, an Italian construction worker. Not the least of her object lessons is the changing loyalty of her best friend, Debbie Malone, as that friendship comes up against pressure from other young people in their circle. Maggie is a special adolescent who will long be remembered by the reader.

*Rachlin, Nahid. *Foreigner*. New York: Norton, 1978. 192pp. LC 78-1603. ISBN 0-393-08819-7. (o.p.) New York: Norton, pap. ISBN 0-393-00961-0.

Feri, unhappy in her marriage to an American, returns to Iran from the United States to visit her father. She suffers both a cultural and an emotional shock. The former is due to her inability to accept the place occupied by women in this Middle Eastern society; the latter is caused when she learns that her mother abandoned her as a child, not to follow a religious vocation but to run off with another man. Mother and daughter find each other and gain insight into one another's life. The author vividly portrays family relationships, Moslem constraints on women, and the sounds and sights of this exotic land.

Rand, Ayn. *Atlas Shrugged*. New York: Random, 1957. 1168pp. ISBN 0-394-41576-0. New York: New Amer. Lib., pap. ISBN 0-451-17192-6.

In a technological civilization Rand's characters remain insecure and look to the government for protection. In exchange they sacrifice their creativity and independence. The heroes, a copper tycoon and an inventor, reject this philosophy and fight for the individualist.

Remarque, Erich Maria. *All Quiet on the Western Front*. Boston: Little, 1929. 291pp. ISBN 0-316-73992-8. New York: Fawcett, pap. ISBN 0-449-21394-3.+

Four German youths are pulled abruptly from school to serve at the front as soldiers in World War I. Only Paul survives, and he contemplates the needless violation of the human body by weapons of war. No longer innocent or lighthearted, he is repelled by the slaughter of soldiers and questions the usefulness of war as a means of adjudication. Although the young men in this novel are German, the message is universal in its delineation of the feelings of the common soldier.

Renault, Mary. *The Bull from the Sea*. New York: Random, 1975. pap. ISBN 0-394-71504-7.

A sequel to *The King Must Die*, this mythological novel begins with Theseus, King of Athens, returning in triumph from Crete, where he has killed the Minotaur. On a subsequent adventure he captures and falls in love with the warrior princess, Hippolyta. Although married to Phaedra of Crete, Theseus continues his relationship with Hippolyta and both women bear him sons. Tragedy occurs when Phaedra is attracted to and spurned by Hippolyta's youthful son.

Renault, Mary. *The King Must Die*. New York: Pantheon, 1958. 338pp. LC 58-7202. ISBN 0-394-43195-2. (o.p.) New York: Random, 1975. ISBN 0-394-71504-7. New York: Bantam, pap. ISBN 0-553-26065-0.

Theseus, the hero king of Athens and son of Aegeus, is the central figure and narrator of this tale based on Greek mythology. A handsome and adventuresome youth, he is constantly challenged by both humans and gods. Renault describes his battles with the sons of Pallas, his conquest of the Marathonian bull, and his valiant rescue of seven youths and seven maidens from the Minotaur.

Renault, Mary. *The Last of the Wine.* New York: Pantheon, 1956. 389pp. (o.p.) New York: Random, pap. ISBN 0-394-71653-1.

This is a fictionalized account of Athens during the years of the Peloponnesian War told by Alexias, a young Athenian of good family background. We learn the details of daily life within the Greek city state, including the literary, cultural, recreational, and political texture of the time. One very memorable account is that of a wrestling match at the Isthmian Games.

Rendell, Ruth. *A Sleeping Life.* Garden City, N.Y.: Doubleday, 1978. 180pp. LC 77-27716. ISBN 0-385-13224-7. (o.p.) New York: Bantam, pap. ISBN 0-553-25969-5.

Chief Inspector Wexford is Rendell's special sleuth and a well-read and wittily humorous one is he. When he is called in to investigate the murder of one Rhoda Comfrey he is baffled to be unable to learn anything at all about her private life, friends, or means of supporting herself. His only clue, an expensive leather wallet, leads him up and down blind alleys until a chance remark by his own daughter, whose marriage is in jeopardy, leads him to Webster's International Dictionary and a brilliant deduction about the motive of the murderer.

Rendell, Ruth. *Speaker of Mandarin.* New York: Ballantine, 1984. 224pp. pap. LC 83-47745. ISBN 0-345-30274-5.

Ruth Rendell is a master mystery writer for her ability to keep the elements of her story constantly in motion and to keep her readers mystified until the final explanation. Rendell's detective, Inspector Wexford, finds himself unexpectedly on a trip to China and meets a group of tourists who later surface as figures in the murder of one of that group. When Adela Kingston is found dead, several others who were in China seem involved in some way. Bit by bit Wexford unravels strange, almost supernatural, events, romantic pasts, criss-crossed paths and a final very surprising ending.

Richard, Adrienne. *Pistol*. Boston: Little, 1965. 245pp. LC 69-17753. ISBN 0-316-74324-0.

Fourteen-year-old Billy Catlett takes a job one summer as a horse wrangler and enjoys the Montana plains life. The Depression hits, however, and the ranchers are ruined. Billy's father loses his job and the family has to move to a tar-paper shack in a town called Deal. Billy, wanting to make his own life choices, strikes out on his own.

Richter, Conrad. *The Light in the Forest*. New York: Knopf, 1953. 179pp. ISBN 0-394-43314-9. New York: Bantam, pap. ISBN 0-553-26878-3.+

John Butler is kidnapped at the age of four and raised by Delaware Indians. Eleven years later, under a truce agreement between the Indians and the colonials, he is forcibly returned to his family. Irrevocably divided in his heart, he escapes and goes back to the Indians but is sent away after the failure of an Indian ambush.

Richter, Conrad. *The Rawhide Knot*. New York: Knopf, 1978. 205pp. LC 78-1637. ISBN 0-394-50208-6. (o.p.) Repr. Lincoln, Neb.: Univ. of Nebraska Press, 1985. 207pp. LC 84-20799. ISBN 0-8032-8916-2.

Throughout these stories the rawhide knot, a symbol for frontier marriage, is the unifying theme. In the title story Sayward Hewett Wheeler, now old and dying, reminisces about her girlhood, when she thwarted the scheme of some drunken men to arrange a marriage for the Hermit, a young recluse, and married him herself. In "The Simple Life" two men feud over a slur involving stolen cattle. One of those men is to be Rudith's husband soon, but she must control her fear as the frontier men control their untamed horses. The sounds and silences, the round-ups, the brawls, and all the other facets of outdoor life are evident in these eight stories. There is also a thread that runs through them attesting to the courage of the frontier women who lived and fought at the side of the pioneer men.

Richter, Hans Peter. *Freidrich*. Trans. from the German by Edite Kroll. New York Holt, 1970. 149pp. LC 78-119098. ISBN 0-03-012721-1. New York: Puffin, pap. ISBN 0-14-032205-1.

Born in 1925, Hans and Freidrich become good friends. Freidrich and his family are middle-class Jews; Hans's parents are poor civil servants.

As Hitler rises to power, Freidrich and his family are persecuted and separated while Hans's family becomes more powerful. With the coming of the Nazi hegemony Freidrich is shunned by his friend and dies outside an air raid shelter.

Robinson, Spider. *Callahan's Crosstime Saloon*. New York: Ace, 1970. 170pp. (o.p.) Repr. Short Hills, N.J.: Enslow Pubs., 1978. LC 78-8529. ISBN 0-89490-014-5. (o.p.) New York: Ace, pap. ISBN 0-441-09043-5.+

In this amusing science fiction story Callahan's saloon is a place where individuals can unburden their problems to a sympathetic crowd. The characters in these tales include an alien ready to order the destruction of the earth, a telekinetic being who plays darts, and other aliens and time travelers. Regular customers of the saloon dispense liberal amounts of wit, wisdom, and common sense.

*Robinson, Marilynne. *Housekeeping*. New York: Farrar, 1980. 219pp. LC 80-24061. ISBN 0-374-17313-3. New York: Bantam, pap. ISBN 0-553-34663-6.

Ruth and Lucille are left on their grandmother's doorstep by their mother, Helen, who, abandoned by her husband, proceeds to drive a borrowed car over a cliff to a watery grave. Death by drowning is a recurrent event or possibility in this strange and beautiful book where feelings and sensitivities are more important than action. When the girl's grandmother dies, two incompetent and helpless great-aunts come to care for them but cannot cope. They are replaced by Aunt Sylvie, Helen's sister, whose low-key, dreamy nature leads to such chaotic housekeeping that the town urges the sheriff to make other arrangements. This is a funny-sad and poetic novel.

Rochman, Hazel, ed. *Somehow Tenderness Survives*. New York: Harper, 1988. 160pp. LC 88-916. ISBN 0-06-025022-4. New York: Trophy, pap. ISBN 0-06-447063-6.

Ten stories about the misery and danger endured by blacks and colored (mixed blood) people in South Africa are by authors, many of whom are well-known. Nadine Gordimer's "Country Lovers" tells of an affair between a black girl and a young white boy and "A Chip of Glass Ruby" portrays the courage of an Indian woman who aids the cause of the fight against apartheid. Peter Abrahams' story "Crackling Day" not only is a vivid picture of the brutality and indignity suffered by South African blacks but is an example of a young boy's courage in fighting against his oppressors. Other noted contributors are Doris Lessing and Mark Mathabane.

Roiphe, Anne. *Lovingkindness*. New York: Summit, 1987. 279pp. ISBN 0-671-64079-8. (o.p.) New York: Warner, pap. ISBN 0-446-35274-8.

Annie Johnson, widowed before the birth of her daughter Andrea, is a modern, successful, professional woman. Her relations with Andrea has been marked with alienation on her daughter's part, as she appears to be intent on destroying her life as a drop-out from schools, an abuser of drugs, and a young woman who has already experienced three abortions. Annie Johnson seeks psychiatric help for Andrea with no success. It is not until Andrea, finding herself a visitor in Israel, is taken into a yeshiva community that some change in her behavior comes about. The rigorous, although warm, Jewish orthodox discipline appears to change Andrea into a submissive young woman living a life completely foreign to anything her mother understands. The destruction inherent in some parent-child conflicts is painfully described here.

Rölvaag, O. E. *Giants in the Earth*. New York: Harper, 1927. 465pp. LC 27-12513. ISBN 0-06-013595-6. (o.p.) New York: Harper, pap. ISBN 0-06-083047-6.

In this epic tale of Norwegian settlers in the plains of South Dakota, the difficulties that they endure give the reader insight into those characteristics often thought of as typically American. Per Hansa and his wife, Beret, expect to make a living and a home for themselves by working the land. Per is pleased with his new life, proud of his successes with his farm and of his leadership in the small community of immigrants. Beret hates the hardships of frontier life and longs for the comforts of her life in Norway. Her religion, which is her chief consolation, gradually becomes an obsession and causes the tragedy with which the book ends.

*Roth, Henry. *Call It Sleep*. New York: Cooper Sq., 1934, 1962. 599pp. LC 60-13694. ISBN 0-8154-0198-1. (o.p.) Repr. New York: Farrar, 1991. ISBN 0-374-11819-1. New York: Avon, pap. ISBN 0-380-01002-X.

The years between the sixth and ninth birthdays of a young boy are described in this vivid, sensitive portrayal of a Jewish childhood in the ghettos of Brownsville and the lower East Side in New York. Because David's father is a violent and bitter man, the child always turns to his mother, with whom he is very close. Her love protects him from the terrors of street gangs, poverty, the sexual conflicts between his parents, and his own initiation into sex by a lame girl. A literary technique that distinguishes between the language used by members of this family when they are speaking their native tongue (Yiddish) and when they speak the broken English they have learned as immigrants in the United States is an unusual feature in this remarkable book.

Roth, Philip. *Good-bye, Columbus and Five Short Stories*. New York: Modern Lib. LC 83-42949. ISBN 0-394-60470-9. New York: Bantam, pap. ISBN 0-553-26365-X.

In the featured story Neil Klugman and Brenda Patimkin are involved in a summer love affair that lacks the substance necessary to sustain a lasting relationship. In another story, "The Conversion of the Jews," Ozzie Freedman is a disruptive element in his Hebrew school. Sgt. Nathan Marx finds himself the "defender of the faith" when he becomes the First Sergeant of a training company that includes Grossbart, an exploiter of people and situations. Trouble brews for Epstein when he begins to emulate the romantic behavior of the young people in his house. In "You Can't Tell a Man by the Song He Sings," a young student learns an early lesson about believing everything he is told. In the last story, Eli becomes a fanatic who assumes the guilt for the Jews in his community in his last law case.

Rushdie, Salman. *Haroun and the Sea of Stories*. Granta Books in association with Viking, Penguin, 1990. 216pp. ISBN 0-670-83804-7. (o.p.) New York: Viking, pap. ISBN 0-14-015737-9.

This delightful fantasy is filled with adventures, amusing characters with names like Iff and Butt, and villains to fight against and defeat. Rushdie's puns and rhymes will be enjoyed by young and old—the catchy tunes by the younger readers and the political allegory by the adults. Rashid is a professional story-teller whose son, Haroun, delights in hearing them. When Rashid's source of stories seems to have disappeared Haroun faces many dangerous opponents to help his father regain his Gift of Gab.

Rylant, Cynthia. *A Kindness*. New York: Orchard, 1988 128pp. LC 88-1454. ISBN 0-531-05767-4. New York: Dell, pap. ISBN 0-440-20579-4.

For 15 years Chip has lived alone with his fragile artist mother Anne, protecting her and managing their lives. Their gentle life is shattered when Anne reveals her pregnancy but refuses to name the father or have an abortion. Chip's reaction forces a separation between him and his mother. Even his girlfriend Jeannie leaves him. After Dusky is born, Chip experiences profound love for his tiny sister and is forced to face the possessiveness that could destroy their family. But will he be able to learn that he can't own other people?

Sachs, Marilyn. *Circles*. New York: Dutton, 1991. 144pp. LC 90-37516. ISBN 0-525-44683-4.

Beebe Clarke, whose aspirations as an actress have been dampened by reality, and Mark Driscoll, who is trying to maintain his absorption with astronomy while encountering changes in his life, meet in the back of their high school auditorium when he stops to comfort her crying. What distinguishes this fictional meeting is that it occurs on the last page of this interesting novel, after Marilyn Sachs has told the stories of the last few weeks of their lives in alternating chapters. Readers should have a feeling of tension and finally of relief as the two bright, serious young people almost meet a number of times. Each is coping with a different background in a single parent family, and those pressures as well as the pressures of school and peers, contribute to their dual story.

*Sagan, Francoise. *Bonjour Tristesse*. Repr. New York: French and European Publications, 1961. 180pp. ISBN 0-686-23927-6.

Cecile, a young French woman, is the voice of this first-person narrative. During her 17th summer her widowed father decides to remarry. That summer Cecile has her first sexual experience and then, in an effort to block her father's marriage to Elsa, uses her lover as a foil to pose as Elsa's romantic interest and arouse her father's jealousy. The ruse ends in tragedy and Cecile must accept the responsibility for it, along with the loss of innocence. Sexual relationships are casually acknowledged by the characters but are appropriate to the society being portrayed.

Saint Exupéry, Antoine de. *The Little Prince*. San Diego, Ca.: Harcourt, 1932. 92pp. LC 67-1144. ISBN 0-15-246503-0. San Diego, Ca.: Harcourt, pap. ISBN 0-15-652820-7.

This many-dimensional fable of an airplane pilot who has crashed in the desert is for readers of all ages. The pilot comes upon the little prince soon after the crash. The prince tells of his adventures on different planets and on Earth as he attempts to learn about the universe in order to live peacefully on his own small planet. A spiritual quality enhances the seemingly simple observations of the little prince.

Saint Exupéry, Antoine de. *Night Flight*. New York: Appleton, 1932. 198pp. (o.p.) New York: Harcourt, pap. LC 73-16016. ISBN 0-15-665605-1.

In a story that captures the adventures of early aviation, Rivière, chief of the airport at Buenos Aires, supervises the night flights of airmail in South America. He challenges his crew to meet any and all obstacles. When one of his three mail planes crashes over the Andes, he dispatches the European mail plan on schedule anyway.

Saki (Hector Hugh Munro). *The Best of Saki*. New York: Modern Lib., 1930. 715pp. (o.p.) Repr. Mattituck, N.Y.: Amereon, ISBN 0-89190-115-9. New York: Penguin, pap. ISBN 0-14-004484-1.

Saki's stories are characterized by wit, whimsicality, an acute sense of humor, and an amiable acceptance of some of the flaws of human nature. Some of his best-known stories, such as "The Open Window," and "Sredni Vashtar," delve into the realms of terror and the supernatural, with chilling effect. Saki's typical protagonist is a young person or child who uses his or her imagination and wits as weapons against the oppression of social ritual, obtuseness, or moral insensitivity.

Salinger, J. D. *The Catcher in the Rye*. Boston: Little, 1951. 277pp. ISBN 0-316-76953-3. Boston: Little, pap. ISBN 0-316-76948-7.+

Holden Caulfield, recovering from a breakdown, reminisces about his life at Pencey Prep, from which he departed abruptly before being expelled, and about the three days he spent wandering in New York City. Holden, always polite and deferential in his direct relationships with adults, is actually irreverent and critical as he shares his real feelings about them. His adventures include a stay in a seedy hotel, a serio-comic and brief encounter with a prostitute, and some wild doings in the company of a girlfriend. Despite his zany behavior and ambivalent attitudes, some things remain constant: his feelings about his family, specifically his pride in his brother, D.B.; his love for his sister, Phoebe; and his painfully concealed grief for a younger brother long dead.

Salinger, J. D. *Franny and Zooey.* Boston: Little, 1961. 201pp. ISBN 0-316-76954-1. New York: Bantam, pap. ISBN 0-553-20348-7.

At 20, Franny Glass is experiencing desperate dissatisfaction with her life and seems to be looking for help via a religious awakening. Her brother Zooey tries to help her out of this depression. He recalls the influence on their growth and development of their appearance as young radio performers on a network program called "It's a Wise Child." An older brother, Buddy, is also an important component of the interrelationships in the Glass family.

Samuels, Gertrude. *Run, Shelley, Run.* New York: Harper, 1974. 192pp. LC 73-12310. ISBN 0-690-00295-5. New York: New Amer. Lib., pap. ISBN 0-451-15635-8.

From the time that she was 13 years old, Shelley had been running from juvenile institutions. She alternated between being classified as a PINS (person in need of supervision) and being in the custody of her mother, who could neither handle her nor cared to.

Sandoz, Mari. *Winter Thunder.* Philadelphia: Westminster, 1954. 61pp. ISBN 0-664-30053-7. (o.p.) Repr. Lincoln, Neb.: Univ. of Nebraska Press, 1986. 61pp. LC 85-20977. ISBN 0-8032-4167-4. Lincoln, Neb.:Univ. of Nebraska Press, pap. ISBN 0-8032-9161-2.

A school bus becomes lost in a blizzard in a rural area of Nebraska. The bus driver, a 16-year-old boy, the 23-year-old teacher, and seven young students have to leave the bus. For eight days they are forced to withstand the blizzard in a makeshift shelter, with little food and insufficient clothing.

Saroyan, William. *The Human Comedy.* New York: Harcourt, 1943. 291pp. Rev. ed. LC 43-51036. ISBN 0-15-142301-6. New York: Dell, pap. ISBN 0-440-33933-2.

Homer, the narrator, identifies himself in this novel as a night messenger for the Postal Telegraph office. He creates a view of family life in the

1940s in a small town in California. His mother, Ma Macauley, presides over the family and takes care of four children after her husband dies. Besides Homer, there is Marcus, the oldest, who is in the army; Bess; and Ulysses, the youngest, who describes the world from his perspective as a solemn four-year-old.

Saroyan, William. *My Name Is Aram*. New York: Harcourt, 1940. 220pp. LC 40-34075. ISBN 0-15-163827-6. New York: Dell, pap. ISBN 0-440-36205-9.

These tales are about the multitudinous Garoghlanian clan, Armenian-Americans living in northern California. Aram, the narrator and central figure, tells stories about his uncles, cousins, aunts, and grandparents, and we share the warmth, love, cheerfulness, and charm of this family. Life has a slower pace when there is time to listen to sad Uncle Jorgi play his zither, and Uncle Khasrove can yell at everybody without upsetting anyone. The neighbors can convert Aram first to Roman Catholicism, then Presbyterianism, and finally Mormonism, without changing his basic character at all.

Sarton, May. *As We Are Now*. New York: Norton, 1973. 136pp. LC 73-7555. ISBN 0-393-08372-1. New York: Norton, pap. ISBN 0-393-30049-8.

Here is a devastating picture of the damage visited upon the elderly or very ill left to end their days in loneliness in an institution. Caro Spencer at 76 is taken to a nursing home in a remote country place by her 80-year-old brother who can no longer care for her in his home. He has a younger second wife who will not bear the burden of that care. The author describes in a pitilessly clear way the neglect, the lack of cleanliness, and, above all, the absence of compassion and love that mark many such homes. The aged person in those conditions must fight to retain both mental stability and the courage to survive. At a time when more and more people live to old age, this novel presents a possibility that many face. Even young people in their teens must be aware of the prospect as their grandparents search for ways to live out their lives in dignity and companionship.

Sayers, Dorothy. *The Nine Tailors*. New York: Harcourt, 1934. 331pp. LC 34-6048. ISBN 0-15-165897-8. New York: Harcourt, pap. ISBN 0-15-665899-2.

The author combines descriptions of a noble church in the fenland with a most ingenious detective tale involving the ringing of the church's bells. Lord Peter Wimsey, caught in a snowstorm on New Year's Eve, is the guest of the rector and later finds the solution to a mystery that involves the discovery of a mutilated corpse in another man's grave.

Schaefer, Jack. *Shane*. Boston: Houghton, 1949. 214pp. ISBN 0-395-07090-2. New York: Bantam, pap. ISBN 0-553-27110-5.+

Wyoming in 1889 is the scene of conflict between cattlemen and homesteaders when Shane mysteriously appears. He works hard as a hired hand for the Starrett family, and young Bob Starrett grows to love him, unaware that he is a feared gunfighter escaping his past.

Schaeffer, Susan Fromberg. *Anya*. New York: Avon, 1976. pap. ISBN 0-380-00573-5.+

The world of a Russian-Jewish family living in Poland turns into a nightmare. The bombing of Warsaw and the violence of the Nazis directed against Anya and her family are part of this devastating story of the Holocaust in Poland from the 1930s through World War II. The story continues through the post-war period in the United States.

*Schaeffer, Susan Fromberg. *Falling*. New York: Ivy, pap. ISBN 0-8041-0741-6.

Elizabeth Kamen is the daughter in a Jewish family in which the relationships are failed and frustrating. Intelligent, despairing, and with little self-esteem, she attempts suicide. The alternative to punishment by law is to seek psychiatric help. In the course of the therapy we learn about Elizabeth's childhood, which is often violent, her relationships with her mother, father, and grandmother, her school life, and her great success as a teacher. It is a sad story filled with pain but also with humor. Dr. Greene is one of the more likable psychiatrists in literature.

*Schwarz-Bart, Andre. *The Last of the Just*. New York: Atheneum, 1960. 374pp. pap. LC 60-11947. ISBN 0-689-70365-1.

A painful story of the persecution of the Jews from the pogrom in New York in 1185 to the crematoria of Auschwitz in 1944, this book follows the Levy family through these centuries, with Ernie Levy as the major character. The thread that runs through the narration is the ancient Jewish tradition of the Lamed-Vov, according to which the world reposes upon 36 Just Men, who often are not aware themselves of the position they hold. These men represent the hearts of the world, and all our griefs are poured into them. The final chapters, in which Ernie, of his own will, enters a concentration camp to seek out his beloved Golda, are chilling. They describe the transport of Jews by cattle-car to death in the infamous gas showers. Harrowing as the book is, it is a valuable addition to the titles on the Holocaust, lest we forget how inhumane man can be.

Scoppettone, Sandra. *Happy Endings Are All Alike.* New York: Harper, 1978. LC 78-2976. ISBN 0-06-025239-1. Boston: Alyson, 1991. 202pp. ISBN 1-55583-177-X.

Jaret Tyler and Peggy Danziger are in love with each other and try to understand and handle this lesbian relationship. Mid Summers, a disturbed young boy, "gets even" with Jaret, whom he considers to act superior, by raping her, certain that she will not report the assault because he knows about and threatens to tell of her relationship with Peggy. Jaret does report it, and the consequences for Peggy's family as well as the attitude of the police ring true.

Scoppettone, Sandra. *The Late Great Me.* New York: Bantam, 1984. 256pp. pap. ISBN 0-553-25910-5.+

Coping was not easy for Geri, a junior in high school, who had a "perfect" older brother, a father who rarely talked and a mother whose attitudes were those of the 1950s. After meeting Dave Townsend, Geri began to see life differently. Unfortunately, she did not always see it clearly, because drinking had become an increasingly important part of her life. An alcoholic at 17, her deterioration was swift and led her family to seek help from Alcoholics Anonymous.

*Scott, Paul. *Staying On.* New York: Morrow, 1977. 216pp. LC 77-1491. ISBN 0-688-03205-2. (o.p.) New York: Avon, pap. ISBN 0-380-46045-9.

After India succeeds in obtaining independence from Britain, Tusker and Lucy Smalley, part of the British colonial army, stay on in the country where almost all their married life has been spent. The book describes their relationships with the Indians who, at this point, constitute all of their daily and social contacts. Those who figure prominently in their lives include the Smalleys' landlords—Mr. Bhoolabhoy and his monstrous, bullying, huge wife—and Ibrahim, their loyal, competent, and infinitely patient servant. By means of flashbacks and in communications that Lucy holds with herself or in letters to friends, we learn about her early days in England, her meeting with Tusker, the snobbery of the British colonial system, and the failures of her marriage. There is humor in the informative portrayals of the relationships between the British and the Indians, and the final scene is as simple and moving a description of loss as has ever been written.

Sebestyen, Ouida. *IOUs*. Boston: Little, 1982. 192pp. LC 82-124. ISBN 0-316-77933-4. New York: Dell, pap. ISBN 0-440-93986-0.

Stowe, at 13, is a responsible young man who has a warm and loving relationship with his mother. She has been deserted by her husband and disowned by her father because of her marriage. A relative telephones to report the imminent death of Stowe's grandfather, who has never seen or wanted to see his grandson. The dying man has asked to see Stowe, but not his mother, and the young man is furious. He keeps the message a secret while he tries to reach some independent decision about what he will do. When one of the children for whom Stowe's mother cares as a means of earning money accidentally destroys the $100 Stowe has secretly saved, there is a confrontation between mother and son. The incident becomes a catalyst that evokes serious revelations between them.

Sevela, Ephraim. *Why There Is No Heaven on Earth*. Trans. from the Russian by Richard Lourie. New York: Harper, 1982. 224pp. LC 81-47736. ISBN 0-06-025502-1.

This story of poor Jewish people in Russia before World War II is told by a young narrator living on Invalid Street. His best friend is Berele Mats whose goodness is beyond description and whose early death makes a heaven on earth an impossibility. Berele is so eager to be kind to his friends that he steals money in order to buy them the unusual treat of ice cream. He schemes ways to get them into the circus without tickets since pocket-money is as scarce as everything else in their lives. The narrator poses the question of what the world has lost when such an extraordinary young fellow as Berele is not able to live out a full lifetime. In the tradition of the famous Sholem Aleichem this is a bittersweet, wryly humorous, touching story of people struggling against poverty and tyranny.

Seymour, Gerald. *The Glory Boys.* New York: Fawcett, 1978. pap. ISBN 0-449-23392-8.

Famy, an inexperienced Palestinian terrorist, goes to England to team up with intelligent IRA killer McCoy. Their target is an aging Israeli nuclear physicist who is to deliver a speech in England. Suspense mounts as the British and Israeli secret agencies—and later French security men—try to trace the two terrorists.

Shannon, George. *Unlived Affections.* New York: HarperCollins, 1989. 144pp. LC 88-31470. ISBN 0-06-025304-5.

After the death of the grandmother who had raised him, angry and lonely 18-year-old Willie Ramsey finds a box of correspondence between his father and mother, whom he had never known. His grandmother had hardly revealed anything about his parents except to remark that his (unfit) father was dead, and to share slight stories about his mother's childhood. Through reading the letters, Willie discovers dark family secrets—that his father was gay and that he had never been told about the birth of his son. The startling revelations of the letters prompt Willie to search his feelings and come to terms with his own insecurities and bitterness.

*Shaw, Irwin. *The Young Lions.* New York: Modern Lib., 1948. 689pp. LC 58-6365. ISBN 0-394-60809-7. (o.p.) New York: Dell, pap. ISBN 0-440-39794-4.

World War II changes the lives of Christian, ex-Communist and Nazi; Michael, a Broadway stage manager; and Noah, an American Jew married to a Christian woman. We follow their lives during the years 1938 to 1945 as they experience frustrations, hardships, and the dangers of the war. The three fight, and two are killed.

Shute, Nevil (Nevil Shute Norway). *On the Beach.* New York: Morrow, 1957. 320pp. LC 57-9158. ISBN 0-688-02223-5. New York: Ballantine, pap. ISBN 0-345-31148-5.

A nuclear war annihilates the world's Northern Hermisphere, and as atomic wastes are spreading southward, residents of Australia try to come to grips with their mortality. In spite of the inevitability of death, these people face their end with courage and live from day to day. They even plant trees they may never see mature.

Sillitoe, Alan. *The Loneliness of the Long-Distance Runner*. New York: Knopf, 1960. 176pp. ISBN 0-394-43389-0. New York: New Amer. Lib., pap. ISBN 0-451-16026-6.

This collection of short stories portrays life from the point of view of the English working class. The unnamed narrator in the title story, which is probably the best known in the book, is a roguish young man who has been in trouble with authority all his life. He is told by the head of a Borstal institution where he is an inmate that he can reform himself by training to be a long-distance runner. He enters into training, and during practice runs, his thoughts go back to the circumstances that led to his detention. The climax of the story is in a track meet between his penal institution and a private school. The boy easily outruns his competitors but pulls up at the finish line and refuses to cross it, thus revenging himself against the head of the institution and spoiling the victory of the other school.

Silverberg, Robert. *Letters from Atlantis*. New York: Atheneum, 1990. 144pp. LC 90-562. ISBN 0-689-31570-8. New York: Warner, pap. ISBN 0-446-36286-7.

Roy and Lora, a young idealistic couple from our future, have perfected time travel by crossing centuries and entering the minds of selected individuals. Choosing to explore the legend of Atlantis, Roy ventures almost 2000 years before Christ and lodges in a corner of the royal prince's subconscious. Meanwhile, Lora chooses to live somewhere around modern Poland. When their hosts sleep, the two create in them a dazed state in which each body writes letters to the other, thus allowing Roy and Lora to communicate. What Roy discovers is that Atlantis is not a legend, but a truly advanced society on the brink of catastrophe. What plagues Roy is his responsibility: Should he interfere with the almost sure decline of civilization?

Simak, Clifford. *City*. New York: Macmillan, 1952. 288pp. pap. ISBN 0-02-025391-5.

Starting at a point thousands of years into the future, when people are but a dim legend and the world is populated by an intelligent dog species and timeless robots, 10,000 years of earth's history is traced through one family, the Websters, along with their dogs and robots. From the dissolution of the city because of changing social pressures in the story "City" to people's transcendence into an alien life form on Jupiter in the tale "Desertion," Simak constructs an allegory of human-kind's future that is both enthralling and provocative.

Simak, Clifford. *Way Station*. New York: Woodhill, 1963. 190pp. pap. ISBN 0-532-15305-7. (o.p.) Repr. Cambridge, Mass.: Bentley, 1980. LC 79-20182. ISBN 0-8376-0440-0. New York: Ballantine, pap. ISBN 0-345-33246-6.

Enoch Wallace, keeper of the way station, a transfer point for aliens traveling across the galaxy, is the only earth person aware of the existence of friendly aliens. He lives a hermit's life deep in rural Wisconsin, alone with his thoughts and the many aliens he serves. Others, however, notice an oddity about this lonely man: he never ages. The chance of discovery grows ever greater. In this story Simak examines one of his favorite themes; namely, can mankind reach moral maturity?

Simenon, Georges. *Maigret in Court*. San Diego: Harcourt, 1983. 147pp. LC 83-4341. ISBN 0-15-155561-3. (o.p.) New York: Avon, pap. ISBN 0-380-70411-0.

Simenon, author of innumerable mystery novels, has introduced to the public his dignified and humane detective, Chief Inspector Maigret. In this story Gaston Meurant is accused of having killed his aunt Léontine and a young child for whom she was caring. Maigret, convinced of Meurant's innocence, introduces testimony relating to the infidelity of Gaston's wife, Givette. The suspense and mystery deepen when Gaston is acquitted and begins a search for one of the men linked to Givette. The emphasis is on a study of character rather than the usual violence and gore.

*Simpson, Mona. *Anywhere But Here*. New York: Knopf, 1986. ISBN 0-394-55283-0. New York: Random, pap. LC 87-40088. ISBN 0-679-73738-3.

Many voices including sisters, grandparents, and cousins are heard in this novel depicting a difficult and volatile relationship between a daughter and her mother. Ann's mother Adele never sees life as it really is. She vacillates between showering gifts on Ann from childhood on and neglecting her in more important ways. She borrows money, squanders it and seldom repays what she owes. Shoplifting is a kind of game into which she initiates Ann. Adele's first husband, Ann's father, leaves her as does her second husband. Far-fetched plans of owning a beautiful house are never realized and any home that Ann has known is usually not furnished. Her daughter's beauty is for Adele simply a way to fame and fortune—for both of them. This is a thought-provoking portrayal of the mixed emotions a daughter can have toward a mother to whom she seems to cling for some need, but who is also a person whom she can hate because of the hurt she has suffered at her mother's hands.

Sinclair, Upton. *The Jungle.* Repr. Cutchogue, N.Y.: Buccaneer. ISBN 0-89966-415-6. New York: New Amer. Lib., pap. ISBN 0-451-52210-9.+

Jurgis Rudkus, an immigrant from Lithuania, arrives in Chicago with his father, his fiancée, and her family. He is determined to make a life for his bride in the new country. The deplorable conditions in the stock-yards and the harrowing experiences of impoverished workers are vividly described by the author.

Singer, Isaac Bashevis. *A Crown of Feathers.* New York: Farrar, 1973. 342pp. ISBN 0-374-13217-8. New York: Farrar, pap. ISBN 0-374-51624-3.

Nobel Prize winner Isaac Singer reflects the melancholy, tempered by humor, that is traditional in Yiddish literature. Whether the stories are set in Eastern Europe or America, they attempt to cope with the difficulty of getting at the truth about individuals or events. Often the stories involve the occult or supernatural—telepathy, clairvoyance, demons, premonitions. Even when the characters are eccentric, such as the bearded lady in one of the tales, they also seem to be very human as they try to manage their daily existence.

*Singer, Isaac Bashevis. *The Manor.* New York: Farrar, 1967. 442pp. ISBN 0-374-20225-7. (o.p.) New York: Farrar, pap. ISBN 0-374-52080-1.

The action of this novel occurs in the period between the Polish insurrection of 1863 and the end of the nineteenth century. The manor is the estate of Count Jambloski, appropriated by the Russians and leased to Calman, a religious Jewish grain merchant. The novel relates the financial success story of Calman against a background of family life and changing times that draw his children away from traditional ways.

Sleator, William. *The Boy Who Reversed Himself*. New York: Dutton, 1986. 176pp. LC 86-19700. ISBN 0-525-44276-6. New York: Bantam, pap. ISBN 0-553-28570-X.

When Omar moves next door to Laura, he is immediately recognized by her friends as creepy: short, strangely dressed, secretive about his past. But he leads Laura into 4-space, another dimension beyond our 3-space world. One of the hazards of travelling there is that one may return reversed, a mirror image of oneself. In spite of Omar's stern warnings and threats, Laura takes the boy she wants to impress into that strange, blurry world, where they are imprisoned. William Sleator provides distinctive characters, reassuring humor, and a plot that can prickle a spine.

Sleator, William. *House of Stairs*. New York: Dutton, 1974. 176pp. LC 73-17417. ISBN 0-525-32335-X. New York: Puffin, pap. ISBN 0-14-034580-9.

Five 16-year-old orphans are imprisoned in an artificial environment of stairs and landings. Quickly they realize that they are guinea pigs in a behavioral experiment in which rewards are given for their responses. Unknown to them, they are being prepared for a future society in which they will be robots serving a master class.

*Smiley, Jane. *A Thousand Acres*. New York: Knopf, 1991. 371pp. LC 91-52720. ISBN 0-394-57773-6.

This tragic novel describes step by step the destruction of a family through jealousy, sibling rivalry, adultery and madness. Larry Cook is a stubborn tyrannical and abusive Iowa farmer. A widower, he decides on impulse to give over his farm lands to his three daughters. Ginny, the oldest, and Rose, second in age, are married to two good men who work the farm willingly; but the youngest daughter, Caroline, a lawyer about to be married, rejects the idea. That split begins the unravelling of the dream to add more and more to their land and ends with only Ginny and Rose's two children surviving the almost complete dissolution of this family and the death of the grandiose—and greedy—plan for "a thousand acres."

Smith, Betty. *Joy in the Morning*. New York: Harper, 1963. 308pp. LC 62-14560. ISBN 0-06-013931-5. (o.p.) New York: Harper, pap. ISBN 0-06-080368-1.

When their families find out that Annie McGairy and Carl Brown have married, the two are cut off without a cent. Carl, a law student, takes a full-time job and goes to law school at night. Annie, who had dropped out of school to help her family, longs to be at college. She is given a chance to audit a course in literature because of her abiding interest in it. Her pregnancy, however, increases the pressure on their lives, and only their deep love sees them through their difficulties.

Smith, Betty. *A Tree Grows in Brooklyn*. New York: Harper, 1943. 443pp. LC 47-11189. ISBN 0-06-013935-8. (o.p.) Repr. Cutchogue, N.Y.: Buccaneer, 1981. 321pp. ISBN 0-89966-303-6. New York: Harper, pap. ISBN 0-06-080126-3.+

Life in the Williamsburg section of Brooklyn during the early 1900s is rough, but the childhood and youth of Francie Nolan is far from somber. Nurtured by a loving mother, Francie blossoms and reaches out for happiness despite poverty and the alcoholism of a father whose weakness is somewhat compensated for by his lovable disposition.

Smith, Martin Cruz. *Nightwing*. New York: Jove, pap. ISBN 0-515-6124-7.+

The Hopi Indians are in a vulnerable state, weakened by the Navajos encroaching on their lands and by the petroleum companies ripping apart the sacred mesa for its oil-impregnated shale. Their medicine man paints an intricate, powerful picture with his colored sands and tells the Hopi deputy, Youngman Duran, that his painting will end the world that day. The old man is found dead the next morning, drained of blood, lying in the center of his painting. Each night after his death, vampire bats sweep the mesa and the desert, bringing more death. When Hayden Paine, a scientist, teams up with Duran to find and destroy the hiding place of the bats, they discover that it is a Hopi holy place and cannot be destroyed.

Solzhenitsyn, Alexander. *One Day in the Life of Ivan Denisovich*. New York: Farrar, 1971. 160pp. LC 63-12266. ISBN 0-374-22643-1. New York: Farrar, pap. ISBN 0-374-52195-6.+

Drawing on his own experiences, the author writes of one day, from reveille to lights-out, in the prison existence of Ivan Denisovich Shukhov. Innocent of any crime, he has been convicted of treason and sentenced to ten years in one of Stalin's notorious slave-labor compounds. The protagonist is a simple man trying to survive the brutality of a totalitarian system.

Spark, Muriel. *The Prime of Miss Jean Brodie*. New York: New Amer. Lib., 1984. pap. LC 84-6771. ISBN 0-452-26179-1.

Miss Jean Brodie, teacher at the Marcia Blaine School for Girls in Edinburgh in the 1930s, gathers around herself a group of young girls who are set apart from other students as the Brodie set: Monica Douglas, who will be famous for her mathematical ability; Rose Stanley, who will be famous for her sex appeal; Eunice Gardiner, of great swimming and gymnastic ability; Sandy Stranger, of the small eyes and outstanding vowel sounds; and Mary MacGregor, who is considered a silent lump. Miss Brodie will make these girls the "crème," especially if they will follow her advice to recognize their prime. Her teaching is unorthodox and her relationship with the students most informal, so that they are privy to her affair with the school's music teacher. We get glimpses into the future of these young girls and are made aware that students are capable of treachery as well as teacher-worship.

Speare, Elizabeth George. *The Sign of the Beaver*. Boston: Houghton, 1983. 144pp. LC 83-118. ISBN 0-395-33890-5. New York: Dell, pap. ISBN 0-440-47900-2.

Matt, young in years but older in the responsibility his father places upon him, must remain alone in his cabin while his father goes off to bring back the rest of the family. The story, which takes place in America after the French and Indian War, portrays the difference in values considered important by the Indians and the white settlers. After disasters that might have caused his death, Matt is helped by a young Indian boy whose respect he desperately wants and finally does win.

Spencer, Elizabeth. *The Light of the Piazza*. New York: McGraw, 1960. 110pp. (o.p.) New York: Viking, pap. ISBN 0-14-008712-5.

Clara, a young woman in her twenties, has the mentality of a child as the result of an accident. Her mother is delighted when Fabrizio, a young Italian, begins to court Clara, and she rationalizes that the marriage will be a successful one in spite of Clara's handicap. The union is arranged with Fabrizio's father—at a price.

Stafford, Jean. *The Mountain Lion*. Repr. Austin, Tx.: Univ. of Texas Press. 1992. 240pp. ISBN 0-292-75136-2.+

Molly and Ralph are two younger children in a family headed by their widowed mother. Two older siblings, Leah and Rachel, are elegant and beautiful. Molly's lack of beauty and charm moves her to solitary pursuits and to a sharply developed mind—and tongue. When their mother's stepfather dies suddenly on one of his visits to them, life changes radically for Ralph and Molly. They are sent from their home in California to spend more and more time at a ranch belonging to their uncle. This divided life turns Molly into more of an introvert with even her former attachment to her brother changing to hatred. This introspective novel explodes into a finale that is both shocking and tragic.

Stegner, Wallace. *Crossing to Safety*. New York: Random, 1987. 288pp. LC 87-20482. ISBN 0-394-56200-3. New York: Penguin, ISBN 0-14-013348-8.

The Langs and the Morgans, young couples who meet when their husbands begin teaching at a Wisconsin university, forge bonds of wonderful, lasting friendship. Charity Lang and Sally Morgan are unlike in personality but see each other through devastating crises because of that friendship. Sid Lang is a frustrated poet whose life is over-directed by his wife; Larry Morgan, much less financially secure than Sid, realizes a slow but successful climb to a position of noted writer. This novel has no violence, explicit sex or ugliness. Instead it is a hymn to solid marriages and loyalty in friendship. The dramatic events are those that occur in the lives of ordinary people.

Stegner, Wallace. *The Spectator Bird*. Garden City, N.Y.: Doubleday, 1976. 214pp. LC 75-38171. ISBN 0-385-07890-0. Lincoln, Neb.: Univ. of Nebraska, pap. LC 78-26789. ISBN 0-8032-9107-8.+

The aging process is analyzed by a 70-year-old literary agent relocated in California after his retirement. Humoring his wife, Ruth, by promising her to write his memoirs, he begins a search through his past. Twenty years before, he had traveled through Denmark, his mother's birthplace. Now he rereads a journal written during that journey. He relives the experience with Ruth, and the past brings new resolution into their lives.

Steinbeck, John. *The Grapes of Wrath.* New York: Viking, 1939. 619pp. LC 88-40296. ISBN 0-670-82638-3. New York: Penguin, pap. ISBN 0-14-004239-3.

Tom Joad and his family, "Okie" tenant farmers, are lured to California in the hope of finding work. The grandparents die on the journey and the Joads are harassed by the police and become involved in a violent strike. Tom, pursued by the police for having killed a man during that time, leaves the family to devote himself to improving the life of the poor and the downtrodden.

Steinbeck, John. *Of Mice and Men.* New York: Viking, 1937. 186pp. ISBN 0-670-52071-3. (o.p.) New York: Random, LC 38-6023. ISBN 0-394-60472-5. New York: Bantam, pap. ISBN 0-553-27824-X.+

Two uneducated laborers dream of a time when they can share the ownership of a rabbit farm in California. George is a plotter and a schemer, while Lennie is a mentally deficient hulk of a man who has no concept of his physical strength. As a team they are not particularly successful, but their friendship is enduring.

Steinbeck, John. *The Pearl.* New York: Viking, 1947. 122pp. ISBN 0-670-54575-9. New York: Penguin, pap. (Bound with *The Red Pony.*) ISBN 0-14-004232-6.+

Kino, a poor pearl-fisher, lives a happy albeit spartan life with his wife and their child. When he finds a magnificent pearl, the Pearl of the World, he is besieged by dishonest pearl merchants and envious neighbors. Even a greedy doctor ties his professional treatment of their baby when it is bitten by a scorpion to the possible acquisition of the pearl. After a series of disasters, Kino throws the pearl away since it has brought him only unhappiness.

Steinbeck, John. *The Red Pony*. New York: Viking, 1937. 120pp. ISBN 0-670-59184-X. New York: Penguin, pap. (Bound with *The Pearl*.) ISBN 0-14-004232-6.+

Jody Tiflin, ten years old, begins to grow up in these four vignettes describing his life on a farm in California. He takes responsibility for his red pony and suffers when it dies. An old man arouses Jody's curiosity about what is beyond the mountains, and he anxiously awaits the birth of a colt. His grandfather's tales are a source of interest and wonder for Jody.

Stewart, George. *Earth Abides*. Issaquah, Wash.: Archive Press, 1974. ISBN 0-910720-00-2.

Secluded in an isolated California mountain cabin, Isherwood Williams escapes death from a pestilence that has ravaged the world's population. He is one of a small group of survivors who call themselves The Tribe and work to form some kind of community. As the best-educated member of the group, Ish inherits the responsibility and respect accorded to leaders.

Stewart, Mary. *The Crystal Cave*. New York: Fawcett, 1984. pap. ISBN 0-449-20644-0.

Presumed to be the offspring of the daughter of the King of Wales and the devil himself, Merlin spends a difficult childhood in the court of the king. He learns much that is mystical under the tutelage of a learned wizard and gains a knowledge of several languages. Escaping to "Less Britain," Merlin becomes an important element in the struggle to unite all Britain. The book is rich in descriptions of fifth-century Britain and Brittany, the Druids and their fearful rites, and the superstitions surrounding pagan worship.

Stewart, Mary. *Nine Coaches Waiting*. New York: Fawcett, 1987. pap. ISBN 0-449-21572-5.

Linda Martin had come to the Chateau Valmy in France to be governess to the young Comte Philippe de Valmy. Although the position was pleasant and the student intelligent, Linda soon realizes that there is deadly tension between the nine-year-old Philippe and his Uncle Leon, who runs the estate from his wheelchair. Only Leon's son, Raoul, seems to be able to stand up to him, but Raoul finds the situation at the Chateau so distasteful that he refuses to live there and confines his activities to managing the vineyards of Bellevigne. As the tension increases, Linda finds herself caught in the conflict between the two strong men.

Stewart, Mary. *The Wicked Day*. New York: Morrow, 1983. 453pp. LC 83-12091. ISBN 0-688-02507-2. (o.p.) New York: Fawcett, pap. ISBN 0-449-20519-3.

Using as sources Monmouth's *History of the Kings of Britain* and Malory's *Le Morte D'Arthur*, Stewart has again given the reader a colorful and action-filled story in which King Arthur figures. The focus here is on Mordred, the King's son by his half-sister, Morgause. Mordred has been raised by a poor couple and for the first 12 years of his life is ignorant of his true lineage. When he learns the truth, he is taken into the Court of the King. At Camelot jealousy causes strife among the half-brothers of Mordred and other knights. In a final tragedy jealousy even pits father against son. The customs and pageantry of that period plus the vivid characterizations of those ambitious queens, Morgan and Morgause, make this an exciting story.

Stewart, Michael. *Monkey Shines*. New York: Freundlich, 1983. 256pp. ISBN 0-88191-001-5.

When Allan Mann, great collegiate athlete, becomes a paraplegic after a motorcycle accident, he wishes only to die. In his university's Department of Experimental Medicine, there is an on-going project related to the intelligence of some monkeys. The doctor in charge "lends" one to Allan and the relationship between monkey and man gradually changes from a pleasant, helpful one for Allan to something dangerous and evil. There is much of a scientific nature in the story, but it is the framework of a provocative thriller and leaves the reader pondering the possible application of some of today's scientific experimentation.

Stone, Irving. *Lust for Life*. Garden City, N.Y.: Doubleday, 1957. 399pp. ISBN 0-385-04270-1. New York: New Amer. Lib., pap. LC 83-24666. ISBN 0-451-26249-6.+

Vincent Van Gogh lived a turbulent life but throughout it he was loved and supported by his brother, Theo. Sons of a Dutch Protestant minister,

Vincent and Theo were raised rather strictly, but Vincent's love of color and movement led him into the life of an artist. He always felt challenged to fill a blank canvas with light and color. Vincent's search for meaning and fulfillment in his life took him all over Europe but only toward the end of his life did he meet other artists who shared his artistic views, and it was not until after his death that his work began to be appreciated.

*Styron, William. *Lie Down in Darkness*. New York: Random, 1951. 400pp. ISBN 0-394-50659-6.

In a novel that owes something in its mood to William Faulkner, we follow the degeneration of a Southern family in Port Warwick, Virginia, in the 1940s. The narration revolves around the day on which Milton Loftis is following the hearse that is carrying the body of his daughter, Peyton, to her grave. She was much loved and indulged by her father but bitterly estranged from her mother. Peyton's death, a suicide, echoed the self-destructive way she had lived. Flashbacks in the form of Milton's thoughts describe the weakness in his character that led him to excessive drinking, an adulterous relationship with Dolly Bonner, and to foolish and costly arguments with his neighbors. Also woven into the story are perceptive portrayals of the culture of the blacks in the South at that time and their relationship with the white people among whom they lived and worked.

Sumii, Sué. *The River With No Bridge*. Boston: Tuttle, 1990. 359pp. LC 89-51715. ISBN 0-8048-1590-9.

A river that has no bridge describes the feeling of isolation and exile felt by a class of Japanese people known as "burakumin." This novel, covering the early decades of the twentieth century, portrays a minority called "etas" through the Hatanaka family. Koji, the younger son, questions the divine status of the Emperor and the imperialism of Japan's government. He suffers the contempt of many of his classmates who are of a higher social class and is afraid even to walk through neighborhoods where non-etas live. The family, consisting of his older brother Seitaro, his mother and his grandmother, are hard-working, kind and moral, unlike many of their Japanese oppressors. Their way of life, how they earn a living and their customs are a valuable part of the novel and much in it will remind the reader of the condition of apartheid in South Africa.

Sutcliff, Rosemary. *The Shining Company*. New York: Farrar, 1990. 294pp. LC 89-46142. ISBN 0-374-35807-4.

Approximately 600 years after the death of Christ, Prince Gorthyn arrives in what is now Scotland to hunt and kill the white hart. One of Gorthyn's subjects, a young man named Prosper, tries to save the creature, and when his efforts are brought to Gorthyn's attentions, Prosper is praised, rather than censured, for his bravery. He pledges to support the prince, and two years later when Mynydogg, King of the Gododdin, raises an army to fight the Saxon, Gorthyn calls for Prosper to serve as his shield bearer. Based on "The Gododdin," the earliest known poem from North Britain, Prosper's story covers two thrilling, treacherous, and bloody years fighting the enemies both outside and within the royal camps.

Swarthout, Glendon. *Bless the Beasts and Children*. New York: Simon & Schuster, pap. ISBN 0-671-72644-7.

Six rich teenagers, rejected by their parents and avoided by their peers, group together at Box Canyon Summer Boys' Camp. Fragile egos and self-destructive personalities begin to heal under the leadership of Cotton, who gently pokes fun at their soft spots while building up their self-esteem. An effort on the part of the group to stop the wanton slaughter of buffalo provides a high point of suspense.

Tan, Amy. *The Joy Luck Club*. New York: Putnam, 1989. 288pp. ISBN 0-399-13420-4. New York: Ivy Books, pap. ISBN 0-8041-0630-4.+

Four aging Chinese women who knew life in China before 1949 and now live in San Francisco meet regularly to play mah-jongg and share thoughts about their American-born children. In alternating sections we learn about the cultural differences between the elderly "aunties" and the younger generation. When one of the older women dies, her daughter is pressed to take her place in the Joy Luck Club. Her feeling of being out of place gradually gives way to an understanding of the need to retain cultural continuity and an appreciation for the strength and endurance of the older women.

Tan, Amy. *The Kitchen God's Wife*. New York: Putnam, 1991. 320pp. LC 91-7828. ISBN 0-399-13578-2.

This novel has an underlying theme that portrays the difficulty and pain in mother and daughter relationships. Although the characters are

Chinese—both those born in China and those who are Chinese-Americans—the differences are generational as well as cultural and, therefore, of universal interest. Pearl, the daughter, is married to a non-Chinese man and has a secret kept from her mother: she has multiple sclerosis. Her mother, Winnie, also has a secret—the identity of Pearl's father. The novel is mainly the mother's story of her life in China, her marriage to Wen Fu, a sadistic bully, and her survival during the Sino-Japanese War. Stories of family disagreements and friendships among the women offer some relief from the heavy burdens of Winnie's life.

Taylor, Peter. *Happy Families Are All Alike.* New York: Astor-Honor. 305pp. LC 59-15376. ISBN 0-8392-1045-0.

These ten short stories take place, for the most part, in urban middle-class Southern households during the 1930s. The author analyzes the reasons that families so often are in conflict and depicts what children learn from these experiences. Taylor pays particular attention to the differences between urban and country people. He indicates that several stories are autobiographical.

Taylor, Peter. *Summons to Memphis.* New York: Knopf, 1986. 224pp. LC 86-45417. ISBN 0-394-41062-9. New York: Ballantine, pap. ISBN 0-345-34660-2.

A son, now a grown man, recounts the family's subservience to a strong-willed father. Against a background of Southern manners in Memphis and Nashville, the Carver daughters and sons experience frustration of their hopes to marry and enjoy family lives of their own. The mother, soon after her marriage to George Carver, withdraws from resisting his authority. The daughters never find suitors who suit their father. One brother, escaping to war, is killed and the narrator, Philip, a bachelor still at 49, is summoned home by his sisters to prevent their father, at 81, from remarrying. The seemingly selfless care given by the daughters might stem from self-interest rather than filial devotion.

Tey, Josephine. *Daughter of Time.* Cutchogue, N.Y.: Buccaneer, 1951. ISBN 0-89966-184-X. New York: Macmillan, pap. ISBN 0-02-054550-9.

British police inspector Alan Grant, injured and hospitalized, is bored. He comes across a picture of Richard III, known in literature as the murderer of the princes in the Tower. With the invaluable help of a research student, Grant takes advantage of his convalescence to probe the truth of this crime in the records of Richard's time.

Thane, Elswyth. *Tryst*. Mattituck, N.Y.: Amereon, 1974 (1939). 256pp. LC 74-4544. ISBN 0-88411-956-4.

In a romance that blends the two worlds of spirit and reality, Sabrina finds a strange fascination in the locked room at the top of the house that her father has leased. He is busy with his research into prehistoric Britain, so Sabrina spends more and more time among the books and belongings of the man who had lived in that room at one time. Hilary Shenstone, killed on a mission for his government, returns in spirit to his room and finds a binding link to this young girl who has come to love him. Since their love is not of this world, an inevitable conclusion brings the two together in the only way possible.

Theroux, Paul. *The Mosquito Coast*. Boston: Houghton, 1982. 416pp. LC 81-6787. ISBN 0-395-31837-8. New York: Avon, pap. ISBN 0-380-61945-8.

Allie Fox is a cantankerous and clever inventor. He is also a cynic who believes that everything in the United States is going to wrack and ruin. For that reason he uproots his family from their Massachusetts home to bring them to a primitive island, leaving all their possessions behind. The story of the hardships endured by the family is told by Charlie, the oldest of the four children, whose courage and strength are constantly tested by a father who takes no heed of the suffering he causes his family. That obstinacy finally brings destruction on the father himself as well as others. This is a kind of nightmarish *Swiss Family Robinson*.

Tolkien, J. R. R. *The Hobbit*. Boston: Houghton, 1938. 320pp. ISBN 0-395-07122-4. New York: Ballantine, pap. ISBN 0-345-36858-4.+

This fantasy features the adventures of hobbit Bilbo Baggins, who joins a band of dwarves led by Gandalf the Wizard. Together they seek to recover the stolen treasure that is hidden in Lonely Mountain and guarded by Smaug the Dragon. This book precedes the *Lord of the Rings* trilogy.

*Tolkien, J. R. R. *The Lord of the Rings*. Boston: Houghton, 1954. 1200pp. ISBN 0-395-59511-8. 3 vols. *The Fellowship of the Ring*. 428pp. ISBN 0-395-48931-8. pap. ISBN 0-395-27223-8. *The Two Towers*. 356pp. ISBN 0-395-48933-4. pap. ISBN 0-395-27222-X. *The Return of the King*. 450pp. ISBN 0-395-48930-X. pap. ISBN 0-395-27221-1. Complete with *The Hobbit*. ISBN 0-395-07122-4. pap. ISBN 0-395-28265-9.

Written by a professor of medieval English literature, this is a tale of imaginary gnomelike creatures who battle against evil. Led by Frodo, the hobbits embark on a journey to prevent a magic ring from falling into the grasp of the powers of darkness. The forces of good succeed in their fight against the Dark Lord of evil, and Frodo and Sam bring the Ring to Mount Doom, where it is destroyed.

Toomer, Jean. *Cane*. Magnolia, Mass.: Peter Smith, ISBN 0-8446-6367-0. New York: Liveright, pap. ISBN 0-87140-104-5.+

Weaving short stories that are written in beautiful, lyrical prose, Toomer explores various dimensions of black life in the South. In "Karintha," "Becky," "Fern," and "Esther," the author has created mood pieces that reflect different personalities.

Trevanian. *The Summer of Katya*. New York: Crown, 1983. 242pp. LC 83-1790. ISBN 0-517-54829-1. (o.p.) New York: Ballantine, pap. ISBN 0-345-31486-7.

The time is 1914 and the story takes place in a small French Basque village. Dr. Jean-Marc Montjean, young and newly graduated from medical school, meets and falls in love with Katya, a beautiful young girl. Their encounter comes by way of an accident that befalls Katya's brother Paul, to whom she is very attached. Jean-Marc becomes involved with their family and begins to pay court to Katya. He is warned that any romantic attachment is out of the question because of her delicate health. A mystery in the background of the family hangs over all their relationships, and in a final meeting there is a shocking climax that leaves the reader stunned.

Trevor, William. *Fools of Fortune*. New York: Viking, 1983. LC 83-47867. ISBN 0-670-32355-1. (o.p.) New York: Penguin, pap. ISBN 0-14-006982-8.

Willie Quinton lives with his Protestant family and is shockingly thrown into the violence of the Irish "Troubles" in 1918. With the sudden death of his father and siblings through an act of terrorism, he is brought up by a maid, Josephine, while his mother becomes a hopeless alcoholic and finally a suicide. He meets a cousin, Marianne, with whom he has a brief love affair. When she learns that she is pregnant she tries to find Willie but he has exiled himself because he has committed a crime of vengeance. Although the couple is finally united after long years of separation their happiness is marred.

Truman, Margaret. *Murder at the National Cathedral*. New York: Random, 1990. 304pp. LC 89-43433. ISBN 0-394-57603-9. New York: Fawcett, pap. ISBN 0-449-21939-9.

Mac Smith, Washington lawyer, and Annabel Reid, his attractive and independent lover, are married by their friend, Canon Singletary, and before they can depart for their honeymoon Singletary is found murdered in one of the chapels of the National Cathedral. The Canon's involvement in a peace organization might have some significance, especially when a British priest who is also part of that organization is found murdered in England. Smith assists in the pursuit of the guilty party. A young boy who had witnessed the first crime is an important factor in the solution. Ms. Truman, daughter of a president and wife of a distinguished journalist, is knowledgeable about Washington, D.C. and its government. Her other mysteries have used other Washington locales such as the Smithsonian, Kennedy Center and the White House.

Trumbo, Dalton. *Johnny Got His Gun*. Philadelphia, Pa.: Lippincott, 1939. 309pp. (o.p.) Repr. New York: Carol, 1970. ISBN 0-884-0110-9. New York: Bantam, pap. ISBN 0-553-27432-5.+

Far more than an antiwar polemic, this compassionate description of the effects of war on one soldier is a poignant tribute to the human instinct to survive. Badly mutilated, blind, and deaf, Johnny fights to communicate with an uncomprehending medical world debating his fate.

Tryon, Thomas. *The Other*. New York: Dell, pap. ISBN 0-440-16736-1.

Bizarre events occur in and around the once-prosperous Perry family in Connecticut during the 1930s. The men have all died mysteriously and brutally. Niles and Holland, 12-year-old twins, seem to be linked to the ghastly deaths and disasters. A compassionate Russian grandmother plays along with Niles's deception and tries to protect him.

*Tyler, Anne. *Dinner at the Homesick Restaurant*. New York: Knopf, 1982. 303pp. LC 81-13694. ISBN 0-394-52381-4. New York: Ivy, pap. ISBN 0-8041-0882-X.

Pearl Tull, an angry woman who vacillates between excesses of maternal energy and spurts of terrifying rage, has been deserted by her husband and has brought up her three children alone. Cody, the eldest, is handsome, wild, and in a lifelong battle of jealousy with his young brother, the sweet-tempered and patient Ezra. Their sister Jenny tries, through three marriages, to find a stability which was never present in Pearl's home. Ezra also tries to achieve a permanence through his homey Homesick Restaurant in Baltimore, but he is cruelly tricked by his brother and is unable to establish any unity in the family.

Tyler, Anne. *Saint Maybe*. New York: Knopf, 1991. 337pp. LC 91-52704 ISBN 0-679-40361-2.

The Bedloe family living in Baltimore in the 1960s is an ideal family. That pleasant domestic scene changes when Danny, after a very brief courtship, marries Lucy, a divorcee with two children. Ian, Danny's younger brother, in a careless remark casting suspicion on Lucy's behavior, brings destruction upon Danny and his family. When Ian becomes involved with the Church of the Second Chance, he decides that he must atone for his guilt by accepting responsibility for the children Danny has left behind. The story describes both the trials and satisfactions of Ian's experience as a parent for all the years until the children are adults. The ending brings special happiness to Ian when he himself finds fulfillment in marriage.

Tyler, Anne. *A Slipping-Down Life*. New York: Berkley, 224pp. pap. ISBN 0-425-10362-5.

Evie Decker, unattractive and unpopular, and Drumsticks Casey, an unknown rock musician, are misfits living in a small Southern town. They are drawn together in a union that is more bizarre than romantic. It is a union, however, that seems to fulfill the needs of each and makes for a marriage that is marked by quiet desperation.

*Undset, Sigrid. *Kristin Lavransdatter*. New York: Knopf, 1935. 3 vols. in 1. ISBN 0-394-43262-2. *The Bridal Wreath*. New York: Random, 1987. ISBN 0-394-75299-6. *The Mistress of Husaby*. ISBN 0-394-75293-7. *The Cross*. ISBN 0-394-75291-0.

Although this trilogy was originally published in 1920-1922 and the action takes place in the fourteenth century, the lives of the characters are marked by almost the same problems depicted in modern novels; passion, adultery, premarital pregnancy, ambition, conflict. Kristin, daughter of Lavrans and Ragnfrid, is betrothed to Simon Andressön but falls in love with Erlend Nilulassön and finally wins her father's approval to marry him. Her father realizes on their wedding night that they are already lovers. The book follows Kristin's life as she tries to manage her estate and as her husband loses his lands and leaves her after a bitter quarrel. After several attempts at reconciliation, Erlend returns, only to be killed in a fight. The six sons of Kristin follow different paths. Two die during the Black Plague, which was so dreadful a scourge in that era. The portrayal of this Norwegian woman is vivid and human.

*Updike, John. *The Centaur*. New York: Knopf, 1963. 302pp. LC 63-7873. ISBN 0-394-41881-6.

Utilizing a contemporary setting in Olinger, Pennsylvania, Updike attempts to retell the myth of Chiron, wisest of the centaurs, a creature who gave up his immortality on behalf of Prometheus. In this modern version, Chiron is a high-school science teacher, George Caldwell, and Prometheus is his 15-year-old son, Peter. The story revolves around three critical days in their lives. The book's sexual explicitness makes this a title for the more mature reader.

Updike, John. *Pigeon Feathers, and Other Stories*. New York: Knopf, 1969. 279pp. ISBN 0-394-44056-0. New York: Fawcett, pap. ISBN 0-449-21132-0.

This is a collection of 19 stories, most of which deal with memories and the way they tie our lives together. The young couple in "Walter Briggs" while away time on a long automobile trip by playing a version of "trivia." In "Should the Wizard Hit Mommy?" the same couple is featured as Jack goes through the naptime ritual of making up a story for his four-year-old daughter. In "A&P" the young man behind the cash register watches with fascination the progress of three girls who have come into the store in bathing suits. When the store manager reprimands them for their attire, the clerk quits and then wonders how the world will treat him if he reacts to such a small incident in such an overdramatic way.

Uris, Leon. *Exodus*. Garden City, N.Y.: Doubleday, 1958. 626pp. LC 62-16691. ISBN 0-385-05082-8. New York: Bantam, pap. ISBN 0-553-25847-8.

Following World War II the British forbade immigration of the Jews to Israel. European Jewish underground groups, aided by Palestinian agent Ari Ben Canaan, made every effort to aid these unfortunate victims of Nazi persecution. The novel provides insight into the heritage of the Jews and understanding of the danger involved in helping them reach a safe haven. It also includes the warm love story of Ari and a gentile nurse, Kitty Fremont, who cares very much for the welfare of the Jewish children caught in this nightmare.

Vidal, Gore. *Burr*. New York: Random, 1975. 430pp. LC 73-3985. ISBN 0-394-48024-4. (o.p.) New York: Ballantine, pap. ISBN 0-345-00884-7.+

Aaron Burr was a man both revered and despised in his lifetime, during the early days of America's history. A hero of the Revolution and vice-president under Thomas Jefferson, Burr gained notoriety when he killed Alexander Hamilton in a duel and was tried for treason. In this fictionalized account a young reporter becomes friendly with the elderly Burr, gains access to his memoirs, and augments them.

Voigt, Cynthia. *Dicey's Song*. New York: Atheneum, 1982. 211pp. LC 82-3882. ISBN 0-689-30944-9. New York: Fawcett, pap. ISBN 0-449-70276-6.

Dicey's father, who had never married her mother, had also not bothered to stay around to take care of his family. The children included James, Sammy and Maybeth, in addition to Dicey. When their mother becomes helplessly ill and is hospitalized, Dicey takes charge and, by way of a long journey, gets them to Gram's house. It is no easy addition for Gram, whose money is limited and whose personality does not seem affectionate. Problems exist in Sammy's explosive behavior and Maybeth's learning difficulties but Dicey has things to learn, too—especially how to hold onto the family while, at the same time, letting them go so that they can mature.

Voigt, Cynthia. *Homecoming.* New York: Atheneum, 1981. 320pp. LC 80-36723. ISBN 0-689-30833-7. New York: Fawcett, pap. ISBN 0-449-70254-5.

Four children are abandoned by their mother, who has told them she was taking them to a cousin Eunice in Bridgeport. Dicey, 13 years old, becomes responsible for the other three children: James, a little younger than she; Maybeth, who appears to be retarded; and Sammy, whose independence and stubbornness make him more difficult to manage than most six-year-olds. With no money and no idea of how to find Bridgeport or their cousin, they take off on foot. Their adventures are many, both benign and dangerous, and they meet both those who will help and those who will hurt. After an unhappy stay with Eunice they leave to seek an unknown grandmother in Maryland. The confrontation between her and the children is painful but leads, at last, to some mutual understanding. This is a story of survival and stubborn ingenuity.

Vonnegut, Kurt. *Cat's Cradle.* Repr. New York: Holt, 240pp. LC 63-10930. ISBN 0-8050-1319-9. New York: Dell, pap. ISBN 0-385-28126-9.

In this mordant satire on religion, research, government, and human nature, a free-lance writer becomes the catalyst in a chain of events that unearths the secret of ice-nine. This is an element potentially more lethal than that produced by nuclear fission. The search leads to a mythical island, San Lorenzo, where the writer also discovers the leader of a new religion, Bokonon.

*Vonnegut, Kurt. *Slaughterhouse Five.* Repr. Magnolia, Mass.: Peter Smith, ISBN 0-8446-6366-2. New York: Dell, pap. ISBN 0-440-18029-5.+

Through a series of randomly related events Billy Pilgrim describes his three lives: as an American soldier in World War II who survives the Dresden bombing, as a postwar happily married optometrist, and as a person kidnapped and transplanted to the planet Trafalmador, where he is on exhibit in a zoo. This is a satirical condemnation of war and violence and the people responsible for both. The language is earthy and explicit.

Walker, Alice. *In Love and Trouble*. New York: Harcourt, 1973. 138pp. pap. LC 73-15987. ISBN 0-15-644450-X.

This is a collection of short stories about black women. In one we read of Roselily, a Mississippi woman, who is rethinking her life during a wedding ceremony as she is about to marry a Black Muslim who will take her away to Chicago. In "Her Sweet Jerome" we meet a beauty-shop owner who has married a much younger man and finds she cannot win him away from the books he reads constantly. "We Drink the Wine in France" is a segmented story about the relationship, characterized by distance, between a Jewish professor of French and Harriet, a young black woman in his class.

Walker, Margaret. *Jubilee*. Boston: Houghton, 1966. 416pp. ISBN 0-395-08288-9. (o.p.) New York: Bantam, pap. ISBN 0-553-27383-3.

Vyry was a slave and the daughter of a slave. She suffered slavery's tribulations and looked forward to the time of freedom to bring her a home of her own and provide an education for her children. The Civil War and the Reconstruction period brought the possibility of that day of jubilation, but the attainment of her two desires still seemed remote. The author gives a clear picture of the everyday life of slaves, their modes of behavior, and the patterns and rhythms of their speech.

*Wallant, Edward L. *The Pawnbroker*. San Diego, Ca.: Harcourt, 1961. 279pp. LC 78-7101. (o.p.) Repr. Cutchogue, N.Y.: Buccaneer, 1979. ISBN 0-686-92468-1. San Diego, Ca.: Harcourt, pap. ISBN 0-15-671422-1.+

Sol Nazerman is a survivor of the Holocaust. In the past he had been a university teacher in Poland; now he runs a pawnshop in Harlem in which Murillio, a ruthless racketeer, has a financial interest. Into Nazerman's shop come people who are sad, sick, or criminal. He also meets Marilyn Birchfield, a friendly social worker who tries to get past the frozen outward indifference of the pawnbroker. In flashbacks that describe the horror and torture suffered by Nazerman and his family, the reader begins to understand his withdrawal from humanity. The relationship between him and his young, ambitious, and confused assistant, Jesus Ortiz, provides the novel's shattering climax.

Walsh, Jill Paton. *Goldengrove*. New York: Farrar, 1985. 130pp. LC 72-81484. ISBN 0-374-32696-7. New York: Farrar, pap. ISBN 0-374-42587-6.

Madge looks forward each year to her summer visits to Goldengrove, her grandmother's seaside home. Not only are the gardens and the beach lovely but it brings Madge together with her much loved cousin, Paul, despite her mother's efforts to keep them apart. Then a summer comes when Madge makes the acquaintance of Ralph Ashton, a blind professor, and learns of things that cannot be mended. She also discovers a surprising revelation about Paul. This brief story is beautiful in its mood, its sensitivity, and its love.

Walsh, Jill Paton. *Unleaving.* New York: Farrar, 1976. 160pp. LC 76-8857. ISBN 0-374-38042-2. New York: Farrar, pap. ISBN 0-374-48068-0.

In this sequel to *Goldengrove* the past and the present are interwoven. Madge has inherited her grandmother's house and has leased it to a group of university students for a summer reading seminar in philosophy. Madge stays on at the house and enjoys the company of several students, especially that of Patrick Tregeagle. Patrick's little sister, Molly, is retarded and becomes the focus of the action in the story. The descriptions of the sea are beautiful and the character portrayals memorable. The author lulls the reader with poetic prose and then shocks with the realization that tragedy often lurks beneath a peaceful scene.

Wangerin, Walter J. *The Book of the Dun Cow.* New York: Harper, 1978. 241pp. LC 77-25641. ISBN 0-06-026346-6.

In a story that is partly allegorical, partly lyrical, and partly mystical, animals can talk. Rooster Chaunticleer rules his coop and the animal world uneventfully until Mundo Cani Dog comes crying for acceptance into this community. The animals are keepers of the monstrous evil serpent Wyrm, which strives to break out of the earth that imprisons it. Wyrm makes use of the equally evil Cockatrice—part cock, part snake, whose offspring, brooded by a toad, are basilisks with poisonous bites—to pillage, destroy, and kill the animals in Chaunticleer's domain. Though faith, loyalty, and courage ultimately win out, it is not without painful loss. There is much to ponder in this story of the conflict between good and evil. It also includes a love story between Chaunticleer and his bride.

Warren, Robert Penn. *All the King's Men.* San Diego, Ca.: Harcourt, 1946 (1982). 438pp. LC 46-6144. ISBN 0-15-104772-3.

In the South during the 1920s a young journalist, Jack Burden, becomes involved in the drive for political power by soon-to-be governor Willie

Stark. The journey is a rocky, disillusioning one, and involves exploitation, deceit, and violence. When asked by Stark to uncover a scandal in the past of Judge Irwin, Jack must weigh the many consequences of such action.

Waugh, Evelyn. *The Loved One.* Boston: Little, 1948. 164pp. ISBN 0-316-92618-3. Boston: Little, pap. ISBN 0-316-92608-6.

Depicting romance in a mortuary could be gruesome but the author succeeds both in poking satirical fun at the maudlin pretentiousness of the funeral industry and in delighting the reader with a hilarious love story.

Webb, Mary. *Precious Bane.* Notre Dame, Ind.: Univ. of Notre Dame, 1980, 320pp. LC 80-50272. ISBN 0-268-01541-4. New York: Viking, pap. ISBN 0-14-013217-1.

Superstition was a strong ruling element in the lives of nineteenth-century country people in England. When Prue Sarn was born with a disfiguring harelip, people blamed it on the same force that had struck down her father with lightning earlier. Prue's brother, Gideon, vowed not to be dominated by fate and enticed his sister into helping him in his pursuit of wealth. This narrow focus interfered with love interests, destroyed family ties, and even pushed Gideon to murder.

Wells, Rosemary. *None of the Above.* New York: Dial, 1974. 192pp. LC 74-2879. ISBN 0-8037-6148-1.

Marcia's new stepfamily is ambitious, intelligent, determined, and elitist. Her easygoing nature and simple values are forced to change if she is to create peace at home and happiness in her father's second marriage. Her own identity must submit to the academic pressures with which she is never comfortable. Although unsure of her love for Raymond, she chooses him over college because he values her for her gentle self and does not press her to change. This is a sensitively written novel that explores the themes of sexuality, teenage marriage, abortion, and family relationships.

Welty, Eudora. *Losing Battles.* New York: Random, 1970. 436pp. . ISBN 0-394-43421-8. New York: Random, pap. ISBN 0-394-72668-5.

At a large family gathering in Banner, Mississippi, the Renfro and Beecham families have assembled to celebrate Granny's ninetieth birthday. They are also celebrating Jack Renfro's return from the prison farm. As one might expect, the day is made up of reminiscences and recountings of earlier events, so that the novel actually spans many years. One of the key figures is Gloria, an orphan. She is frequently teased about being the daughter of another orphan, Rachel Sojourner, and of one of the Beecham boys who died in World War I. Gloria, who had married Jack just prior to his imprisonment, feels that they must get away from the clan, all of whom seem proud of their ignorance in spite of Miss Julia Mortimer's lifelong struggle to teach them something. It was a losing battle, probably even for Gloria.

Welty, Eudora. *The Optimist's Daughter*. New York: Random, 1969. 180pp. ISBN 0-394-48017-1. New York: Random, pap. ISBN 0-394-72667-7.

Winner of the Pulitzer prize, this novel is considered the high point of Welty's lengthy career. The strong character study examines 45-year-old Laurel McKelva Hand, who returns from Chicago to Mississippi, where her father is dying. She is forced to consider her complex and ambiguous emotions about her powerful and dynamic father, the impact of this relationship on her life, and her puzzlement at his late marriage to a coarse and shallow woman who is Laurel's own age.

Werfel, Franz. *The Forty Days of Musa Dagh*. Mattituck, N.Y.: Amereon. ISBN 0-88411-719-7. New York: Carroll & Graf, pap. ISBN 0-88184-668-6.

Gabriel Bagradian returns to his ancestral village in Syria, where he learns that the Turks are disarming the Armenians and sending them into exile. Gabriel plans the resistance to the Turks and directs the fortification of the mountain Musa Dagh. The Turks are successfully repulsed a number of times but at great cost in lives to the Armenians on the mountain. On the fortieth day the remnant of the Armenian force is rescued by the French.

West, Jessamyn. *The Friendly Persuasion*. San Diego, Ca.: Harcourt, 1945. 216pp. LC 45-35221. ISBN 0-15-133605-9.

The Birdwell family of Indiana led a quiet life until the Civil War came into their lives. They were Quakers and tried to live according to the teaching of William Penn. Jess Birdwell, a nurseryman, loved a fast horse as well as his trees and the people he knew. Eliza, his wife, was a Quaker minister and a gentle, albeit strict, soul. When the war reached Indiana, Josh, the oldest son, was torn between his Quaker upbringing and his belief in the rightness of the Union cause; Mattie was at that difficult age between childhood and womanhood; and Little Jess, the youngest, ran into trouble with Eliza's geese. This is a wonderful family chronicle, with the laughter, tears, and tenderness that can be found in many families.

West, Jessamyn. *The Massacre at Fall Creek.* New York: Harcourt, 1975. 373pp. LC 74-30377. ISBN 0-15-157820-6. (o.p.) Repr. Magnolia, Mass: Peter Smith, ISBN 0-8446-6274-7. San Diego, Ca.: Harcourt, pap. ISBN 0-15-657681-3.

White settlers on the Indian frontier in 1824 slaughter nine Indians, mostly women and children. They are brought to trial and hanged. Interwoven with this tale is the love story of Hannah Cape, a 17-year-old girl, and Charles Fort, the defense lawyer. The Indians' attitudes and philosophies are sympathetically presented in this story of rendering justice equally for the red man as for the white.

*West, Nathanael. *Miss Lonelyhearts.* (Bound with *The Day of the Locust.*) New York: New Directions, 1962 pap. LC 62-16924. ISBN 0-8112-0215-1.

Miss Lonelyhearts, a male journalist, answers letters and provides advice in a newspaper column. The human pain in and strange quality of the letters become entangled with tragic episodes in the life of the journalist. He can no more find solutions to the problems of others than he can to his own, and he loses his sense of reality in an ambiguous final scene.

Westall, Robert. *The Machine Gunners.* New York: Greenwillow, 1976. 186pp. LC 76-13630. ISBN 0-688-80055-6. New York: David McKay, pap. ISBN 0-679-80130-8.

Garmouth, England, is under constant bombing attack by the Germans in World War II. Charles McGill finds a machine gun in a downed German plane and, with that weapon as protection, he and his friends construct a fortress in preparation for an enemy attack. They capture a

German soldier who becomes their friend. Instead of the expected Nazis, other gangs and their families become the enemy. An attack mistakenly thought to be by Nazis leaves their one ally, the German soldier, dead.

Wharton, Edith. *The Age of Innocence*. New York: Appleton, 1920. 365pp. (o.p.) Repr. New York: Scribner, 1968. LC 68-027785. ISBN 0-684-14659-2. New York: Scribner, pap. ISBN 0-684-71925-8.+

New York City in the 1920s was a place of tight social stratification with rituals for everything from romance to etiquette at the opera. The young attorney Newland Archer was engaged to lovely, socially acceptable May Welland. He faced the power of family and social mores when he became attracted to May's bohemian cousin, Ellen.

Wharton, Edith. *Ethan Frome*. New York: Scribner, 1911. Repr. ISBN 0-684-15326-2. New York: Scribner, pap. ISBN 0-684-71927-4.+

In a quiet New England village Ethan endures life as a farmer and is in constant conflict with his hypochondriacal wife, Zeena. Only when her young cousin Mattie comes to live with them does Ethan's life brighten. Against all wisdom, they fall in love, but the romance sours when a bobsled accident leaves the lovers crippled and forces them to depend all the more on Zeena. This is a grim story of retribution.

Wharton, Edith. *Summer*. New York: Harper, 1917. 291pp. pap. LC 79-5266. ISBN 0-06-080507-2.+

Charity Royall, brought down from the Mountain when she was an infant, is a ward of Lawyer Royall. Lucius Harney becomes Charity's lover and the father of her child, but he clearly is not destined to be her husband. Lawyer Royall, despised by Charity at first, becomes the key to the security of her future, a future that will not include the passionate love she experienced with Harney but will, at least, be completely unlike the lives of the people of the Mountain. Edith Wharton has written with sensitivity of a young girl's sexuality and growth into maturity.

White, Robb. *Deathwatch*. New York: Dell, 1973. 224pp. pap. ISBN 0-440-91740-9.

Hired as a guide for a hunting expedition, Ben refuses to ignore the accidental and fatal shooting for which Mr. Madec is responsible.

Stripped of his clothes and belongings, Ben becomes a target and struggles to survive in the desert. Despite his success in turning the tables on Madec and capturing him, he is jailed by the police because of the plausible story concocted by Madec and his two lawyers. There is a serious question whether Ben will be able to prove his innocence.

White, T. H. *The Once and Future King*. New York: Putnam, 1958. 677pp. (o.p.) New York: Berkley, pap. ISBN 0-425-09116-3.+

White's contemporary retelling of Malory's *Le Morte d'Arthur* is romantic and exciting. From the time of his youth, when he absorbed Merlyn's high ideals through magical lessons, Arthur matured into a king who suffered when his friend, Lancelot, and his wife, Guinevere, abused his principles of justice. This omnibus volume includes the complete story of the Arthurian epic.

Wibberley, Leonard. *The Mouse That Roared*. Boston: Little, 1955. 279pp. ISBN 0-316-93872-6. (o.p.) New York: Bantam, pap. ISBN 0-553-24969-X.

The "Tiny Twenty" overtake the major powers of the world after plotting a bold maneuver to steal the atomic secrets of the United States. Centuries of industrialization and sophistication separate the tiny European nation from the enraged larger countries, who must acquiesce to the will of the former. Underneath this lighthearted tale is a serious warning about the dangers of nuclear power.

Wicker, Tom. *Unto This Hour*. New York: Viking, 1984. 642pp. LC 83-47865. ISBN 0-670-52193-0. (o.p.) New York: Berkley, pap. ISBN 0-425-07583-4.

The literature on the American Civil War is so extensive that one would scarcely expect that more could be said. Wicker, however, has written a long, detailed novel, meticulously researched, which describes the five days in August 1862 when the Second Bull Run (called in the South the Second Manassas) was fought. President Lincoln and Generals Lee, Pope, and Jackson are among the several historical figures that appear. The many fighting men on both sides—the foolhardy, the brave, the patriotic, and the frightened—and the women they love are also portrayed in this thorough account of a military event that is so much a part of our country's history.

*Wideman, John Edgar. *Philadelphia Fire*. New York: Holt, 1990. LC 90-30590. ISBN 0-8050-1266-4. New York: Random, pap. LC 91-50219. ISBN 0-679-73650-6.

On May 13, 1985 a terrible event took place in the city of brotherly love, Philadelphia. A house that a radical group called Move occupied was bombed by the city when they refused to vacate the premises. That caused a fire that destroyed many other homes and killed 11 people, including five children. The narrator in the novel is a man who had left the city, and his family, some years before. The fire draws him back to write about it and, through that event, to recall his early life among other black youth as well as about racism. The style is challenging since it is not straight narrative but a form of stream-of-consciousness writing with complex ideas and strong language. This is a title for the most mature readers.

Wiesel, Elie. *Dawn*. Trans. from the French by Frances Frenaye. New York: Hill & Wang, 1961. 89pp. (o.p.) New York: Bantam, pap. ISBN 0-553-22536-7.

Elisha, a young Jewish terrorist fighting for the creation of Israel in the 1940s, is faced with an agonizing moral dilemma. He is to be the executioner of a British officer in reprisal for the hanging of a captured terrorist. A survivor of the concentration camps and a victim all of his life, Elisha considers whether he is any different from his oppressors if he can execute a helpless prisoner in cold blood.

Wilder, Thornton. *The Bridge of San Luis Rey*. New York: Harper, 1927. 148pp. LC 67-22516. ISBN 0-06-014631-1. (o.p.) Repr. New York: Harper, 1986. 160pp. LC 85-45925. ISBN 0-06-091341-X.

On Friday, July 20, 1714, high in the Andes of Peru, the famous bridge of San Luis Rey collapsed, killing the five people who were crossing it. A priest who was witness to the event decided that the tragedy provided the chance to prove the wisdom of God in that instance, and thereafter spent years investigating the lives of the people who had been killed.

Wilhelm, Kate. *Where Late the Sweet Birds Sang*. New York: Harper, 1976. 251pp. LC 75-6379. ISBN 0-06-014654-0. (o.p.) New York: Collier, pap. ISBN 0-02-026482-8.

Pollution and pestilence are the consequences of a war that destroys most of the earth and its inhabitants. The elder Sumners have created a scientific research center whose goal is to perfect a technique for cloning since, among the other results of the world disaster, men and women have become sterile. The younger Sumners are victimized by these clones, who perpetuate the form of humans but have no humaneness or humanity.

Wilkinson, Brenda. *Ludell*. New York: Harper, 1975. 176pp. LC 75-9390. ISBN 0-06-026492-6. New York: Bantam, pap. ISBN 0-553-26433-8.

For Ludell Wilson, a black girl in the rural town of Waycross, Georgia, life was not easy materially. Because her mother was living up north in New York, Ludell's grandmother took care of her. The warmth of her love made up for the discipline she imposed, which was much too strict, in Ludell's opinion. We follow Ludell for three years, observing her in school and seeing her become interested in a boyfriend and involved with neighboring families and their troubles. The changes in Ludell afford the reader both laughs and sighs.

Wilkinson, Brenda. *Ludell and Willie*. New York: Harper, 1977. 182pp. LC 76-18402. ISBN 0-06-026488-8. New York: Bantam, pap. ISBN 0-553-24995-9.

Ludell and Willie, her sweetheart of several years, are seniors in high school, in the Southern town of Waycross, Georgia. They have declared their love for one another and dream with hope and idealism of a happy future. They have to contend, however, with the over-strictness of Mama, Ludell's grandmother, and with the problem of Ludell's moving to New York.

Winthrop, Elizabeth. *A Little Demonstration of Affection*. New York: Harper, 1975. 160pp. LC 74-20390. ISBN 0-06-026557-4.

John, age 16, Charley, 14, and Jenny, 12, are siblings. In their family the parents are rarely physically demonstrative to each other or their children. During the summer when this story takes place, each adolescent is experiencing the difficulties associated with growing up. Their emotional development provokes a brief erotically charged moment between Charley and Jenny.

Wister, Owen. *The Virginian.* New York: Macmillan, 1902. 434pp. (o.p.)
Repr. Mattituck, N.Y.: Amereon, ISBN 0-89190-537-5. New York: New
Amer. Lib., pap. ISBN 0-451-52325-3.+

This classic of the American West is in the style that made Gary Cooper
the ideal (and idol) he was. Its hero is a graceful, upright, and self-
contained cowboy who made famous those words "When you call me
that, smile." We read about gun fights, confrontations with the Indians,
cow rustling, and a feud between the Virginian and his implacable
enemy Trampas. The novel also includes the obligatory romance between the cowboy and the young schoolteacher Molly Wood. She even
gets him to read and finally marries him after a misunderstanding about
his part in a lynching is cleared up. In spite of its age, *The Virginian*
remains fun to read.

*Woiwode, Larry. *Beyond the Bedroom Wall.* New York: Farrar, 1975.
620pp. LC 75-6922. ISBN 0-374-11237-1. New York: Viking, pap. ISBN
0-14-012186-2.

This family saga describes the lives of the Neumillers in North Dakota
and Illinois. It concentrates on Martin, the father, a devout Catholic and
a man of a great personal integrity, and Alpha, the mother of five
children who, although not born a Catholic, strives to take part in her
husband's commitment. Her life, hemmed in by the provincialism of
small-town mores, is over too soon, and Martin tries to keep his brood
together after her death. As is not uncommon in family stories, there are
painful events, such as the accidental death of a child and a good deal of
moving from place to place, which is necessary in order for Martin to
make a living. Varying interpretations of events are presented through
different characters; Jerome and Charles, two of the sons, give their
versions and Alpha's diary gives us another perspective. This is as
personal a story as one's own life history.

Wolfe, Thomas. *Look Homeward, Angel.* Repr. Cutchogue, N.Y.: Buccaneer, 1981. 359pp. ISBN 0-89966-293-5. New York: Scribner, pap. ISBN
0-684-71941-X.+

The childhood and youth of Eugene Gant, reared in the fictitious town
of Altamont, are described in this autobiographical novel. Eugene
begins to study the various relationships between the members of his
family, meets eccentric townspeople, discovers the world of literature,

goes to college, has his first love affair, and finally embarks on a romantic pilgrimage.

*Woolf, Virginia. *Mrs. Dalloway.* New York: Harcourt, 1925. 296pp. LC 25-9749. ISBN 0-15-162862-9. San Diego, Ca.: Harcourt, pap. ISBN 0-15-662870-8.

In this stream-of-consciousness novel all action takes place on a single day. By probing the thoughts and memories of various characters, the author has encompassed several people's lives. Clarissa has a party planned for the evening and is thinking of her daughter's involvement with a religious fanatic. Also in her thoughts are old friends like Sally Seton, who drops by at the party, and Clarissa's former lover, Peter Walsh, who is drawn to Sally, much to Clarissa's chagrin. When a noted psychiatrist arrives late at the party because one of his patients, Septimus Smith, has committed suicide, Clarissa is affected, not because she knew the victim, but because suicide is tantamount to wastefulness.

Wouk, Herman. *The Caine Mutiny.* New York: Doubleday, 1951. 494pp. LC 51-9977. ISBN 0-385-04053-9. Repr. Annapolis, Md.: Naval Institute Press, 1987. 648pp. ISBN 0-87021-010-6.

The old American mine sweeper *Caine* patrols the Pacific during World War II. The action shifts from the bridge of the ship to the wardroom, and from scenes of petty tyranny on the part of the skipper to incidents of fierce action and heroism on the part of the men. Ensign Willie Keith is assigned to the ship and leads a mutiny against paranoid Captain Queeg, who is eventually brought to trial in a scene that poses the difficulty of weighing evidence to prove that the takeover by the men was justifiable.

Wouk, Herman. *City Boy: The Adventures of Herbie Bookbinder and His Cousin, Cliff.* New York: Simon & Schuster, 1948. 306pp. (o.p.) Repr. Garden City, N.Y.: Doubleday, 1969. LC 69-10961. ISBN 0-385-04072-5.

This somewhat autobiographical story recounts the adventures of an 11-year-old boy from the Bronx named Herbie—small, fat, and likable—as he bounds through New York City public schools and summer camp in the Coolidge era. The author describes Herbie's campaigns against the adults in his life in a style that reviewers have called a mixture of Booth Tarkington and Sinclair Lewis.

Wren, Percival Christopher. *Beau Geste*. Philadelphia, Pa.: Lippincott, 1925. 421pp. (o.p.) Repr. Laurel, N.Y.: Lightyear. ISBN 0-89968-135-2.

A foreign-legion column comes upon a desert fortress manned entirely by dead men. One of the corpses, a sergeant, has apparently been bayoneted by one of his own men. A flashback unravels the mystery of the three English Geste brothers. They confess to a jewel theft and enlist in the French Foreign Legion, which sends them to North Africa, where they encounter the tyrannical sergeant.

*Wright, Richard. *Native Son*. New York: Harper, 1940. 398pp. LC 79-86654. ISBN 0-06-014762-8. New York: Harper, pap. ISBN 0-06-083055-7.

Bigger Thomas is black. He is driven by anger, hate, and frustration, which are born out of the poverty that has dominated his life. When he gets a job with the Daltons, a white family, he is confused by their behavior and misinterprets their patronizing friendship. Tragedy follows when he accidently kills Mary Dalton and escalates when Bigger murders his black girlfriend, Bessie.

Wyndham, John. *The Day of the Triffids*. Garden City, N.Y.: Doubleday, 1951. 222pp. (o.p.) New York: Ballantine, pap. ISBN 0-345-32817-5.

The radiation from a spectacular meteor shower leaves most of the population blinded. The thin veneer of civilization disintegrates rapidly and is replaced by a quasi-feudal and brutal social order. The Triffids, a mobile meat-eating plant, run amok, adding to the danger. Although threatened by the Triffids, the people are their own worst enemy. Wyndham uses the plot to make a social statement about Western society.

Yep, Laurence. *Child of the Owl*. New York: Harper, 1977. 217pp. LC 76-24314. ISBN 0-06-440336-X. New York: Dell, pap. ISBN 0-440-91230-X.

Casey, a 12-year-old Chinese American girl, is more American than Chinese. When her father, a compulsive gambler, is hospitalized after a severe beating, Casey moves in with her grandmother in San Francisco's Chinatown. Although she is a street-smart child, Casey finds that she is an outsider in this community. Her grandmother teaches her something of her heritage and what it means to be "a child of the owl."

Yep, Laurence. *Dragonwings*. New York: Harper, 1975. 248pp. LC 74-2625. ISBN 0-06-026738-0. New York: Harper, pap. ISBN 0-06-440085-9.

In 1903 Moon Shadow, eight years old, leaves China for the "Land of the Golden Mountains," San Francisco, to be with his father, Windrider, a father he has never seen. There, beset by the trials experienced by most foreigners in America, Moonrider shares his father's dream—to fly. This dream enables Windrider to endure the mockery of the other Chinese, the poverty he suffers in this hostile place—the land of the white demons—and his loneliness for his wife and his own country.

*Yourcenar, Marguerite. *A Coin in Nine Hands*. Trans. from the French by Dori Katz. New York: Farrar, 1982. 174pp. LC 82-9324. ISBN 0-374-12522-8. New York: Farrar, pap. ISBN 0-374-51953-6.

Through the lives of a cross-section of Italian society during Mussolini's dictatorship, a plan to assassinate the tyrant is revealed. In the relationships, not all political, of nine people, the reader is exposed to varying philosophies of life in this fascist period. The brutality of those in power and the mounting tension as a woman terrorist sets out on a doomed mission to kill the dictator make this a provocative novel.

Zamyatin, Yevgeny. *We*. New York: Avon, 1983. 256pp. pap. LC 83-90620. ISBN 0-380-63313-2.

The author, exiled from Russia for his anti-Stalinist views, has written a book that predated and influenced Orwell's *1984*. In this grim novel people have numbers, not names. The main character, D-503, is an engineer and quite adjusted to the mathematically ordered life the inhabitants follow. There is a Table of Hours which mandates all activity, from a daily walk (four abreast and at a set tempo) to the time allowed for sexual encounters. When D-503 meets an exciting woman, I-330, he becomes involved in an attempted revolution. In this totalitarian society there is a nucleus of persons who do not fear freedom as a disorderly mode of existence. The punishment for such action is terrible, and D-503 is torn between his adherence to the regulated life he leads and his passion for the woman who leads the revolutionary movement. The book is frightening because its theme is believable.

Zelazny, Roger. *My Name Is Legion*. New York: Ballantine, 1976. 224pp. pap. LC 75-44242. ISBN 0-345-29522-6.

This is a collection of three novellas, including the Hugo- and Nebula-award-winner "Home Is the Hangman." All three stories concern the exploits of the no-name detective, a man who has been erased from the International Data Bank, a man with a thousand disguises and personalities. His futuristic detection would make Sam Spade wince as he clears a school of dolphins of a murder charge and battles a super-robot out to kill its creators.

*Zelazny, Roger. *This Immortal*. New York: Garland, 1966. 174pp. LC 75-443. ISBN 0-8240-1445-6. (o.p.) Riverdale, N.Y.: Baen, pap. ISBN 0-671-69848-6.

A time in the future finds a strange earth threatened with destruction by the Vegans. The plot, however, is secondary to the fantastic gallery of humans and ghouls who prowl the planet. From the perhaps immortal and always enigmatic Conrad, to Hasan the Assassin, to Cort Myshtigo, the Vegan tourist, *This Immortal* has the feel of myth and contains the echoes of dreams and nightmares. Fascinatingly written but quite violent, this Hugo winner presents a different kind of science fiction.

Zindel, Paul. *The Pigman*. New York: Harper, 1968. 192pp. LC 68-10784. ISBN 0-06-026827-1. New York: Bantam, pap. ISBN 0-553-26321-8.

John Conlan and Lorraine Jensen, high school sophomores, are both troubled young people who have problems at home. They become friendly with an elderly widower, Mr. Pignati, who welcomes them into his home and shares with them his simple pleasures, including his collection of ceramic pigs, of which he is proud. When the Pigman, as the young people call him, goes to the hospital after a heart attack, they take advantage of his absence and use his house for a party that becomes destructive. The consequences are tragic and propel the two young friends into more responsible behavior.

Zolotow, Charlotte, ed. *An Overpraised Season: 10 Stories of Youth.* New York: Harper, 1973. 204pp. LC 73-5499. ISBN 0-06-026954-5.

Selected from the works of such writers as Kurt Vonnegut, John Updike, Doris Lessing, and Jessamyn West, these short stories are sensitive portrayals of intergenerational connections and separations. In "The Lie" we see the corrosiveness of too much pressure on a child to succeed in his father's footsteps; in "Father's Day" we watch the sudden and frightening impact on a father whose son has to read aloud in class a description of his father; a John Updike story describes a chance meeting between an old flame and the father of a boy who sees that father in a startlingly different light. The collection might lead readers to the longer works of these authors.

Obituaries: Out-of-Print Titles

Continuing a tradition established in the first edition of *Fiction for Youth*, this section suggests for revival some titles that are now unavailable because they are out of print. In the second edition I pointed out that, out of 17 titles that had been so listed in the first edition, eight had become available—perhaps because of some notice that they were mourned.

Again in this edition nine worthwhile titles, formerly unavailable, are back in print and are included in the main body of the book. Now I am listing the titles below in the hope that their publishers will see fit to bring them back. In the second edition I referred to the fact that a film based on *At Play in the Fields of the Lord* by Peter Matthiessen was being considered. That film has been produced—and so has a new edition of the book. A beautifully presented program based on *Where Pigeons Go to Die* was a recent television production. This may encourage the publisher to re-issue that title.

My gone-but-not-forgotten list for this edition follows:

Bor, Josef. *The Terezin Requiem*. Trans. from the Czech by Edith Pargeter. New York: Knopf, 1963. 112pp. New York: Avon, pap. ISBN 0-380-33449-9.

Raphael Schächter, one among many inmates in Terezin, a concentration camp in Czechoslovakia, is a young and talented conductor. The

Nazis allow him to form an orchestra. Working against the obstacles of death, illness, and the movement of inmates out of the camp to unknown destinations, the constantly changing group rehearses the Verdi *Requiem*. In the final irony, it performs the piece for Adolf Eichmann. The book is a paean to human endurance.

Boulle, Pierre. *The Whale of the Victoria Cross*. New York: Vanguard, 1983. 182pp. LC 83-14641. ISBN 0-8149-0873-X.

A convoy of British ships is on its way to the Falkland Islands to recapture them from Argentina. Lieut. Commander Clark of the destroyer *Daring* receives the message from the Duke of Edinburgh (who is President of the World Life Fund): "Watch out. Whales on the radar are frequently taken for submarines." This poses a serious problem in understanding what the blips on radar really are. A pair of blue whales do appear and one is brutally killed and eaten by killer whales. The crew is unanimous in wanting to save the remaining whale which then becomes their mascot, named by them Auntie Margot, and which begins to show rare intelligence and courage. The reader will learn some fascinating things about marine life through Bjorg, an ex-whaler and member of the crew. There is also great humor in this whale of a story.

Brown, Joe. *Addie Pray*. New York: Simon & Schuster, 1971. 313pp. *Paper Moon*. New York: New Amer. Lib., pap. ISBN 0-451-09940-0.

During the Depression, two Southern con artists, 11-year-old Addie Pray and Long Boy, Addie's putative father, set off to live by their wits and make money by imaginative swindles. With the help of Major Carter Lee, Addie is set up as an heiress to become the "richest little girl in the world." Addie's feeling for life on the run and her relationship with Long Boy eventually win out over the life of luxury. Through the author's vivid dialogue and descriptions Addie becomes a memorable heroine.

Campbell, R. Wright. *Where Pigeons Go to Die*. New York: Rawson, 1978. 156pp. ISBN 0-89256-058-4.

Reminiscing as an adult on a visit home, Hugh Baudoum recalls the events of his tenth year, which was a turning point in his passage from childhood to maturity. Hugh recounts the memories of the day on which he entered his favorite pigeon in a long-distance race from which the bird did not return, and on which his grandfather suffered a stroke.

Greenberg, Joanne. *In This Sign*. New York: Avon, pap. ISBN 0-380-00941-2.

The life of deaf-mutes Abel and Janice Ryder is followed from their marriage to their old age. After they leave the cloistered world of the institution for those with their handicap, they are plunged, unprepared, into the terrifying world of the hearing. They are never fully assimilated into that society. When they have a daughter who can hear, they gain new perspectives, but poverty and personal tragedy—the death of a son—further separate them from others, even from other deaf people. Greenberg's insights into the lives of the deaf are sensitive and painful.

Lee, Mildred. *The People Therein*. Boston: Houghton, 1980. 320pp. LC 80-12968. ISBN 0-395-29434-7. New York: New Amer. Lib., pap. ISBN 0-451-11355-1.

Eighteen-year-old Ailanthus Farr lives in the Great Smoky Mountains. The time is 1910. Although she is handicapped and withdrawn, she refuses to marry Cecil Higgins, whom she does not love. When she meets Drew Thorndike, a naturalist from Boston who is visiting the area, they begin a relationship that is mutually loving. The love affair results in a pregnancy but at a time that Drew has left to care for a dying relative. When he finally returns, his love for Lanthy is affirmed, and the story ends with her words, "It's a glory."

Roberts, Kenneth. *Oliver Wiswell*. Garden City, N.Y.: Doubleday, 1940. 836pp. LC 40-34073. ISBN 0-385-04793-2. New York: Fawcett, pap. ISBN 0-449-24446-6.

Unlike the customary Revolutionary War fiction, this novel presents an alternative point of view, that of the Tories. Because of his Loyalist views, Oliver Wiswell, son of a prominent Milton, Massachusetts, lawyer, is committed to the cause of the English government. He hopes that war will not be necessary to resolve the problems of the American colonies. After the war, Wiswell finds his childhood sweetheart and looks forward to a brighter future in Nova Scotia.

Rogers, Thomas. *At the Shore*. New York: Simon & Schuster, 1980. LC 80-36839. ISBN 0-671-24969-X.

Jerry Engels, coming of age in the 1940s near Lake Michigan, is worried about his future but even more worried about women. His mother, his older sister, and the girl next door are important in his developing romantic ideas. Other girls influence him but it is finally Rosalind whom he truly loves and with whom he wishes to bring that love to fulfillment. The pain and uncertainties related to adolescence and sexuality are written about with understanding and affection. The reader will smile and suffer with Jerry.

Straight, Michael. *A Very Small Remnant*. New York: Knopf, 1963. 232pp. (o.p.) Albuquerque, N.M.: Univ. of New Mexico Press, pap. LC 76-21507. ISBN 0-8263-0433-8.

In 1864 a tribe of Cheyennes surrenders its weapons after a truce negotiated by Major Edward Wynkoup. His superior, Colonel Chivington, leads his troops in a surprise massacre of the Indians at Sandy Creek, Colorado. Feeling that he has betrayed the Indians, Wynkoup resigns his commission and becomes an Indian agent.

Street, James. *Goodbye, My Lady*. New York: Archway, pap. ISBN 0-671-42890-X.

For Claude (Skeeter) Jackson, the primitive and poverty-stricken life he led with his old Uncle Jesse held little that was special. Then a strange sound coming out of the Mississippi swamp heralded the arrival of Lady, a dog that made a great difference in Skeeter's life. Lady's bark was like a laugh; she ran with the speed of the wind and cried rather than whined. When they had to part, Skeet showed the courage and dignity that he had learned from Uncle Jesse.

Title Index

The Abduction. Newth, M.
Absalom, Absalom! Faulkner, W.
Admission to the Feast. Beckman, G.
Advise and Consent. Drury, A.
The African Queen. Forester, C.S.
After the First Death. Cormier, R.
The Age of Innocence. Wharton, E.
Alas, Babylon. Frank, P.
The Aleph and Other Stories. Borges, J.L.
The Alexandria Quartet. Durrell, L.
The Alfred G. Graebner Memorial H.S. Handbook. Conford, E.
All Quiet on the Western Front. Remarque, E.M.
All the King's Men. Warren, R.P.
An American Tragedy. Dreiser, T.
And Then There Were None. Christie, A.
Andersonville. Kantor, A.
The Andromeda Strain. Crichton, M.
Animal Dreams. Kingsolver, B.
Animal Farm. Orwell, G.
Annie John. Kincaid, J.
The Anodyne Necklace. Grimes, M.
Anthills of the Savannah. Achebe, C.
Anya. Schaeffer, S.F.
Anywhere But Here. Simpson, M.
Appointment in Samarra. O'Hara, J.

April Morning. Fast, H.
Are You in the House Alone? Peck, R.
Arizona Kid. Koertge, R.
Arrowsmith. Lewis, S.
As We Are Now. Sarton, M.
The Assistant. Malamud, B.
At Play in the Fields of the Lord. Matthiessen, P.
Atlas Shrugged. Rand, A.
The Autobiography of Miss Jane Pittman. Gaines, E.J.

The Bad Lands. Hall, O.
Bang the Drum Slowly. Harris, M.
Barren Ground. Glasgow, E.
Baumgartner's Bombay. Desai, A.
The Bean Trees. Kingsolver, B.
Beau Geste. Wren, P.C.
Beauty. McKinley, R.
Behind the Attic Wall. Cassedy, S.
Being There. Kosinski, J.
A Bell for Adano. Hersey, J.
The Bell Jar. Plath, S.
Beloved. Morrison, T.
Bendigo Shafter. L'Amour, L.
The Bent Twig. Canfield, D.
Berlin Game. Deighton, L.
The Berlin Stories. Isherwood, C.
Bert Breen's Barn. Edmonds, W.D.
The Best of Saki. Saki (H.H. Monro)
Bethlehem Road. Perry, A.
Beyond the Bedroom Wall. Woiwode, L.
Beyond the Curve. Abe, K.
The Big Sky. Guthrie, A.B.
The Big Time. Leiber, F.
Bitter Medicine. Paretsky, S.
Bless the Beasts and Children. Swarthout, G.
Blood Brother. Arnold, E.
Bobby Rex's Greatest Hit. Gingher, M.
Bonjour Tristesse. Sagan, F.
The Book of Daniel. Doctorow, E.L.
The Book of Fantasy. Borges, J.L.
The Book of the Dun Cow. Wangerin, W.
The Boy Who Reversed Himself. Sleator, W.
The Boys from Brazil. Levin, I.

A Coin in Nine Hands. Yourcenar, M.
Cold Comfort Farm. Gibbons, S.
Cold River. Judson, W.
Cold Sassy Tree. Burns, O.
Collected Stories Vol. 4. Dick, P.
The Collector. Fowles, J.
Comeback. Francis, D.
The Compass Rose. Le Guin, U.K.
The Contender. Lipsyte, R.
Crazy Weather. McNichols, C.
Creek Mary's Blood. Brown, D.
The Crime of My Life. Garfield, B.
Crossing to Safety. Stegner, W.
A Crown of Feathers. Singer, I.B.
The Cruel Sea. Monsarrat, N.
A Cry of Angels. Fields, J.
Cry, the Beloved Country. Paton, A.
The Crying of Lot 49. Pynchon, T.
The Crystal Cave. Stewart, M.
A Cure for Dreams. Gibbons, K.
The Curious Case of Sidd Finch. Plimpton, G.

Darkness at Noon. Koestler, A.
Daughter of Time. Tey, J.
Daughters. Marshall, P.
Dawn. Wiesel, E.
A Day No Pigs Would Die. Peck, R.N.
The Day of the Jackal. Forsyth, F.
The Day of the Triffids. Wyndham, J.
Dear Bill, Remember Me? Mazer, N.F.
A Death in the Family. Agee, J.
Death of a Mystery Writer. Barnard, R.
The Death of the Heart. Bowen, E.
Deathwatch. White, R.
Deliverance. Dickey, J.
Denny's Tapes. Meyer, C.
Dicey's Song. Voigt, C.
Dinner at the Homesick Restaurant. Tyler, a.
The Dispossessed. Le Guin, U.K.
Doctor Zhivago. Pasternak, B.
The Dollmaker. Arnow, H.S.
Dragonsong. McCaffrey, A.
Dragonwings. Yep, L.

The Folded Leaf. Maxwell, W.
Fools of Fortune. Trevor, W.
For Whom the Bell Tolls. Hemingway, E.
Foreigner. Rachlin, N.
A Formal Feeling. Oneal, Z.
The Forsyte Saga. Galsworth, J.
The Forty Days of Musa Dagh. Werfel, F.
The Foundation Trilogy. Asimov, I.
Franny and Zooey. Salinger, J.D.
Freidrich. Richter, H.P.
The French Lieutenant's Woman. Fowles, J.
Friend of My Youth. Munro, A.
The Friendly Persuasion. West, J.
The Friends. Guy, R.

Gabriela, Clove and Cinnamon. Amado, J.
Ganesh. Bosse, M.
The Garden of the Finzi-Continis. Bassani, G.
Gateway. Pohl, F.
A Gathering of Days. Blos, J.W.
A Gathering of Old Men. Gaines, E.J.
Gentlehands. Kerr, M.E.
Gentleman's Agreement. Hobson, L.
The German Lesson. Lenz, S.
Giant. Ferber, E.
Giants in the Earth. Rölvaag, O.E.
The Glory Boys. Seymour, G.
Go Tell It on the Mountain. Baldwin, J.
Going After Cacciato. O'Brien, T.
Goldengrove. Walsh, J.P.
Gone With the Wind. Mitchell, M.
The Good Earth. Buck, P.
The Good Soldier: Schweik. Haek, J.
Good-bye, Columbus. Roth, P.
Good-bye, Mr. Chips. Hilton, J.
Gorilla, My Love. Bambara, T.C.
The Grapes of Wrath. Steinbeck, J.
The Grass Harp. Capote, T.
The Great Gatsby. Fitzgerald, F.S.
The Great Train Robbery. Crichton, M.
Green Mansions. Hudson, W.H.
The Green Years. Cronin, A.J.
Grendel. Gardner, J.C.

Intrigue. Ambler, E.
Intruder in the Dust. Faulkner, W.
The Invisible Man. Ellison, R.
The Ipcress File. Deighton, L.
Is That You, Miss Blue? Kerr, M.E.
Island of the Blue Dolphins. O'Dell, S.
It Can't Happen Here. Lewis, S.

Jack Gance. Just, W.
Jack the Bear. McCall, D.
Jacob Have I Loved. Paterson, K.
Jazz Country. Hentoff, N.
Johnny Got His Gun. Trumbo, D.
Johnny Tremain. Forbes, E.
Joy in the Morning. Smith, B.
The Joy Luck Club. Tan, A.
Jubilee. Walker, M.
Julie of the Wolves. George, J.C.
July's People. Gordimer, N.
The Jungle. Sinclair, U.
Jurassic Park. Crichton, M.
The Just and the Unjust. Cozzens, J.G.

The Keepers of the House. Grau, S.A.
A Kindness. Rylant, C.
The King Must Die. Renault, M.
Kiss, Kiss. Dahl, R.
The Kitchen God's Wife. Tan, A.
Kristin Lavransdatter. Undset, S.

The Language of Goldfish. Oneal, Z.
The Last Angry Man. Green, G.
The Last Hurrah. O'Connor, E.
The Last of the Just. Schwarz-Bart, A.
The Last of the Wine. Renault, M.
The Last Unicorn. Beagle, P.
The Late George Apley. Marquand, J.F.
The Late Great Me. Scoppettone, S.
Laughing Boy. LaFarge, O.
The Learning Tree. Parks, G.
The Left Hand of Darkness. Le Guin, U.K.
The Leopard. Lampedusa, G.
Letters from Atlantis. Silverberg, R.

Mama's Bank Account. Forbes, K.
The Man in the High Castle. Dick, P.K.
The Man Without a Face. Holland, I.
Manchurian Candidate. Condon, R.
Manhattan Transfer. Dos Passos, J.
The Manor. Singer, I.B.
Man's Fate. Malraux, A.
Marathon Man. Goldman, W.
The Martian Chronicles. Bradbury, R.
The Massacre at Fall Creek. West, J.
The Member of the Wedding. McCullers, C.
Metamorphosis. Kafka, F.
Middle Passage. Johnson, C.
Miss Lonelyhearts. West, N.
Mr. Bedford and the Muses. Godwin, G.
Mister Johnson. Cary, J.
Mister Roberts. Heggen, T.
Mr. Sammler's Planet. Bellow, S.
Mrs. Bridge. Connell, E.S.
Mrs. Dalloway. Woolf, V.
Mrs. Mike. Freedman, R.
Mrs. Pollifax on the China Station. Gilman, D.
Monkey Shines. Stewart, M.
Monkeys. Minot, S.
Monsignor Quixote. Greene, G.
A Month in the Country. Carr, J.L.
The Moon and Sixpence. Maugham, W.S.
Morte d'Urban. Powers, J.F.
The Mosquito Coast. Theroux, P.
A Mother and Two Daughters. Godwin, G.
Mountain Lion. Stafford, J.
The Mouse That Roared. Wibberley, L.
The Moving Toyshop. Crispin, E.
Murder at the National Cathedral. Truman, M.
Murder on the Orient Express. Christie, A.
The Murders of Richard III. Peters, E.
Mutiny on the Bounty. Nordhoff, C.
My Antonia. Cather, W.
My Brilliant Career. Franklin, M.
My Brother Sam Is Dead. Collier, J.L.
My Name Is Aram. Saroyan, W.
My Name Is Asher Lev. Potok, C.
My Name Is Legion. Zelazny, R.

The Peacock Spring. Godden, R.
The Pearl. Steinbeck, J.
The People: No Different Flesh. Henderson, Z.
Permanent Connections. Bridgers, S.E.
Philadelphia Fire. Wideman, J.E.
Pictures From an Institution. Jarrell, R.
Pigeon Feathers and Other Stories. Updike, J.
The Pigman. Zindel, P.
Pistol. Richard, A.
The Plague. Camus, A.
Planet of the Apes. Boulle, P.
Portrait of Jennie. Nathan, R.
Portrait of the Artist as a Young Man. Joyce, J.
The Postman Always Rings Twice. Cain, J.M.
The Power and the Glory. Greene, G.
Praisesong for the Widow. Marshall, P.
Precious Bane. Webb, M.
The Prime of Miss Jean Brodie. Spark, M.
Princess Ashley. Peck, R.
The Princess Bride. Goldman, W.
The Promise. Potok, C.

The Queen of October. Mickle, S.F.
The Question of Max. Cross, A.

Ragtime. Doctorow, E.L.
Ratha's Creature. Bell, C.
The Rawhide Knot. Richter, C.
Rebecca. Du Maurier, D.
The Red Pony. Steinbeck, J.
Red Sky at Morning. Bradford, R.
The Refugee Summer. Fenton, E.
Remains of the Day. Ishiguro, K.
Rendezvous with Rama. Clarke, A.C.
Return. Levitin, S.
Ringworld. Niven, L.
A River Runs Through It. MacLean, N.
The River With No Bridge. Sumii, S.
Rogue Male. Household, G.
Rosemary's Baby. Levin, I.
The Rough Road. MacPherson, M.
Rumors of Peace. Leffland, E.
Rumpole for the Defense. Mortimer, J.

Run, Shelley, Run. Samuels, G.
Run Silent, Run Deep. Beach, E. L.

SS-GB. Deighton, L.
Saint Maybe. Tyler, A.
The Salzburg Connection. MacInnes, H.
The Scarlet Pimpernel. Orczy, E.
Schindler's List. Keneally, T.
Season of Yellow Leaf. Jones, D.C.
Seaward. Cooper, S.
Secret Pilgrim. Le Carré, J.
Selected Stories. Gordimer, N.
The Sentinel. Clarke, A.C.
A Separate Peace. Knowles, J.
Seven Days in May. Knebel, F.
Seven Gothic Tales. Dinesen, I.
Shane. Schaefer, J.
The Shawl. Ozick, C.
The Sheltered Life. Glasgow, E.
The Shepherd. Forsyth, F.
The Shining Company. Sutcliff, R.
The Shooting Party. Colegate, I.
Siddhartha. Hesse, H.
The Sign of the Beaver. Speare, E.G.
The Silver Kiss. Klause, A.C.
Sister Carrie. Dreiser, T.
Slake's Limbo. Holman, F.
Slaughterhouse Five. Vonnegut, K.
The Slave Dancer. Fox, P.
The Slave Girl. Emecheta, B.
A Sleeping Life. Rendell, R.
A Slipping-Down Life. Tyler, A.
Snow Bound. Maxer, H.
The Snow Goose. Gallico, P.
So Long, See You Tomorrow. Maxwell, W.
The Solid Gold Kid. Mazer, N.F.
Somehow Tenderness Survives. Rochman, H.
Something Out There. Gordimer, N.
Something Wicked This Way Comes. Bradbury, R.
The Son of Someone Famous. Kerr, M.E.
Song of Solomon. Morrison, T.
Sons and Lovers. Lawrence, D.H.
The Sound of Waves. Mishima, Y.

Sounder. Armstrong, W.H.
The Space Merchants. Pohl, F.
Spartina. Casey, J.
Speaker of Mandarin. Rendell, R.
The Spectator Bird. Stegner, W.
Spring Snow. Mishisma, Y.
The Spy Who Came in from the Cold. Le Carré, J.
The Spyglass Tree. Murray, A.
Stand on Zanzibar. Brunner, J.
Staying On. Scott, P.
Steppenwolf. Hesse, H.
Stones for Ibarra. Doerr, H.
Stotan! Crutcher, C.
The Strange Affair of Adelaide Harris. Garfield, L.
The Stranger. Camus, A.
Summer. Wharton, E.
The Summer of Katya. Trevanian.
Summer of My German Soldier. Greene, B.
Summons to Memphis. Taylor, P.
The Sweet Hereafter. Banks, R.
Sweet Whispers, Brother Rush. Hamilton, V.
The Sword of Shannara. Brooks, T.

Talking God. Hillerman, T.
Teacup Full of Roses. Mathis, S.B.
Tell Me a Riddle. Olsen, T.
Tell Me That You Love Me, Junie Moon. Kellogg, M.
The Terminal Man. Crichton, M.
Testing the Current. McPherson, W.
Them. Oates, J.C.
The Thin Man. Hammett, D.
Things Fall Apart. Achebe, C.
The Things They Carried. O'Brien, T.
The Thirty-Nine Steps. Buchan, J.
This Immortal. Zelazny, R.
A Thousand Acres. Smiley, J.
Thousand Cranes. Kawabata, Y.
The Throwing Season. French, M.
Tiger in the Well. Pullman, P.
Tim. McCullough, C.
Time and Again. Finney, J.
The Tin Drum. Grass, G.
Tirra Lirra by the River. Anderson, J.

Where Late the Sweet Birds Sang. Wilhelm, K.
Where the Lilies Bloom. Cleaver, V.
Whip Hand. Francis, D.
The White Castle. Pamuk, O.
White Peak Farm. Doherty, B.
Whitewater. Horgan, P.
Why There Is No Heaven on Earth. Sevela, E.
The Wicked Day. Stewart, M.
Widows. Dorfman, A.
Wild in the World. Donovan, J.
Wind From an Enemy Sky. McNickle, D.
Winesburg, Ohio. Anderson, S.
Winter Thunder. Sandoz, M.
Winterkill. Lesley, C.
The Wizard of Earthsea Trilogy. Le Guin, U.K.
The Woman in the Dunes. Abé, K.
A Woman of Independent Means. Hailey, E.F.
The Women of Brewster Place. Naylor, G.
World's End. Boyle, T.C.
A Wreath for Udomo. Abrahams, P.

Yellow Raft in Blue Water. Dorris, M.
The Young Lions. Shaw, I.
Young Man with a Horn. Baker, D.

Z for Zachariah. O'Brien, R.C.
Zen and the Art of Motorcycle Maintenance. Pirsig, R.M.
Zorba the Greek. Kazantzakis, N.

Subject Index

ABORTION
Anderson, J. *Tirra Lirra by the River*
Marshall, P. *Daughters*
Paretsky, S. *Bitter Medicine*
Wells, R. *None of the Above*

ACCIDENTS
Agee, J. *A Death in the Family*
Banks, R. *The Sweet Hereafter*
Cain, J. *The Postman Always Rings Twice*
Horgan, P. *Whitewater*
Stafford, J. *The Mountain Lion*

ADOLESCENCE AND YOUTH
Atwood, M. *Cat's Eye*
Baldwin, J. *Go Tell It on the Mountain*
Bradford, R. *Red Sky at Morning*
Bridgers, S.E. *Home Before Dark*
Cole, B., *Celine*
Degens, T. *Transport 7-41-R*
Donovan, J. *I'll Get There. It Better Be Worth the Trip*
Fast, H. *April Morning*
Fenton, E. *The Refugee Summer*
George, J.C. *Julie of the Wolves*
Horgan, P. *Whitewater*

Joyce, J. *A Portrait of the Artist as a Young Man*
Kadohata, C. *The Floating World*
Kerr, M.E. *The Son of Someone Famous*
Kincaid, J. *Annie John*
Knowles, J. *A Separate Peace*
Koertge, R. *The Arizona Kid*
Lee, H. *To Kill a Mockingbird*
McCorkle, J. *Ferris Beach*
McCullers, C. *The Member of the Wedding*
McNichols, C. *Crazy Weather*
Maxwell, W. *The Folded Leaf*
Mazer, N.F. *Dear Bill, Remember Me?*
Mickle, S.F. *The Queen of October*
Miller, J.W. *Newfound*
Munro, A. *Lives of Girls and Women*
Oates, J.C. *Where Are You Going? Where Have You Been?*
Oneal, Z. *The Language of Goldfish*
Peck, R.N. *A Day No Pigs Would Die*
Peck, R. *Princess Ashley*
Powell, P. *Edisto*
Price, R. *Tongues of Angels*
Quindlen, A. *Object Lessons*
Sachs, M. *Circles*
Salinger, J.D. *The Catcher in the Rye*
Sillitoe, A. *The Loneliness of the Long-Distance Runner*
Spark, M. *The Prime of Miss Jean Brodie*
Speare, E.G. *The Sign of the Beaver*
Stafford, J. *The Mountain Lion*
Swarthout, G. *Bless the Beasts and Children*
Wharton, E. *Summer*
Winthrop, E. *A Little Demonstration of Affection*
Wouk, H. *City Boy*
Zolotow, C. *An Overpraised Season*

ADOPTION
DeVries, P. *The Tunnel of Love*

ADVENTURE
Adams, R. *Watership Down*
Buchan, J. *The Thirty-Nine Steps*
Coetzee, J.M. *Foe*
Crichton, M. *The Great Train Robbery*
Forester, C.S. *The African Queen*

Household, G. *Rogue Male*
MacLean, A. *The Guns of Navarone*
Orczy, E. *The Scarlet Pimpernel*
Wren, P.C. *Beau Geste*

AFRICA. *See also* APARTHEID; SOUTH AFRICA
Abrahams, P. *A Wreath for Udomo*
Achebe, C. *Anthills of the Savannah; Things Fall Apart*
Caputo, P. *Horn of Africa*
Cary, J. *Mister Johnson*
Coetzee, J.M. *The Life and Times of Michael K.*
Emecheta, B. *The Slave Girl*
Forester, C.S. *The African Queen*
Gordimer, N. *Selected Stories*
Paton, A. *Cry, the Beloved Country*
Wren, P.C. *Beau Geste*

AIDS
Koertge, R. *The Arizona Kid*

AIR PILOTS
Forsyth, F. *The Shepherd*
Heller, J. *Catch-22*
Michener, J.A. *The Bridges at Toko-ri*
Saint-Exupéry, A. *Night Flight*

ALABAMA
Lee, H. *To Kill a Mockingbird*

ALASKA AND ARCTIC REGIONS
Le Guin, U.K. *The Left Hand of Darkness*
London, J. *The Call of the Wild*

ALCOHOLISM
Carter, A.R. *Up Country*
Donovan, J. *I'll Get There. It Better Be Worth the Trip*
Lowry, M. *Under the Volcano*
McCall, D. *Jack the Bear*
Minot, S. *Monkeys*
Moore, B. *The Lonely Passion of Judith Hearne*
O'Hara, J. *Appointment in Samarra*
Samuels, G. *Run, Shelley, Run*
Scoppettone, S. *The Late Great Me*

ALLEGORIES
Abé, K. *The Woman in the Dunes*
Beagle, P. *The Last Unicorn*
Bell, C. *Ratha's Creature*
Camus, A. *The Fall*
Golding, W. *Lord of the Flies*
Hesse, H. *Siddhartha*
Kafka, F. *Metamorphosis*
Lewis, C.S. *Out of the Silent Planet; Perelandra; That Hideous Strength*
Orwell, G. *Animal Farm*
Tolkien, J.R.R. *The Fellowship of the Ring; The Hobbit*
Wangerin, W. *The Book of the Dun Cow*

ANIMAL EXPERIMENTS
Dickinson, P. *Eva*
Stewart, M. *Monkey Shines*

ANIMALS. *See also* **CATS; DOGS**
Bell, C. *Ratha's Creature*
Burnford, S. *The Incredible Journey*
Donovan, J. *Wild in the World*
Swarthout, G. *Bless the Beasts and Children*

ANTI-SEMITISM. *See also* **JEWS; NATIONAL SOCIALISM**
Bassani, G. *The Garden of the Finzi-Continis*
Hobson, L. *Gentleman's Agreement*
Malamud, B. *The Fixer*
Schwarz-Bart, A. *The Last of the Just*

APARTHEID
Coetzee, J.M. *The Life and Times of Michael K.*
Gordimer, N. *July's People; My Son's Story; Something Out There*
Paton, A. *Cry, the Beloved Country*
Rochman, H. *Somehow Tenderness Survives*

APES
Boulle, P. *The Planet of the Apes*
Donovan, J. *Family*

APPALACHIA
Marshall, C. *Christy*
Miller, J.W. *Newfound*

ARIZONA
Arnold, E. *Blood Brother*

ARMENIANS
Werfel, F. *The Forty Days of Musa Dagh*

ARMENIANS IN THE UNITED STATES
Saroyan, W. *My Name is Aram*

ARTISTS
Atwood, M. *Cat's Eye*
Carr, J.L. *A Month in the Country*
Cary, J. *The Horse's Mouth*
Durrell, L. *Clea (in The Alexandria Quartet)*
Gallico, P. *The Snow Goose*
Maugham, S. *The Moon and Sixpence*
Nathan, R. *Portrait of Jennie*
Potok, C. *My Name is Asher Lev*
Price, R. *Tongues of Angels*
Stone, I. *Lust for Life*

ASSASSINATION
Forsyth, F. *The Day of the Jackal*
Household, G. *Rogue Male*

ATHLETES
French, M. *The Throwing Season*
Sillitoe, A. *The Loneliness of the Long-Distance Runner*
Stewart, M. *Monkey Shines*

ATOMIC BOMB. *See also* **END OF THE WORLD**
Bograd, L. *Los Alamos Light*
Burdick, E. *Fail-Safe*
Frank, P. *Alas, Babylon*
Golding, W. *Lord of the Flies*
Niven, L. *Ringworld*
Shute, N. *On the Beach*
Vonnegut, K. *Cat's Cradle*
Wibberley, L. *The Mouse That Roared*
Wilhelm, K. *Where Late the Sweet Birds Sang*

AUSTRALIA
Anderson, J. *Tirra Lirra by the River*

Franklin, M. *My Brilliant Career*
Shute, N. *On the Beach*

AUSTRIA
MacInnes, H. *The Salzburg Connection*

AVARICE
Webb, M. *Precious Bane*

BASEBALL
Harris, M. *Bang the Drum Slowly*
Malamud, B. *The Natural*
Plimpton, G. *The Curious Case of Sidd Finch*

BASKETBALL
Deuker, C. *On the Devil's Court*

BATS
Smith, M.C. *Nightwing*

BELGIUM
Stone, I. *Lust for Life*

BLACKS
Armstrong, W.H. *Sounder*
Baldwin, J. *Go Tell It on the Mountain; If Beale Street Could Talk*
Bambara, T.C. *Gorilla, My Love*
Barrett, W.E. *Lilies of the Field*
Childress, A. *A Hero Ain't Nothin' But a Sandwich*
Ellison, R. *The Invisible Man*
Faulkner, W. *The Intruder in the Dust*
Gaines, E.J. *The Autobiography of Miss Jane Pittman; A Gathering of Old
    Men*
Hamilton, V. *Sweet Whispers, Brother Rush*
Johnson, C. *Middle Passage*
Lipsyte, R. *The Contender*
Marshall, P. *Daughters; Praisesong for the Widow*
Mathis, S.B. *Listen for the Fig Tree; Teacup Full of Roses*
Meyer, C. *Denny's Tapes*
Morrison, T. *Beloved; Song of Solomon*
Murray, A. *The Spyglass Tree; Train Whistle Guitar*
Naylor, G. *The Women of Brewster Place*
Parks, G. *The Learning Tree*

Powell, P. *Edisto*
Toomer, J. *Cane*
Walker, A. *In Love and Trouble*
Wideman, J.E. *Philadelphia Fire*
Wilkinson, B. *Ludell; Ludell and Willie*
Wright, R. *Native Son*

BOATING
Casey, J. *Spartina*

BOXING
Lipsyte, R. *The Contender*

BRAINWASHING
Cormier, R. *I Am the Cheese*
Koestler, A. *Darkness at Noon*

BRAZIL
Amado, J. *Gabriela, Clove and Cinnamon*

BUDDHA AND BUDDHISM
Hesse, H. *Siddhartha*

BURR, AARON
Vidal, G. *Burr*

CALIFORNIA
Leffland, E. *Rumors of Peace*
Norris, F. *The Octopus*
O'Dell, S. *Island of the Blue Dolphins*
Pynchon, T. *The Crying of Lot 49*
Saroyan, W. *The Human Comedy; My Name Is Aram*
Steinbeck, J. *Of Mice and Men; The Red Pony*

CANADA
Craven, M. *I Heard the Owl Call My Name*
Davies, R. *Fifth Business*
Freedman, B. *Mrs. Mike*

CAPITALISTS AND FINANCIERS
Durrell, L. *Justine (in The Alexandria Quartet)*
Rand, A. *Atlas Shrugged*

CARNIVAL
Bradbury, R. *Something Wicked This Way Comes*

CATHOLIC FAITH
Barrett, W. *Lilies of the Field*
Cronin, A.J. *The Green Years*
Greene, G. *The Heart of the Matter; The Power and the Glory; Monsignor Quixote*
Guareschi, G. *The Little World of Don Camillo*
Joyce, J. *Dubliners; A Portrait of the Artist as a Young Man*
Percy, W. *Love in the Ruins*
Power, J.F. *Morte d'Urban*
Wilder, T. *The Bridge of San Luis Rey*
Woiwode, L. *Beyond the Bedroom Wall*

CATS
Burnford, S. *The Incredible Journey*

CEMETERIES
Beagle, P. *A Fine and Private Place*

CHICAGO
Dreiser, T. *Sister Carrie*
Maxwell, W. *The Folded Leaf*
Sinclair, U. *The Jungle*
Wright, R. *Native Son*

CHILD ABUSE
Crutcher, C. *Stotan!*
Kellogg, M. *Like the Lion's Tooth*
Kingsolver, B. *The Bean Trees*
Oates, J.C. *Them*
Samuels, G. *Run, Shelley, Run*

CHINA
Buck, P. *The Good Earth*
Gilman, D. *Mrs. Pollifax on the China Station*
Malraux, A. *Man's Fate*
Rendell, R. *Speaker of Mandarin*
Tan, A. *The Joy Luck Club; The Kitchen God's Wife*

CHINESE IN THE UNITED STATES
Jen, G. *Typical American*

Tan, A. *The Joy Luck Club; The Kitchen God's Wife*
Yep, L. *Child of the Owl; Dragonwings*

CHIVALRY
White, T.H. *The Once and Future King*

CHRISTMAS STORIES
Forsyth, F. *The Shepherd*

CHURCHES
Carr, J.L. *A Month in the Country*

CIVIL WAR. *See* **UNITED STATES**

CLONES. *See also* **GENETICS**
Crichton, M. *Jurassic Park*
Levin, I. *The Boys from Brazil*
Wilhelm, K. *Where Late the Sweet Birds Sang*

COAL MINING
Llewellyn, R. *How Green Was My Valley*

COLLEGE LIFE
Amis, K. *Lucky Jim*
Jarrell, R. *Pictures from an Institution*
Maxwell, W. *The Folded Leaf*
Salinger, J.D. *Franny and Zooey*

COMMUNISM
Doctorow, E.L. *The Book of Daniel*
Koestler, A. *Darkness at Noon*
Malraux, A. *Man's Fate*
Pasternak, B. *Doctor Zhivago*
Solzhenitsyn, A. *One Day in the Life of Ivan Denisovich*

COMPUTERS
Crichton, M. *The Terminal Man*
Francis, D. *Twice Shy*
Menick, J. *Lingo*

CONCENTRATION CAMPS
Schaffer, S.F. *Anya*
Schwarz-Bart, A. *The Last of the Just*

Wallant, E.L. *The Pawnbroker*

CONFEDERATE STATES OF AMERICA
Kantor, M. *Andersonville*

CONNECTICUT
De Bries, P. *The Tunnel of Love*
Hobson, L. *Gentleman's Agreement*

COWBOYS
Clark, W.V. *The Ox-bow Incident*
Richard, A. *Pistol*
Wister, O. *The Virginian*

CRETE
Kazantzakis, N. *Zorba the Greek*
Renault, M. *The King Must Die*

CUBA
Hemingway, E. *The Old Man and the Sea*

CULTURE CONFLICT
Jones, D.C. *Season of Yellow Leaf*
Rachlin, N. *Foreigner*
Richter, C. *The Light in the Forest*

DEAF
McCullers, C. *The Heart Is a Lonely Hunter*

DEATH
Agee, J. *A Death in the Family*
Banks, R. *The Sweet Hereafter*
Beagle, P. *A Fine and Private Place*
Beckman, G. *Admission to the Feast*
Blos, J.W. *A Gathering of Days*
Cooper, S. *Seaward*
Craven, M. *I Heard the Owl Call My Name*
Doerr, H. *Stones for Ibarra*
Donovan, J. *I'll Get There. It Better Be Worth the Trip*
Godwin, G. *Father Melancholy's Daughter*
Gordon, M. *Final Payments*
Guest, J. *Ordinary People*
Hughes, M. *Hunter in the Dark*

Jackson, S. *We Have Always Lived in the Castle*
McCorkle, J. *Ferris Beach*
Oneal, Z. *A Formal Feeling*
Peck, R. *Father Figure*
Peck, R.N. *A Day No Pigs Would Die*
Price, R. *Tongues of Angels*
Shute, N. *On the Beach*
Stegner, W. *Crossing to Safety*
Styron, W. *Lie Down in Darkness*
Thane, E. *Tryst*
Waugh, E. *The Loved One*
Welty, E. *The Optimist's Daughter*
Zindel, P. *The Pigman*

DETECTIVE AND MYSTERY STORIES. *See also* SUSPENSE

Barnard, R. *Death of a Mystery Writer*
Buchan, J. *The Thirty-nine Steps*
Christie, A. *And Then There Were None; Murder on the Orient Express*
Crispin, E. *The Moving Toyshop*
Cross, A. *The Question of Max*
Dexter, C. *The Wench Is Dead*
Farris, J. *When Michael Calls*
Francis, D. *Comeback; Trial Run; Twice Shy; Whip Hand*
Garfield, B. *The Crime of My Life*
Grafton, S. *"C" is for Corpse*
Grimes, M. *The Anodyne Necklace*
Hammett, D. *The Maltese Falcon; The Thin Man*
Hillerman, T. *Talking God*
Innes, M. *The Case of the Journeying Boy*
James, P.S. *An Unsuitable Job for a Woman*
Langton, J. *Emily Dickinson is Dead*
Mortimer, J. *Rumpole for the Defense*
Paretsky, S. *Bitter Medicine*
Perry, A. *Bethlehem Road*
Peters, E. *The Murders of Richard the III*
Pullman, P. *The Tiger in the Well*
Rendell, R. *A Sleeping Life; Speaker of Mandarin*
Sayers, D. *The Nine Tailors*
Simenon, G. *Maigret in Court*
Truman, M. *Murder at the National Cathedral*

DICTATORSHIP

Achebe, C. *Anthills of the Savannah*

Atwood, M. *The Handmaid's Tale*

DINOSAURS
Crichton, M. *Jurassic Park*

DISASTERS
Burdick, E. *Fail-Safe*
Crichton, M. *The Andromeda Strain*
Frank, P. *Alas, Babylon*
Sandoz, M. *Winter Thunder*
Shute, N. *On the Beach*
Stewart, G. *Earth Abides*
Wilhelm, K. *Where Late the Sweet Birds Sang*

DIVORCE
Cole, B. *Celine*
Donovan, J. *I'll Get There. It Better Be Worth the Trip.*
Peck, R. *Father Figure*
Powell, P. *Edisto*
Sachs, M. *Circles*

DOGS
Armstrong, W. *Sounder*
Burnford, S. *The Incredible Journey*
Gipson, S. *Old Yeller*
London, J. *The Call of the Wild*

DRUGS
Bridgers, S.E. *Permanent Connections*
Childress, A. *A Hero Ain't Nothin' But a Sandwich*
Mathis, S.B. *A Teacup Full of Rose*

DUNKIRK, BATTLE OF
Gallico, P. *The Snow Goose*

ECOLOGY
Herbert, F. *Dune*

EDUCATION
Hersey, J. *The Child Buyer*

EGYPT
Durrell, L. *The Alexandria Quartet (Balthazar; Clea; Justine; Mountolive)*

END OF THE WORLD (AND AFTER...)
Boulle, P. *Planet of the Apes*
Leiber, F. *The Wanderer*
Miller, W. *A Canticle for Liebowitz*
O'Brien, R. *Z for Zachariah*
Percy, W. *Love in the Ruins*
Rand, A. *Atlas Shrugged*
Shute, N. *On the Beach*
Wyndham, *The Day of the Triffids*

ENGLAND
Colegate, I. *The Shooting Party*
Galsworthy, J. *The Forsyte Saga*
Ishiguro, K. *The Remains of the Day*
Monsarrat, N. *The Cruel Sea*
Pullman, P. *The Tiger in the Well*
Stewart, M. *The Crystal Cave; The Wicked Day*
Tey, J. *The Daughter of Time*
Webb, M. *Precious Bane*
Westall, R. *The Machine Gunners*

ENVIRONMENTAL ISSUES
Kingsolver, B. *Animal Dreams*

ESCAPES
Hersey, J. *The Wall*
Household, G. *Rogue Male*

ESKIMOS
George, J.C. *Julie of the Wolves*
Newth, M. *The Abduction*

ESPIONAGE
Ambler, E. *Intrigue*
Buchan, J. *The Thirty-nine Steps*
Cormier, R. *I Am the Cheese*
Deighton, L. *Berlin Game; The Ipcress File; SS-GB*
Doctorow, E.L. *The Book of Daniel*
Durrell, L. *Mountolive (in The Alexandria Quartet)*
Forsyth, F. *The Day of the Jackal*
Gilman, D. *Mrs. Pollifax on the China Station*
Goldman, W. *Marathon Man*
Greene, G. *The Human Factor*

Higgins, J. *The Eagle Has Flown*
Innes, M. *The Case of the Journeying Boy*
Le Carré, J. *The Secret Pilgrim; The Spy Who Came in from the Cold*
MacInnes, H. *The Salzburg Connection*

EUROPEAN WAR, 1914-1918
Carr, J. L. *A Month in the Country*
Hemingway, E. *A Farewell to Arms*
Remarque, E.M. *All Quiet on the Western Front*
Trumbo, D. *Johnny Got His Gun*

FACTORIES
Paterson, K. *Lyddie*

FAMILY RELATIONSHIPS. *See also* FATHERS AND DAUGHTERS; FATHERS AND SONS; MOTHERS AND DAUGHTERS; MOTHERS AND SONS
Agee, J. *A Death in the Family*
Anderson, S. *Winesburg, Ohio*
Arnow, H. *The Dollmaker*
Atwood, M. *Cat's Eye*
Bellow, S. *Mr. Sammler's Planet*
Blos, J.W. *A Gathering of Days*
Bowen, E. *The Death of the Heart*
Boyle, T.C. *World's End*
Bridgers, S.E. *Home Before Dark; Permanent Connections*
Burns, O.A. *Cold Sassy Tree*
Canin, E. *Emperor of the Air*
Capote, T. *The Grass Harp*
Chase, J. *During the Reign of the Queen of Persia*
Childress, A. *A Hero Ain't Nothin' But a Sandwich*
Cleaver, V. *Where the Lilies Bloom*
Connell, E. *Mrs. Bridge*
Craven, M. *Walk Gently This Good Earth*
Cronin, A.J. *The Green Years*
Davies, R. *Fifth Business*
Desai, A. *Clear Light of Day*
Edmonds, W. *Bert Breen's Barn*
Galsworthy, J. *The Forsyte Saga*
Glasgow, E. *The Sheltered Life*
Godwin, G. *A Mother and Two Daughters*
Gordon, M. *Final Payments; The Other Side*
Guest, J. *Ordinary People*

Tyler, A. *Dinner at the Homesick Restaurant; Saint Maybe*
Voigt, C. *Dicey's Song; Homecoming*
Walsh, J.P. *Goldengrove; Unleaving*
Webb, M. *Precious Bane*
West, J. *The Friendly Persuasion*
Wilkinson, B. *Ludell*
Winthrop, E. *A Little Demonstration of Affection*
Woiwode, l. *Beyond the Bedroom Wall*
Wolfe, T. *Look Homeward, Angel*

FANTASIES
Beagle, P. *A Fine and Private Place; The Last Unicorn*
Bell, C. *Ratha's Creature*
Borges, J.L. *The Book of Fantasy*
Brooks, T. *The Sword of Shannara*
Cassedy, S. *Behind the Attic Wall*
Cooper, S. *Seaward*
Dickinson, P. *The Blue Hawk*
Finney, J. *Time and Again*
Goldman, W. *The Princess Bride*
Hilton, J. *Lost Horizon*
Hudson, W.H. *Green Mansions*
Jones, D.W. *Castle in the Air*
Klause, A.C. *The Silver Kiss*
Le Guin, U.K. *The Wizard of Earthsea Trilogy*
McKinley, R. *Beauty*
Nathan, R. *Portrait of Jennie*
O'Brien, T. *Going After Cacciato*
Rushdie, S. *Haroun and the Sea of Stories*
Tolkien, J.R.R. *The Hobbit; The Lord of the Rings*
White, T.H. *The Once and Future King*
Wibberley, L. *The Mouse That Roared*

FARM LIFE
Carter, A.R. *Up Country*
Chase, J. *During the Reign of the Queen of Persia*
Doherty, B. *White Peak Farm*
Edmonds, W. *Bert Breen's Barn*
Glasgow, E. *Barren Ground*
Hamsun, K. *Growth of the Soil*
Peck, R.N. *A Day No Pigs Would Die*
Rolvaag, O.E. *Giants in the Earth*
Smiley, J. *A Thousand Acres*

Steinbeck, J. *The Red Pony*
Undset, S. *Kristin Lavransdatter*
Webb, M. *Precious Bane*
Wharton, E. *Ethan Frome*

FASCISM
Bassani, G. *The Garden of the Finzi-Continis*
Ishiguro, K. *The Remains of the Day*
Lewis, S. *It Can't Happen Here*
Yourcenar, M. *A Coin in Nine Hands*

FATHERS AND DAUGHTERS
Bellow, S. *Mr. Sammler's Planet*
Bograd, L. *Los Alamos Light*
Dickinson, P. *Eva*
Godden, R. *The Peacock Spring*
Godwin, G. *Father Melancholy's Daughter*
Gordon, M. *Final Payments*
Kingsolver, B. *Animal Dreams*
Konigsburg, E.L. *Father's Arcane Daughter*
Marshall, P. *Daughters*
Sagan, F. *Bonjour Tristesse*
Schaeffer, S.F. *Falling*
Styron, W. *Lie Down in Darkness*
Taylor, P. *Summons to Memphis*
Undset, S. *The Bridal Wreath (in Kristin Lavransdatter)*
Wells, R. *None of the Above*
Welty, E. *The Optimist's Daughter*
Yep, L. *Child of the Owl*

FATHERS AND SONS
Boyle, T. C. *World's End*
Canin, E. *Emperor of the Air*
Deuker, C. *On the Devil's Court*
Gold, H. *Fathers*
Gordimer, N. *My Son's Story*
Just, W. *Jack Gance*
Lenz, S. *The German Lesson*
Lesley, C. *Winterkill*
McCall, D. *Jack the Bear*
Peck, R. *Father Figure*
Peck, R.N. *A Day No Pigs Would Die*
Potok, C. *My Name Is Asher Lev; The Promise*

Rushdie, S. *Haroun and the Sea of Stories*
Taylor, P. *Summons to Memphis*
Updike, J. *The Centaur*
Yep, L. *Dragonwings*

FIRES
Wideman, J.E. *Philadelphia Fire*

FISHING
Casey, J. *Spartina*
Maclean, N. *A River Runs Through It*

FLORIDA
Frank, P. *Alas, Babylon*

FOREIGN SERVICE
Lederer, W. *The Ugly American*

FOREST FIRES
Maclean, N. *A River Runs Through It.*

FRANCE
Orczy, E. *The Scarlet Pimpernel*
Stewart, M. *Nine Coaches Waiting*

FRIENDSHIP
Atwood, M. *Cat's Eye*
Bosse, M. *Ganesh*
Brookner, A. *Brief Lives*
Crutcher, C. *Stotan!*
Degens, T. *Transport 7-41-R*
Fields, J. *A Cry of Angels*
Gingher, M. *Bobby Rex's Greatest Hit*
Godden, R. *An Episode of Sparrows*
Greene, B. *Summer of My German Soldier*
Harris, M. *Bang the Drum Slowly*
Holland, I. *The Man Without a Face*
Horgan, P. *Whitewater*
Kerr, M.E. *Is That You, Miss Blue?*
Kingsolver, B. *The Bean Trees*
Le Guin, U.K. *Very Far Away from Anywhere Else*
McCullers, C. *The Heart Is a Lonely Hunter*
MacPherson, M. *The Rough Road*

Maxwell, W. *The Folded leaf*
Mishima, Y. *Spring Snow*
Munro, A. *Friend of My Youth*
Potok, C. *The Promise*
Stegner, W. *Crossing to Safety*
Steinbeck, J. *Of Mice and Men*
Swarthout, G. *Bless the Beasts and Children*
Zindel, P. *The Pigman*

FRONTIER AND PIONEER LIFE
Berger, T. *Little Big Man*
Cather, W. *My Antonia*
Ferber, E. *Cimarron*
Freedman, B. *Mrs. Mike*
Gipson, F. *Old Yeller*
Guthrie, A.B. *The Big Sky*
L'Amour, L. *Bendigo Shafter*
Michener, J. *Centennial*
Portis, C. *True Grit*
Richter, C. *The Light in the Forest; The Rawhide Knot*
Rölvaag, O.E. *Giants in the Earth*
Speare, E.G. *The Sign of the Beaver*

FUNERALS
Agee, J. *A Death in the Family*
Beagle, P. *A Fine and Private Place*
Styron, W. *Lie Down in Darkness*
Waugh, E. *The Loved One*
Welty, E. *Losing Battles; The Optimist's Daughter*

GARIBALDI
Lampedusa, G. *The Leopard*

GAUGUIN, PAUL
Maugham, W.S. *The Moon and Sixpence*

GENETICS. See also CLONES
Herbert, F. *Dune*
Levin, I. *The Boys from Brazil*

GENIUS
Hersey, J. *The Child Buyer*

GENOCIDE. *See also* **HOLOCAUST**
Werfel, F. *The Forty Days of Musa Dagh*

GEORGIA
Fields, J. *A Cry of Angels*

GERMANY
Degens, T. *Transport 7-41-R*
Deighton, L. *Berlin Game*
Forsyth, F. *The Odessa File*
Grass, G. *The Tin Drum*
Hesse, H. *Steppenwolf*
Isherwood, C. *The Berlin Stories*
Just, W. *The Translator*
Vonnegut, K. *Slaughterhouse Five*

GOGH, VINCENT VAN. *See* **VAN GOGH, VINCENT**

GREECE
Fenton, E. *The Refugee Summer*
Kazantzakis, N. *Zorba the Greek*

GREECE, ANCIENT
Renault, M. *The Bull from the Sea; The King Must Die; The Last of the Wine*

THE HANDICAPPED
Kellogg, M. *Tell Me That You Love Me, Junie Moon*
Konigsburg, E.L. *Father's Arcane Daughter*
Mathis, S.B. *Listen for the Fig Tree*
Maugham, W.S. *Of Human Bondage*
Stegner, W. *Crossing to Safety*
Stewart, M. *Nine Coaches Waiting*
Stewart, Michael. *Monkey Shines*
Trumbo, D. *Johnny Got His Gun*
Walsh, J.P. *Unleaving*

HASIDISM
Potok, C. *My Name Is Asher Lev*

HIJACKING
Keneally, T. *Flying Hero Class*

HOLOCAUST
Begley, L. *Wartime Lies*
Hersey, J. *The Wall*
Levi, P. *If Not Now, When?*
Ozick, C. *The Shawl*
Schaeffer, S.F. *Anya*
Wiesel, E. *Dawn*

HOMOSEXUALITY
Donovan, J. *I'll Get There. It Better Be Worth the Trip*
Durrell, L. *Clea (in The Alexandria Quartet)*
Holland, I. *The Man Without a Face*
Koertge, R. *The Arizona Kid*
Shannon, G. *Unlived Affections*

HORSE RACING
Francis, D. *Comeback; Trial Run; Twice Shy; Whip Hand*

HOSPITALS
Paretsky, S. *Bitter Medicine*

HUMOR
Amis, K. *Lucky Jim*
Beagle, P. *A Fine and Private Place*
Berger, T. *Little Big Man*
Burns, O.A. *Cold Sassy Tree*
Cary, J. *The Horse's Mouth*
Crispin, E. *The Moving Toyshop*
DeVries, P. *The Tunnel of Love*
Garfield, L. *The Strange Affair of Adelaide Harris*
Gibbons, S. *Cold Comfort Farm*
Guareschi, G. *The Little World of Don Camillo*
Hasek, K. *The Good Soldier: Schweik*
Heggen, T. *Mister Roberts*
Heller, J. *Catch-22*
Koertge, R. *The Arizona Kid*
Mickle, S.F. *The Queen of October*
Portis, C. *True Grit*
Rushdie, S. *Haroun and the Sea of Stories*
Saroyan, W. *My Name Is Aram*
Sevela, E. *Why There Is No Heaven on Earth*
Wibberly, L. *The Mouse That Roared*
Wouk, H. *City Boy*

ILLINOIS
Ferber, E. *So Big*
Woiwode, L. *Beyond the Bedroom Wall*

ILLNESS
Beckman, G. *Admission to the Feast*
Gordon, M. *Final Payments*
Hamilton, V. *Sweet Whispers, Brother Rush*
Harris, M. *Bang the Drum Slowly*
Hughes, M. *Hunter in the Dark*
Mann, T. *The Magic Mountain*

IMMIGRANTS
Cather, W. *My Antonia*
Forbes, K. *Mama's Bank Account*
Gordon, M. *The Other Side*
Jen, G. *Typical American*
Rölvaag, O.E. *Giants in the Earth*
Roth, H. *Call It Sleep*
Sinclair, U. *The Jungle*

INCEST
Banks, R. *The Sweet Hereafter*
Smiley, J. *A Thousand Acres*

INDIA
Desai, A. *Baumgartner's Bombay; Clear Light of Day*
Hesse, H. *Siddhartha*
Godden, R. *The Peacock Spring*
Jhabvala, R. *Heat and Dust*
Markandaya, K. *Nectar in a Sieve*
Scott, P. *Staying On*

INDIANA
West, J. *The Friendly Persuasion*

INDIANS OF NORTH AMERICA
Arnold, E. *Blood Brother*
Berger, T. *Little Big Man*
Borland, H. *When the Legends Die*
Brown, D. *Creek Mary's Blood*
Dorris, M. *Yellow Raft in Blue Water*
French, M. *The Throwing Season*

Fuller, I. *The Loon Feather*
Guthrie, A.B. *The Big Sky*
Hillerman, T. *Talking God*
Hotze, W. *A Circle Unbroken*
Jones, D. *Season of Yellow Leaf*
La Farge, O. *Laughing Boy*
Lesley, C. *Winterkill*
McNichols, C. *Crazy Weather*
McNickle, D. *Wind from an Enemy Sky*
Michener, J. *Centennial*
Momaday, N.S. *House Made Of Dawn*
O'Dell, S. *Island of the Blue Dolphins*
Richter, C. *The Light in the Forest*
Smith, M.C. *Nightwing*
Speare, E.G. *The Sign of the Beaver*
West, J. *The Massacre at Fall Creek*

INDIVIDUALISM
Orwell, G. *Nineteen Eighty-four*
Pasternak, B. *Doctor Zhivago*
Rand, A. *Atlas Shrugged*

INTERRACIAL MARRIAGE
Arnold, E. *Blood Brother*
Brown, D. *Creek Mary's Blood*
Fairbairn, A. *Five Smooth Stones*
Grau, S. *The Keepers of the House*
Jones, D. *Season of Yellow Leaf*

IRAN
Rachlin, N. *Foreigner*

IRELAND
Gordon, M. *The Other Side*
Joyce, J. *Dubliners*
Moore, B. *Lies of Silence; The Lonely Passion of Judith Hearne*
O'Flaherty, L. *The Informer*

IRISH IN AMERICA
Gordon, M. *The Other Side*
O'Connor, E. *The Last Hurrah*

ISRAEL
Roiphe, A. *Lovingkindness*

Uris, L. *Exodus*
Wiesel, E. *Dawn*

ITALY
Bassani, G. *The Garden of the Finzi-Continis*
Guareschi, G. *The Little World of Don Camillo*
Yourcenar, M. *A Coin in Nine Hands*

JAPAN
Boulle, P. *The Bridge Over the River Kwai*
Ishiguro, K. *A Pale View of the Hills*
Kawabata, Y. *Thousand Cranes*
Mishima, Y. *The Sound of Waves; Spring Snow*
Sumii, S. *The River With No Bridge*

JAPANESE-AMERICANS
Kadohata, C. *The Floating World*

JEWS
Agnon, S.Y. *Twenty-one Stories*
Hersey, J. *The Wall*
Levitin, S. *The Return*
Malamud, B. *The Fixer*
Roiphe, A. *Lovingkindness*
Schaeffer, S.F. *Anya*
Schwarz-Bart, A. *The Last of the Just*
Sevela, E. *Why There Is No Heaven on Earth*
Singer, I.B. *A Crown of Feathers*
Uris, L. *Exodus*

JEWS IN THE UNITED STATES
Bellow, S. *Mr Sammler's Planet*
Doctorow, E.L. *The Book of Daniel*
Gold, H. *Fathers*
Hobson, L. *Gentleman's Agreement*
Malamud, B. *The Assistant*
Potok, C. *My Name Is Asher Lev; The Promise*
Roth, H. *Call It Sleep*
Roth, P. *Good-bye, Columbus*
Wallant, E.L. *The Pawnbroker*

JUDAISM
Roiphe, A. *Lovingkindness*

Freedman, B. *Mrs. Mike*
Gallico, P. *The Snow Goose*
Glasgow, E. *The Sheltered Life*
Godden, R. *The Peacock Spring*
Hemingway, E. *A Farewell to Arms; For Whom the Bell Tolls*
Humphreys, J. *Firemen's Fair*
Kawabata, Y. *Thousand Cranes*
Kerr, M.E. *Little, Little*
Le Guin, U. *Very Far Away From Anywhere Else*
McCullough, C. *Tim*
McKinley, R. *Beauty*
Marquez, G. *Love in the Time of Cholera*
Maxwell, W. *So Long, See You Tomorrow*
Mishima, Y. *The Sound of Waves; Spring Snow*
Nathan, R. *Portrait of Jennie*
Pasternak, B. *Doctor Zhivago*
Price, R. *A Long and Happy Life*
Smith, B. *Joy in the Morning*
Thane, E. *Tryst*
Trevanian. *The Summer of Katya*
Trevor, W. *Fools of Fortune*
Wharton, E. *The Age of Innocence; Summer*
Wilkinson, B. *Ludell and Willie*

MACABRE STORIES
Dahl, R. *Kiss, Kiss*
Fowles, J. *The Collector*
Jackson, S. *The Lottery; We Have Always Lived in the Castle*
Tryon, T. *The Other*

MASSACHUSETTS
Marquand, J.P. *The Late George Apley*
O'Connor, E. *The Last Hurrah*

MENTAL ILLNESS
Crichton, M. *The Terminal Man*
Guest, J. *Ordinary People*
Kesey, K. *One Flew over the Cuckoo's Nest*
Neufeld, J. *Lisa, Bright and Dark*
Plath, S. *The Bell Jar*
Schaeffer, S.F. *Falling*
Trevanian. *The Summer of Katya*
Vonnegut, K. *Slaughterhouse Five*

MENTALLY HANDICAPPED
Keyes, D. *Flowers for Algernon*
McCullough, C. *Tim*
Steinbeck, J. *Of Mice and Men*

MEXICO
Doerr, H. *Stones for Ibarra*
Greene, G. *The Power and the Glory*
Lowry, M. *Under the Volcano*

MICHIGAN
Arnow, H. *The Dollmaker*
Oates, J.C. *Them*

MIGRANT WORKERS
Bridgers, S.E. *Home Before Dark*
Steinbeck, J. *The Grapes of Wrath*

MINNESOTA
Lewis, S. *Main Street*
Powers, J.F. *Morte d'Urban*

MISSIONARIES
Archebe, C. *Things Fall Apart*
Forester, C.S. *The African Queen*
Matthiessen, P. *At Play in the Fields of the Lord*

MISSISSIPI
Faulkner, W. *Absalom, Absalom!; Intruder in the Dust*
Welty, E. *Losing Battles; The Optimist's Daughter*

MONASTERIES
Eco, U. *The Name of the Rose*

MONTANA
Craven, M. *Walk Gently This Good Earth*

MORAL ISSUES AND VALUES
Bellow, S. *Mr. Sammler's Planet*
Cain, J. *The Postman Always Rings Twice*
Camus, A. *The Stranger*
Canfield, D. *The Bent Twig*
Cormier, R. *The Chocolate War*

Craven, M. *I Heard the Owl Call My Name; Walk Gently This Good Earth*
Donovan, J. *Family*
Dreiser, T. *An American Tragedy; Sister Carrie*
Eco, U. *The Name of the Rose*
Gardner, J.C. *Grendel*
Greene, G. *The Heart of the Matter; The Human Factor*
Hemingway, E. *The Old Man and the Sea*
Hinton, S.E. *The Outsiders*
Kerr, M.E. *Gentlehands*
Le Guin, U. *The Compass Rose; The Eye of the Heron*
Lenz, S. *The German Lesson*
Pirsig, R.M. *Zen and the Art of Motorcycle Maintenance*
Saint-Exupéry, A. de. *The Little Prince*
Steinbeck, J. *The Pearl*
Theroux, P. *The Mosquito Coast*
Wangerin, W. *The Book of the Dun Cow*

MOSLEMS
Rachlin, N. *Foreigner*

MOTHERS AND DAUGHTERS
Anderson, J. *Tirra Lirra by the River*
Chase, J. *During the Reign of the Queen of Persia*
Connell, E. *Mrs. Bridge*
Dorris, M. *Yellow Raft in Blue Water*
Gibbons, K. *A Cure for Dreams*
Godwin, G. *A Mother and Two Daughters*
Ishiguro, K. *A Pale View of the Hills*
McCorkle, J. *Ferris Beach*
Marshall, P. *Daughters*
Munro, A. *Friend of My Youth; Lives of Girls and Women*
Roiphe, A. *Lovingkindness*
Schaeffer, S. *Falling*
Simpson, M. *Anywhere But Here*
Spencer, E. *A Light in the Piazza*
Tan, A. *The Joy Luck Club; The Kitchen God's Wife*
Tyler, A. *Dinner at the Homesick Restaurant*

MOTHERS AND SONS
Carter, A.R. *Up Country*
Lawrence, D.H. *Sons and Lovers*
Roth, L. *Call It Sleep*
Rylant, C. *A Kindness*

Beagle, P. *A Fine and Private Place*
Bellow, S. *Mr. Sammler's Planet*
Boyle, T.C. *World's End*
Dos Passos, J. *Manhattan Transfer*
Dreiser, T. *An American Tragedy; Sister Carrie*
Ellison, R. *Invisible Man*
Fitzgerald, F.S. *The Great Gatsby*
Goldman, W. *Marathon Man*
Green, G. *The Last Angry Man*
Malamud, R. *The Assistant*
Nathan, R. *Portrait of Jennie*
Plath, S. *The Bell Jar*
Potok, C. *The Promise*
Roth, H. *Call It Sleep*
Salinger, J.D. *The Catcher in the Rye*
Wharton, E. *The Age of Innocence*
Wolfe, T. *Look Homeward, Angel*
Wouk, H. *City Boy*

NIGERIA
Achebe, C. *Things Fall Apart*

NORTH CAROLINA
Cleaver, V. *Where the Lilies Bloom*
Tyler, A. *A Slipping-Down Life*

NORWAY
Hamsun, K. *Growth of the Soil*
Undset, S. *Kristin Lavransdatter (14th cent.)*

NORWEGIANS IN THE UNITED STATES
Rölvaag, O.E. *Giants in the Earth*

NURSING HOMES
Sarton, M. *As We Are Now*

OLD AGE
Bennett, A. *The Old Wives' Tale*
Cary, J. *The Horse's Mouth*
Hemingway, E. *The Old Man and the Sea*
Hilton, J. *Good-bye, Mr. Chips*
Sarton, M. *As We Are Now*
Stegner, W. *The Spectator Bird*

PAWNBROKERS
Wallant, E.L. *The Pawnbroker*

PENNSYLVANIA
Updike, J. *The Centaur*

PERU
Wilder, T. *The Bridge of San Luis Rey*

PETROLEUM INDUSTRY
Ferber, E. *Cimarron; Giant*

PHILOSOPHICAL NOVELS
Bellow, S. *Mr. Sammler's Planet*
Camus, A. *The Fall*
Eco, U. *The Name of the Rose*
Hesse, H. *Siddhartha*
Mann, T. *The Magic Mountain*
Pamuk, O. *The White Castle*
Pirsig, R.M. *Zen and the Art of Motorcycle Maintenance*
Wilder, T.J. *The Bridge of San Luis Rey*
Woolf, V. *Mrs. Dalloway*

PHYSICIANS
Camus, A. *The Plague*
Crichton, M. *The Terminal Man*
Cronin, J. *The Citadel*
Green, G. *The Last Angry Man*
Lewis, S. *Arrowsmith*
Maugham, W.S. *Of Human Bondage*
Pasternak, B. *Doctor Zhivago*

POLAND
Begley, L. *Wartime Lies*
Grass, G. *The Tin Drum*
Hersey, J. *The Wall*
Kosinski, J. *The Painted Bird*
Schaeffer, S.F. *Anya*
Singer, I.B. *The Manor*

POLITICS
Drury, A. *Advise and Consent*
Grau, S.A. *The Keepers of the House*

Gaureschi, G. *The Little World of Don Camillo*
Just, W. *Jack Gance; The Translator*
Knebel, F. *Seven Days in May*
O'Connor, E. *The Last Hurrah*
Warren, R.P. *All the King's Men*

POVERTY
Holman, F. *Slake's Limbo*
McCullers, C. *The Heart Is a Lonely Hunter*
Malamud, B. *The Assistant*
Markandaya, K. *Nectar in a Sieve*
Oates, J.C. *Them*
Roth, H. *Call It Sleep*
Sinclair, U. *The Jungle*
Steinbeck, J. *The Grapes of Wrath; The Pearl*
Welty, E. *Losing Battles*
Wright, R. *Native Son*

PREGNANCY
Baldwin, J. *If Beale Street Could Talk*

PREJUDICE
Sumii, S. *The River With No Bridge*

PRESIDENTS
Burdick, E. *Fail-Safe*
Knebel, F. *Seven Days in May*

QUAKERS
West, J. *The Friendly Persuasion*

RACIAL ISSUES. *See also* APARTHEID
Baldwin, J. *If Beale Street Could Talk*
Ellison, R. *Invisible Man*
Fairbairn, A. *Five Smooth Stones*
Faulkner, W. *Intruder in the Dust*
Forster, E.M. *A Passage to India*
Grau, S. *The Keepers of the House*
Guy, R. *The Friends*
Lee, H. *To Kill a Mockingbird*
O'Connor, F. *Everything That Rises Must Converge*
Parks, G. *The Learning Tree*
Paton, A. *Cry, the Beloved Country*

West, J. *The Massacre at Fall Creek*
Wideman, J.E. *Philadelphia Fire*
Wright, R. *Native Son*

RAILROADS
Norris, F. *The Octopus*
Rand, A. *Atlas Shrugged*

RAPE
Burgess, A. *A Clockwork Orange*
Dickey, J. *Deliverance*
Lee, H. *To Kill a Mockingbird*
Mathis, S.B. *Listen for the Fig Tree*
Peck, R. *Are You in the House Alone?*
Scoppettone, S. *Happy Endings Are All Alike*
Trevanian. *The Summer of Katya*

REFUGEES, JEWISH
Bellow, S. *Mr. Sammler's Planet*
Levitin, S. *The Return*
Schaeffer, S.F. *Anya*
Wallant, E.L. *The Pawnbroker*

RELIGION
Craven, M. *I Heard the Owl Call My Name*
Dickinson, P. *Tulku*
Eco, U. *The Name of the Rose*
Godwin, G. *Father Melancholy's Daughter*
Gordon, M. *Final Payments*
Greene, G. *The Heart of the Matter; The Power and the Glory; Monsignor
    Quixote*
Guareschi, G. *The Little World of Don Camillo*
Kerr, M.E. *What I Really Think of You*
Marshall, C. *Christy*
Moore, B. *The Lonely Passion of Judith Hearne*
Newton, S. *I Will Call It Georgie's Blues*
Pamuk, O. *The White Castle*
Potok, C. *My Name Is Asher Lev*
Powers, J.F. *Morte d'Urban*
Price, R. *Tongues of Angels*

ROME, ANCIENT
Graves, R. *I, Claudius*

RUNAWAYS
Samuels, G. *Run, Shelley, Run*

RUNNING
Sillitoe, A. *The Loneliness of the Long-Distance Runner*

RUSSIA
Koestler, A. *Darkness at Noon*
Malamud, B. *The Fixer*
Pasternak, B. *Doctor Zhivago*
Sevela, E. *Why There Is No Heaven on Earth*
Solzhenitsyn, A. *One Day in the Life of Ivan Denisovich*

SATIRE
Boulle, P. *Planet of the Apes*
Burgess, A. *A Clockwork Orange*
DeVries, P. *The Tunnel of Love*
Gibbons, S. *Cold Comfort Farm*
Goldman, W. *The Princess Bride*
Grass, G. *The Tin Drum*
Guareschi, G. *The Little World of Don Camillo*
Hasek, J. *The Good Soldier: Schweik*
Hersey, J. *The Child Buyer*
Huxley, A. *Brave New World*
Kosinski, J. *Being There*
Lewis, S. *It Can't Happen Here*
Marquand, J.P. *The Late George Apley*
Maugham, W.S. *Cakes and Ale*
Menick, J. *Lingo*
Orwell, G. *Animal Farm; Nineteen Eighty-Four*
Percy, W. *Love in the Ruins*
Powers, J.F. *Morte d'Urban*
Pynchon, T. *The Crying of Lot 49*
Vonnegut, K. *Cat's Cradle*
Waugh, F. *The Loved One*
West, N. *Miss Lonelyhearts*
Wibberley, L. *The Mouse That Roared*

SCHOOL LIFE
Comford, E. *The Alfred G. Graebner Memorial H.S. Handbook of Rules and Regulations*
Hilton, J. *Good-bye, Mr. Chips*
Kerr, M.E. *Is That You, Miss Blue?*

Knowles, J. *A Separate Peace*
Maxwell, W. *The Folded Leaf*
Peck, R. *Princess Ashley*
Spark, M. *The Prime of Miss Jean Brodie*

SCIENCE FICTION

Asimov, I. *Foundation Trilogy; I, Robot; Nightfall*
Benford, G. *If the Stars Are Gods*
Boulle, P. *Planet of the Apes*
Bradbury, R. *Fahrenheit 451; The Illustrated Man; The Martian Chronicles;*
    Something Wicked This Way Comes
Brunner, J. *Stand on Zanzibar*
Clarke, A.C. *Childhood's End; Rendezvous with Rama; The Sentinel*
Crichton, M. *The Andromeda Strain*
Crichton, M. *Jurassic Park*
Dick, P.K. *Collected Stories, Vol. 4; The Man in the Castle*
Dickinson, P. *Eva*
Engdahl, S.L. *Enchantress from the Stars*
Farmer, P.J. *To Your Scattered Bodies Go*
Henderson, Z. *The People: No Different Flesh*
Herbert, F. *Dune*
Le Guin, U. *The Compass Rose; The Dispossessed; The Left Hand of Darkness*
Leiber, F. *The Big Time; The Wanderer*
Lewis, C.S. *Out of the Silent Planet; Perelandra; That Hideous Strength*
McCaffrey, A. *Dragonsong*
McIntyre, V.N. *Dreamsnake*
Miller, W.M. *A Canticle for Leibowitz*
Niven, L. *Ringworld*
Pohl, F. *Gateway; The Space Merchants*
Robinson, S. *Callahan's Crosstime Saloon*
Silverberg, R. *Letters from Atlantis*
Simak, C. *City; Way Station*
Sleator, W. *The Boy Who Reversed Himself; House of Stairs*
Vonnegut, K. *Cat's Cradle*
Wyndham, J. *The Day of the Triffids*
Zelazny, R. *My Name is Legion; This Immortal*

SCOTLAND

Buchan, J. *The Thirty-nine Steps*
Cronin, A. *The Green Years*
MacPherson, M. *The Rough Road*
Spark, M. *The Prime of Miss Jean Brodie*
Sutcliff, R. *The Shining Company*

SEA STORIES
Conrad, J. *Lord Jim*
Heggen, T. *Mister Roberts*
Hughes, R. *A High Wind in Jamaica*
Johnson, C. *Middle Passage*
Monsarrat, N. *The Cruel Sea*
Nordhoff, C. *Mutiny on the Bounty*
Wouk, H. *The Caine Mutiny*

SHORT STORIES
Abe, K. *Beyond the Curve*
Agnon, S.Y. *Twenty-one Stories*
Asimov, I. *I, Robot; Nightfall*
Bambara, T.C. *Gorilla, My Love*
Borges, J.L. *The Aleph and Other Stories; The Book of Fantasy*
Boyle, T.C. *If the River Was Whiskey*
Canin, E. *Emperc⁻ of the Air*
Capote, T. *The Grass Harp*
Clarke, A.C. *The Sentinel*
Dahl, R. *Kiss, Kiss*
Dinesen, I. *Seven Gothic Tales*
Garfield, B. *The Crime of My Life; Favorite Stories by Presidents of the Mystery Writers of America*
Godwin, G. *Mr. Bedford and the Muses*
Gordimer, N. *Selected Stories; Something Out There*
Helprin, M. *Ellis Island and Other Stories*
Jackson, S. *The Lottery*
Joyce, J. *Dubliners*
Le Guin, U. *The Compass Rose*
Maclean, N. *A River Runs Through It*
Maugham, W.S. *Cakes and Ale*
Mazer, N.F. *Dear Bill, Remember Me?*
Munro, A. *Friend of My Youth*
Oates, J.C. *Where Are You Going, Where Have You Been?*
O'Connor, F. *Everything That Rises Must Converge*
Olsen, T. *Tell Me a Riddle*
Paley, G. *Enormous Changes at the Last Minute*
Porter, K.A. *Pale Horse, Pale Rider*
Robinson, S. *Callahan's Crosstime Saloon*
Rochman, H. *Somehow Tenderness Survives*
Roth, P. *Good-bye, Columbus*
Saki (H.H. Munro). *The Short Stories of Saki*
Sillitoe, A. *The Loneliness of the Long-Distance Runner*

Simak, C. *City*
Singer, I.B. *A Crown of Feathers*
Taylor, P. *Happy Families Are All Alike*
Toomer, J. *Cane*
Updike, J. *Pigeon Feathers*
Wlaker, A. *In Love and Trouble*
Zolotow, C., ed. *An Overpraised Season*

SICILY
Hersey, J. *A Bell for Adano*
Lampedusa, G. *The Leopard*

SLAVERY
Blos, J.W. *A Gathering of Days*
Coetzee, J.M. *Foe*
Cooper, J.C. *Family*
Emecheta, B. *The Slave Girl*
Fox, P. *The Slave Dancer*
Johnson, C. *Middle Passage*
Mickle, S.F. *The Queen of October*
Mitchell, M. *Gone with the Wind*
Morrison, T. *Beloved*
Petry, A. *Tituba of Salem Village*
Walker, M. *Jubilee*

SLUM LIFE
Godden, R. *An Episode of Sparrows*
Green, G. *The Last Angry Man*
Lipsyte, R. *The Contender*
Oates, J.C. *Them*
Roth, H. *Call It Sleep*
Smith, B. *A Tree Grows in Brooklyn*
Wallant, E.L. *The Pawnbroker*
Wright, R. *Native Son*

THE SOUTH
Barrett, W.E. *Lilies of the Field*
Faulkner, W. *Absalom, Absalom!; Intruder in the Dust*
Gaines, E. *A Gathering of Old Men*
Glasgow, E. *The Sheltered Life*
Kantor, M. *Andersonville*
Lee, H. *To Kill a Mockingbird*
Mitchell, M. *Gone With the Wind*

Murray, A. *The Spyglass Tree; Train Whistle Guitar*
Styron, W. *Lie Down in Darkness*
Taylor, P. *Summons to Memphis*
Warren, R.P. *All the King's Men*
Welty, E. *Losing Battles; The Optimist's Daughter*

SOUTH AFRICA
Gordimer, N. *July's People; My Son's Story; Something Out There*
Rochman, H. *Somehow Tenderness Survives*

SOUTH DAKOTA
Rölvaag, O.E. *Giants in the Earth*

SPAIN
Hemingway, E. *For Whom the Bell Tolls*

SPY THRILLERS. *See* ESPIONAGE

SUBWAYS
Holman, F. *Slake's Limbo*

SUICIDE
Anderson, J. *Tirra Lirra by the River*
Guest, J. *Ordinary People*
Horgan, P. *Whitewater*
Maxwell, W. *The Folded Leaf*
O'Hara, J. *Appointment in Samarra*
Oneal, Z. *The Language of Goldfish*
Plath, S. *The Bell Jar*
Schaeffer, S.F. *Falling*
Styron, W. *Lie Down in Darkness*

SUPERNATURAL STORIES
Jackson, S. *The Haunting of Hill House*
Klause, A.C. *The Silver Kiss*
Levin, I. *Rosemary's Baby*
Saki (H.H. Munro). *The Best of Saki*
Thane, E. *Tryst*
Tryon, T. *The Other*

SURREALISM
Abe, K. *Beyond the Curve*

SURVIVAL
Adams, R. *Watership Down*
Burnford, S. *The Incredible Journey*
Dickey, J. *Deliverance*
Donovan, J. *Wild in the World*
Frank, P. *Alas, Babylon*
George, J. C. *Julie of the Wolves*
Golding, W. *Lord of the Flies*
Holman, F. *Slake's Limbo*
Household, G. *Rogue Male*
Judson, W. *Cold River*
Kosinski, J. *The Painted Bird*
Malamud, B. *The Fixer*
Mazer, H. *Snow Bound*
Newth, M. *The Abduction*
O'Dell, S. *Island of the Blue Dolphins*
Sandoz, M. *Winter Thunder*
Stewart, G. *Earth Abides*
Theoux, P. *The Mosquito Coast*
Voigt, C. *Homecoming*
White, R. *Deathwatch*

SUSPENSE. *See also* **DETECTIVE AND MYSTERY STORIES**
Burdick, E. *Fail-Safe*
Crichton, M. *The Andromeda Strain*
Farris, J. *When Michael Calls*
Forsyth, F. *The Day of the Jackal; The Odessa File*
Gann, E. K. *The High and the Mighty*
Goldman, W. *Marathon Man*
Higgins, J. *The Eagle Has Flown*
Holt, V. *Bride of Pendorric*
Keneally, T. *Flying Hero Class*
Knebel, F. *Seven Days in May*
Levin, I. *The Boys from Brazil; Rosemary's Baby*
Mazer, N.F. *The Solid Gold Kid*
Moore, B. *Lies of Silence*
Seymour, G. *The Glory Boys*
White, R. *Deathwatch*

SWIMMING
Crutcher, C. *Stotan!*

SYMBOLISM
Abé, K. *The Woman in the Dunes*

Camus, A. *The Plague*
Gallico, P. *The Snow Goose*
Grass, G. *The Tin Drum*
Hesse, H. *Steppenwolf*
Kafka, F. *The Trial*
Kawabata, Y. *Thousand Cranes*
Mann, T. *The Magic Mountain*

TEACHERS AND TEACHING

Amis, K. *Lucky Jim*
Davies, R. *Fifth Business*
Hilton, J. *Good-bye, Mr. Chips*
Kerr, M.E. *Is That You, Miss Blue?*
Knowles, J. *A Separate Peace*
Spark, M. *The Prime of Miss Jean Brodie*
Updike, J. *The Centaur*

TERRORISM

Cormier, R. *After the First Death*
Keneally, T. *Flying Hero Class*
Moore, B. *Lies of Silence*
Seymour, G. *The Glory Boys*

TEXAS

Ferber, E. *Giant*
Gipson, F. *Old Yeller*
Hailey, E.F. *A Woman of Independent Means*
Horgan, P. *Whitewater*

TIME TRAVEL

Finney, J. *Time and Again*
Silverberg, R. *Letters from Atlantis*

TOTALITARIANISM. *See also* COMMUNISM; FASCISM; NATION-AL SOCIALISM

Bradbury, R. *Fahrenheit 451*
Dorfman, A. *Widows*
Koestler, A. *Darkness at Noon*
Lewis, S. *It Can't Happen Here*
Orwell, G. *Animal Farm; Nineteen Eighty-Four*
Zemyatin, Y. *We*

TRIALS

Camus, A. *The Stranger*

VIETNAM WAR
Meyers, W.D. *Fallen Angels*
O'Brien, T. *Going After Cacciato; The Things They Carried*

VIRGINIA
Glasgow, E. *Barren Ground*
Styron, W. *Lie Down in Darkness*

WALES
Llewellyn, R. *How Green Was My Valley*

WAR *See also* VIETNAM WAR, UNITED STATES, WORLD WAR 1939-1945, EUROPEAN WAR 1914-1918
Boulle, P. *Bridge Over the River Kwai*
Caputo, P. *Horn of Africa*
Gardner, J.C. *Grendel*
Myers, W. D. *Fallen Angels*

WASHINGTON, D.C.
Truman, M. *Murder at the National Cathedral*

THE WEST AND WESTERN STORIES
Brown, D. *Creek Mary's Blood*
Clark, W.V. *The Ox-bow Incident*
Hall, O. *The Bad Lands*
L'Amour, L. *Bendigo Shafter*
Lesley, C. *Winterkill*
McMurtry, L. *Buffalo Girls*
Michener, J. *Centennial*
Portis, C. *True Grit*
Richard, A. *Pistol*
Schaefer, J. *Shane*
Wister, O. *The Virginian*

WEST INDIES
Kincaid, J. *Annie John*
Naipaul, V.S. *A House for Mr. Biswas*

WHEAT
Norris, F. *The Octopus*
Walker, M. *Winter Wheat*

WITCHCRAFT
Levin, I. *Rosemary's Baby*
Petry, A. *Tituba of Salem Village*

WOMEN, STATUS OF
Allende, I. *Eva Luna*
Amado, J. *Gabriela, Clove and Cinnamon*
Atwood, M. *Cat's Eye; The Handmaid's Tale*
Connell, E. *Mrs. Bridge*
Franklin, M. *My Brilliant Career*
Gibbons, K. *A Cure for Dreams*
Le Guin, U. *The Dispossessed*
Marshall, P. *Daughters*
Munro, A. *Lives of Girls and Women*
Naylor, G. *The Women of Brewster Place*
Paley, G. *Enormous Changes at the Last Minute*
Paterson, K. *Lyddie*
Perry, A. *Bethlehem Road*
Quindlen, A. *Object Lesson*
Rachlin, N. *Foreigner*
Tan, A. *The Joy Luck Club; The Kitchen God's Wife*

WORLD WAR I, 1914-1918. *See* EUROPEAN WAR, 1914-1918

WORLD WAR II, 1939-1945
Beach, E.L. *Run Silent, Run Deep*
Boulle, P. *The Bridge Over the River Kwai*
Brown, H. *A Walk in the Sun*
Deighton, L. *SS-GB*
Desai, A. *Baumgartner's Bombay*
Heggen, T. *Mister Roberts*
Heller, J. *Catch-22*
Hersey, J. *A Bell for Adano; The Wall*
Higgins, J. *The Eagle Has Flown*
Kosinski, J. *The Painted Bird*
Leffland, E. *Rumors of Peace*
MacLean, A. *The Guns of Navarone*
Mailer, N. *The Naked and the Dead*
Monsarrat, N. *The Cruel Sea*
Sevela, E. *Why There Is No Heaven on Earth*
Shaw, I. *The Young Lions*
Watkins, Y.K. *So Far from the Bamboo Grove*
Westall, R. *The Machine Gunners*
Wouk, H. *The Caine Mutiny*